Classic
Christian
Hymn-writers

Classic Christian Hymn-writers

by Elsie Houghton

CHRISTIAN • LITERATURE • CRUSADE
Fort Washington, Pennsylvania 19034

CHRISTIAN LITERATURE CRUSADE

U.S.A.

P.O. Box 1449, Fort Washington, PA 19034

First published 1982

Reprinted 1984, 1988

First American Edition 1992

Published in Britain by the Evangelical Press of Wales

ISBN 0-87508-966-6

Cover photo: D'Arlen Photo/Superstock

PRINTED IN THE UNITED STATES OF AMERICA

CONTENTS

ILLUSTRATIONS

1

EARLY HYMN-WRITERS

Lord Jesus, think on me,
  And purge away my sin;
From earthborn passions set me free,
  And make me pure within. . . .

Lord Jesus, think on me,
  That, when the flood is past,
I may the eternal brightness see,
  And share Thy joy at last.

Synesius of Cyrene (c.375—c.430)

I T has been said that the Christian Church started on its way singing. In response to such a statement we might well ask what was the nature of its song in those dawn-days of the Faith.

In its earliest days the Church adhered very much to the old Jewish ways of worship, so the Psalter became its first book of praise and was, for a time, sufficient for its purposes. Music and singing had always been in the forefront of Jewish life and worship. When the prophets warned of desolation to come, they said "there would be no singing in the land"; how could they sing when their hearts were full of sadness?

Temple worship must have been very impressive, with large choirs chanting psalms and the worshipers responding with "Hallelujah," or "Amen," or "For His mercy endureth for ever." The psalms which appear in Scripture as the Songs of Degrees (Psalms 120–134) were pilgrim songs, sung stage by stage on the way to Jerusalem; others were processional songs, national hymns, songs for religious festivals; other psalms were for personal use. Calvin says, "All the sorrows, fears, troubles, hopes, doubts, perplexities, stormy outbreaks by which the hearts of men are tossed, are here depicted by the Holy Spirit." So the Psalter became the hymnbook of the Church from the very beginning, and early Christian writers bear witness to the use made of it in private and public worship.

Singing is mentioned only twice in the Gospels. When our Lord made His triumphal entry into Jerusalem He was acclaimed with the Hosanna hymn, "Hosanna. Blessed is the King of Israel that cometh in the name of the Lord." Then, on the night before the crucifixion, before the Lord and the eleven went out, after the supper, to the Mount of Olives, they sang a hymn. This was the Great Hallel, consisting of Psalms 113–118, the great Passover hymn.

In apostolic times, as long as the Christians continued to cling to the old practices of Judaism, no need was felt for a new form of praise. Eventually, however, a new type of song had to be found to give utterance to the new experience. Church history would verify the truth of the statement that there is never a new work of the Spirit, a time of revival in the Church, which is not followed by a great outburst of singing. The earliest examples of Christian hymns are probably the Benedictus, "Blessed be the Lord God of Israel, for He hath visited and redeemed His people"; the Magnificat, "My soul doth magnify the Lord"; and the Nunc Dimittis, "Lord, now lettest Thou Thy servant depart in peace." These hymns reflect the piety and devotion of the earliest Christian community in Palestine. They were in rhythmic prose, for metrical forms, which are more akin to modern poetic form, did not come into use until the fourth century.

When it became evident, at the beginning of the second century, that Christians were not a Jewish sect, they came under imperial suspicion and persecution began. This persecution lasted for three centuries. The Christians used to hold meetings for worship before dawn on Sunday mornings and they "sang a hymn of praise to Christ as God." At that time every act of Christian worship was likely to end in martyrdom.

One hymn from this period is

> Hail, gladdening Light, of His pure glory pour'd,
> Who is the immortal Father, heavenly, blest.

It is one of the very earliest of hymns. In the fourth century it was called the Candlelight Hymn because it was used when the lamps were lit for evening service.

The great creeds which were hammered out in those centuries of persecution were first sung as hymns. One of the greatest was the Te Deum, "We praise Thee, O God, we acknowledge Thee to be the Lord," and it is unsurpassed as a confession of the Church's faith and thanksgiving. The early hymn-writers included Clement of Alexandria and Bar Daisan (unhappily heretical in doctrine) in the second century; Ephraim the Syrian in the fourth century used his gift of poetry to counter the Gnostic heresy as Chrysostom, bishop of Constantinople, used hymns to counter Arianism.

One of the early hymns still found in hymnbooks is that quoted at the head of this chapter. The hymn probably owes much to the skill of its translator, A. W. Chatfield. Synesius was not entirely orthodox in his belief, but this hymn is charged with such true Christian feeling that we are encouraged to think that he was fundamentally sound. Another hymn from the eighth century still in use is based on a theme which Stephen the Sabaite suggested in one of his hymns—

> Art thou weary, art thou languid,
> Art thou sore distressed?
> "Come to Me," saith One, "and, coming,
> Be at rest!"

We are indebted to J. M. Neale for his translation of this and many other hymns.

Stephen was only ten when he accompanied his uncle, John of Damascus, into voluntary exile. The tide of Mohammedanism had submerged the Holy Land. Jerusalem had fallen in 636. Thereafter men of God were almost driven to take refuge from the storm in secluded places. John and his nephew Stephen are said to have lived in the monastery of Mar Saba in "one of the most stricken wildernesses of the world."

The hymn ascribed to Joseph the Hymnographer of the ninth century is also more of an elaboration of a suggestion than an actual translation. It runs—

> *O happy band of pilgrims,*
> *If onward ye will tread,*
> *With Jesus as your Fellow,*
> *To Jesus as your Head!* . . .

Monastery of Mar Saba

O happy band of pilgrims,
Look upward to the skies,
Where such a light affliction
Shall win you such a prize.

As we turn to the Church in the West, it was Ambrose, bishop of Milan in the fourth century, who made hymns popular. He was a great and saintly man. Augustine was one of his converts. He lived during the stormy times of the Arian controversy when hymns were much used. These hymns which were "cradled on the battlefield" quickly spread throughout the Church. Ambrose composed several hymns himself and some are found in recently published hymnbooks. For example, those which begin with the words:

O splendor of God's glory bright

(tr. by R. S. Bridges)

O Jesus, Lord of heavenly grace

(tr. by J. Chandler)

and

Infinite God, to Thee we raise
Our hearts in solemn songs of praise

(tr. by Charles Wesley)

Ambrosian music was also very popular. He introduced simple, sweet melodies for congregational singing. Augustine, however, was so taken up with the tunes that he paid little attention to the wonderful words and was disposed to banish such singing in favor of the simple but dull "plain time." So the practice of congregational singing introduced by Ambrose declined and eventually it was abandoned altogether. Instead there was a return to the severe, ancient style which made church song to a large extent the monopoly of the clergy. The right of the people to a direct share in the Church's praise was not restored until after the Reformation.

It seems, then, that for several dark centuries the Church did not sing. Doubtless, amidst the darkness, there were pockets of light where the voice of singing was still heard, in the monasteries and possibly in small groupings of the true children of God. It was only when the Spirit of God moved mightily again in the Reformation that hymns were again written and sung in Germany and other European countries, including Britain.

2

THE TWO BERNARDS

Jerusalem the golden,
  With milk and honey blest,
Beneath thy contemplation
  Sink heart and voice oppressed:
I know not, O I know not
  What joys await us there,
What radiancy of glory,
  What bliss beyond compare.

Bernard of Cluny

T HE Middle Ages were a time of inexpressible confusion and misery. With the fall of the Roman Empire, order in Europe largely disappeared. It was a wild, lawless world, and for long periods civilization sadly declined.

These conditions contributed to the force of the Monastic Movement which had gathered strength since it was introduced to the West from Egypt. What were believing men to do in such a brutal age? What protest could they make in the name of their faith which would produce any impression? They concluded that the only effective witness was to turn their backs on a system given over to evil and to withdraw into separated communities, thereby showing their Christianity in their lives and by their work.

The monasteries which sprang up all over Europe were oases of law and order amid the surrounding anarchy.

They gave hospitality to the stranger and were a refuge for the hunted and oppressed. They showed the dignity of labor, in the days when the strong lived by plunder, by cultivating the wilderness land around their monasteries. They were the homes of learning and culture and within their seclusion scholars had peace to pursue their tasks.

Many of these men, who looked out from their seclusion to the chaos and iniquity of the world, could see no possibility of remedy except through the return of Christ as the Judge of men.

❧

Bernard of Cluny was representative of this outlook. He saw no gleam of hope, only a world full of anguish. Is it to be wondered at that, in despair of any improvement in this world, he should cast his longing eyes forward to the coming of the Lord of righteousness under whose reign evil would be judged and forever dethroned! The hymn "Jerusalem the Golden," Bernard's best-known hymn, is in keeping with this outlook.

Little is known of Bernard except that he was born in Brittany, of English parents, at a time in the twelfth century when Brittany and Normandy belonged to England. He did not concern himself in the politics of his day, neither did he take part in the Crusades. He spent his life in the great monastery of Cluny in Brittany. The head of the monastery, Peter the Venerable, who was also a poet, was famous for his gentleness and learning. So, under the gentle rule of Peter, Bernard found a happy spot from which he could safely look out at the world in its strife and turmoil. In the end, however, the wealth of the monastery was its undoing, and even in Bernard's time the salt was losing its savor. His sorrow over the corruptions he saw in the world outside was intensified in the later years of his life by what he saw of evils within the monastery. He poured out his soul in a long satire of some 3,000 lines which has been considered the loveliest of medieval poems. J. M. Neale has converted sections of it into classic English hymns of which "Jerusalem the Golden" is the best-known. What longing for the better country is expressed in the verse

> *O sweet and blessed country,*
> *The home of God's elect!*
> *O sweet and blessed country,*
> *That eager hearts expect!*
> *Jesus, in mercy bring us*
> *To that dear land of rest,*
> *Who art, with God the Father*
> *And Spirit, ever blest!*

Bernard's description of heaven has the commendation of those who have found in it adequate expression of what has been called their "heavenly homesickness." His verses have soothed the dying hours of many of God's saints. There is one striking story of a child who suffered almost beyond endurance, but when Bernard's verses were read to him he would lie quietly without a murmur.

Bernard of Clairvaux (1091–1153) was one of the noblest figures in the whole monastic line, and he was probably the most illustrious and powerful personality of his age. Three hundred years after his death Luther wrote that "Bernard was the best monk that ever lived, whom I love beyond all the rest put together." He acquired such a reputation for saintliness that people came from all parts to seek his guidance. His monks loved him as their father and he was a true friend to them and to many others. Even kings and high spiritual dignitaries sought his counsel and bowed to his rebuke. Officially he was never more than the simple Abbot of Clairvaux, but he had the mind of a statesman and power came to him unsought. Clairvaux was only his resting-place during the pauses of a very busy life. He moved freely about the world, and even when he retreated to his abbey he did not have real peace for men and women followed him there, and his retirement took the form of a counseling ministry. He also wrote letters unceasingly to those who sought his help by this means.

Bernard was in the true evangelical succession and fol-

Artist's impression of Bernard of Clairvaux
preaching at the Second Crusade

lowed Augustine in doctrine. He was an evangelist fired by the gospel and delighted to declare that Christ is the sinner's only hope and salvation. He was unsparing in his censure of abuses and corruptions and full of zeal for Christian truth. The hymns attributed to him, written in Latin, are charged with this glowing spirit. There is some doubt as to how many of the hymns attributed to him were actually written by him. The best known of them is

> *Jesus, the very thought of Thee*
> *With sweetness fills my breast;*
> *But sweeter far Thy face to see,*
> *And in Thy presence rest.*

This hymn breathes the very spirit of Bernard, and will probably outlive all others linked with his name.

Bernard was born in Burgundy, a country of high mountains and thick forests. His father was a noble knight, his mother, the Lady Aletta, a devout lady who secretly gave her six sons and one daughter to the Lord. Bernard was sent to a cathedral school, but until her death she herself taught her son the doctrines of the Christian faith and he grew up loving the service of God. He refused to go to Court, choosing instead to go to the most obscure, desolate, and severe monastery he could find. Eventually all his brothers and his father joined him and soon the little monastery at Citeaux was quite unable to contain the numbers who followed Bernard. He was then chosen to found a new monastery—which he did in a valley which was uncleared, untilled and full of bandits. He and his companions nearly starved in the process of building it and were reduced to eating leaves before the peasants, who had come to respect their courage and piety, brought them bread. Bernard studied the Bible under the trees and worked hard with the band of monks to drain the wild, marshy land, until at length the Valley of Wormwood was transformed into the bright Valley of Clairvaux.

Bernard's fame as a preacher spread throughout Europe. He was offered bishoprics but he refused all, preferring to remain Abbot of Clairvaux. He took part in the Second Crusade and its failure broke his heart. At length the early austerities, which he deeply regretted, and the wear and tear of sixty years began to tell upon him; and it was evident that the voice which was never silent when there were any afflicted to comfort, or there was any cause to plead, was soon to be silenced. As he lay dying he said, "I have lived wickedly, Thou loving Lord Jesus, but Thou hast purchased heaven with Thy suffering and death. Thou hast unlocked heaven and presented it to me. . . . In this I have joy and comfort."

> O hope of every contrite heart,
>   O joy of all the meek,
> To those who fall how kind Thou art!
>   How good to those who seek!
>
> But what to those who find? Ah, this
>   Nor tongue nor pen can show:

The love of Jesus, what it is
   None but His loved ones know. . . .

Jesus, our only joy be Thou,
   As Thou our prize wilt be;
Jesus, be Thou our glory now,
   And through eternity.

3

MARTIN LUTHER

(1483–1546)

A mighty fortress is our God,
A bulwark never failing;
Our helper He, amid the flood
Of mortal ills prevailing.
For still our ancient foe
Doth seek to work us woe—
His craft and power are great,
And armed with cruel hate,
On earth is not his equal.

(based on Psalm 46)
(tr. by F. H. Hedge)

ALTHOUGH we are concerned chiefly with Martin Luther's service to the Church of God in reintroducing congregational singing, we will first give an outline of the life of this remarkable man who stood alone against Pope and Emperor in his defence of the truth of God.

Luther was born in Eisleben, in Saxony, in 1483. His father was a copper miner but, although poor, his parents knew the value of education and sent their children to school—at great cost to themselves. They also brought up their children in the fear of the Lord, possibly being too severe on them. Once his father beat Martin so severely that he fled from him, and because he had taken a nut without asking her permission his mother flogged him until the blood flowed. Martin went away to school in Eisenach when he was thirteen, and being too poor to pay his fees he went singing from door to door to earn money. A kind woman took him into her house for the four-year duration of his course and, a lover of music herself, she taught him how to play the lute and flute.

Later, Luther took a degree at the University of Erfurt and began to study law. One day, while going through a forest in a thunderstorm, his companion was struck dead by lightning. Luther vowed to give himself to God, if his life were spared. A few weeks later he left the University and entered a monastery at Erfurt. His parents were angry, as they had hoped he would become a lawyer and be able to help his family financially.

Luther was very diligent in all his duties at the monastery, but he became more and more miserable as, in spite of all his diligence, he seemed to get no nearer to God. His happiest hours were spent in the library where he found a Latin Bible, the first Bible he had ever seen. He read it with delight, and his joy knew no bounds when he discovered in the Bible that God is the loving Father of believers and that Jesus Christ is His express image. He found also that penances, pilgrimages, the veneration of relics and suchlike things are not ordained by God, and that heaven was to be obtained by believing in the Son of God and coming to the Father by Him.

Two years later Luther took priest's orders and went to lecture in Divinity at the University of Wittenberg. At the same time he studied Greek and Hebrew so that he could read the Bible in the original languages. When he visited Rome in 1512 his eyes were opened to the fact that there was much evil in the Church. It is said that, as he was on his knees toiling up the steps of what was claimed to be Pilate's staircase, he heard a voice saying to him, "The just shall live by faith," and that he rose from his knees in possession of the key-word of the Reformation. Ten years passed from the time he first saw a Bible to the time he began to attempt to reform the Church, having learned from God what the true Church ought to be.

In 1517 Tetzel, a Dominican friar, was sent by the Pope to sell indulgences which would reduce the time to be spent in purgatory by those who bought them. Luther determined to oppose this traffic and posted his theses against indulgences on the door of the castle church at Wittenberg, declaring that the indulgences were useless and that the Pope had no power to forgive sins. The University men, whom he had taught in the Scriptures, were delighted at his action, but the rest of Europe was aghast at his boldness. Luther's long controversy with Rome came to a crisis when he burned a papal bull, or edict, in 1520. He was then summoned to go to Worms to be tried by papal authorities in the presence of the Emperor. The Emperor Charles V agreed to deal with the case of Luther at this Diet. Luther's friends warned him not to go, but his reply was, "If there are as many devils in Worms as tiles on the housetops, I will still go there."

Arriving at the hall of assembly he was astounded at the presence of so many people of rank besides the Emperor. Luther was asked by the presiding officer Johann von Eck if he wrote the books displayed and if he was willing to retract the doctrines contained in them. The reformer acknowledged his authorship but asked if he could have time to reflect on how to answer the second question. He spent much of the following night in prayer. The next day, April 18, 1521, was the greatest day in Luther's life. In the Emperor's presence Dr. Eck put the question to him again. Luther refused to withdraw anything he had written, ending his statement with the famous words "Here I stand: I can do no other. So help me God."

As he returned to Wittenberg, trusting in the protection of God, his friend the Duke of Saxony sent a band of horsemen who carried him away to the Castle of Wartburg, out of reach of his enemies. He lived in that lonely fortress for a year and there he began the greatest work of his life, the translation of the Bible into German.

IN SILENTIO
FORTITVDO

ET SPE ERIT
VESTRA.

Martin Luther

After returning to Wittenberg he completed the translation of the New Testament with the help of Melanchthon. It was printed in 1522. The newly discovered power of the printing press had come just in time and soon thousands of copies of the New Testament were pouring from the printing presses of Wittenberg. Luther completed the translation of the whole Bible by 1534.

Three years after the Diet of Worms Luther threw off his monastic garb, and soon afterwards he married Catherine von Bora who had left her convent. In 1529 the Reformed princes assembled at Spires and separated from Rome by a "Protest" against a decree aimed at Lutherans. The following year the Lutherans presented their Confession of Faith at the Diet of Augsburg. Luther spent the rest of his life in comparative quietness at Wittenberg, happy in his home life—writing, lecturing and contending for the Faith. During his later years his sufferings were great, but his last illness continued only for a few hours, so he was able to continue his various labors almost until the day of his death. As he was dying he three times repeated the words "Into Thy hands I commend my spirit; Thou hast redeemed me, O God of Truth." He fell asleep in Jesus on February 18, 1546.

From the time of Pope Gregory I in the sixth century the people had been deprived of taking any direct share in singing during church services. The Roman theory of worship affirmed that all that is essential for the congregation is done by the clergy—strictly speaking, the people need not be there! Against this sacerdotal theory Luther asserted the doctrine of the priesthood of all believers. Every soul has the right of direct access to God by faith in Jesus Christ and can present his own prayers and praises without priestly mediation.

In various parts of Europe some had been trying to make their voices heard before Luther's day. In England the Lollards, the "soft singers," had made a plaintive beginning which soon died. There had been attempts in Finland, Bohemia, and in Germany itself. Doubtless these precursors helped Luther, but his main inspiration came from the Book of Psalms. "It is my intention," he wrote, "to make German psalms for the people; that is, spiritual songs, whereby the Word of God may be kept alive among them by singing." He was determined that the words should be such as could be understood by the common people. He himself gave the lead, other poets came forward, and together they produced simple, strong hymns whose subjects were the simple truths of the Faith.

The hymn "A Mighty Fortress Is Our God," affirming that God is the defence of His people, has been called "the Marseillaise of the Reformation." There is in it an inextinguishable fire of faith that ensures for it a lasting place among Christian hymns. It was written in the year when the Evangelical princes delivered their protest at the Diet of Spires, from which Protestants took their name. Luther often used to sing the hymn when the Diet of Augsburg was sitting, and it soon became a favorite with the German people, cheering armies in conflict and sustaining believers in hours of fiery trial. After Luther's death Melanchthon heard a little girl singing this hymn, and said, "Sing on, my little girl, you don't know what famous people you comfort." The first line of the hymn is inscribed on Luther's tomb in Wittenberg.

During the Diet of Augsburg Luther was one day so overcome with what he had been through that he fainted. On recovering he said to his friends, "Come, let us defy the devil and praise God by singing the hymn—

> *Out of the depths I cry to Thee;*
> *Lord, hear me, I implore Thee:*
> *If Thou shouldst mark iniquity,*
> *Who, Lord, shall stand before Thee?*
> *O may Thine ear attend my cry!*
> *Lord, bid me to Thyself draw nigh,*
> *While now I call upon Thee."*

Luther wrote a Christmas hymn for his five-year-old son Hans, which shows the tenderness which was one of the qualities "blended in the rich humanity of this heroic man."

> *From heaven above to earth I come,*
> *To bear good news to every home;*
> *Glad tidings of great joy I bring,*
> *Whereof I now will say and sing. . . .*
>
> *Ah, dearest Jesus, holy Child,*
> *Make Thee a bed, soft, undefiled,*

Within my heart, that it may be
A quiet chamber kept for Thee.

The hymns would have made little headway if they had not been matched with fitting music. Luther himself was very musical but he wanted other skilled men to give the lead. He and two friends spent several weeks at Wittenberg, experimenting with possible melodies from Roman service books and from popular songs, altering and molding them until they were suitable. *Ein' feste Burg*, the tune to "A Mighty Fortress," is said to have been made up of borrowed fragments. In 1524 the first hymnbook of the Evangelicals in Germany was published; it contained sixteen hymns, most of which were written by Luther himself. By the time of his death, sixty collections of hymns had appeared.

The popular effect was immediate. All over Germany, among all classes of people, the voice of praise was heard. "There broke forth from all lands of the Reformation a great burst of hymns, with the clear notes of the gospel, in the common tongue." The enemies of the Reformation said that Luther had done more harm by his songs than by his sermons.

The truth is that the genius of this man, with the help of God, had forged a powerful new weapon of the Faith, and the conquests won by it were incalculable. Great masses of people, with Luther's hymns and melodies on their lips, sang themselves into the creed of the Protestant Reformation.

4

MARTIN RINKART

(1586–1649)

Now thank we all our God,
  With hearts and hands and voices;
Who wondrous things hath done,
  In whom His world rejoices;
Who, from our mothers' arms,
  Hath blessed us on our way
With countless gifts of love,
  And still is ours today.

THE German pastor and poet, Martin Rinkart, born in 1586, was the son of a cooper of Eilenburg in Saxony. His father worked long hours for poor wages, but sufficient to feed, clothe and house his family until the Thirty Years' War began. Martin was sent to school. He loved books and music and his parents hoped he would become a scholar; perhaps a minister. They had no money to pay for his further education, but in 1601 Martin became a foundation scholar and chorister of St. Thomas's School of Theology at the University, his course including the study of Greek and Latin.

In course of time he became a minister, and after holding several short appointments he became both precentor, because he sang so well, and minister of the little church of Eisleben, famous as the birthplace of Martin Luther. Within a few years he was appointed archdeacon of the parish of Eilenburg, his native town. He had left there a poor scholar: he came back as a much respected minister of the gospel in the year 1618 when peace and prosperity came to an end, for the Thirty Years' War broke out.

The whole of Germany was ravaged by the war, not least the area in which Eilenburg was situated. It was a walled city and fugitives flocked into it for shelter. Rinkart stayed there during the entire period of the war, facing the troubles with the people and helping them in all possible ways. Great armies kept crossing the land, eating all the food, pillaging shops and farms, and leaving ruin and desolation behind them. Then the plague broke out and the people, weary and worn out, could not resist it. Victims died within a few hours. The other two ministers in the town died, but still Rinkart stayed and carried on their work as well as his own. All day long he went from bed to bed, nursing the sick, cheering and praying with the dying. He buried about five thousand people, sometimes reading the funeral service over forty or fifty bodies. Eight thousand people died in one year and his own wife was one of the victims.

When the plague ceased, famine followed, as no seed had been sown and no farming done. The shops were empty, the mills silent, and the marketplaces deserted. People stood outside Rinkart's house, weeping and beseeching him to help them. He gave all he had, even at the expense of his own family. In all these troubles and afflictions the fine courage of Rinkart kept the people from despair. His name is little known, but he was perhaps one of the bravest men of history.

He can have had little time for writing hymns, but whenever there was a breathing space in the long war Rinkart was ready with a song to inspire his flock with fresh hope and trust in God. A year after the war ended Rinkart died. His work had been well and faithfully done. He passed on to that better country where war and pestilence are unknown and where God wipes tears from all faces.

Rinkart's hymn, "Now Thank We All Our God," is sung in Germany on all occasions of national thanksgiving. It is found in most English hymnbooks and is used particularly at times of gratitude for special mercies. It is believed that the hymn was written just before the end of the Thirty Years' War, in prospect of the re-establishment of peace. In view of all the distresses of the war, the plague and the famine, which made conditions for the people so distressing, Rinkart's hymn is remarkable. There is no mention in it of trials and difficulties, only thankfulness and a quiet, joyful resting in God. Surely it is these qualities in Rinkart which, under God, enabled him to minister to the desperate needs of the people at a time when many were at their wits' ends!

> *O may this bounteous God*
>   *Through all our life be near us,*
> *With ever joyful hearts*
>   *And blessed peace to cheer us,*
>   *And keep us in His grace,*
>   *And guide us when perplexed,*
>   *And free us from all ills*
>   *In this world and the next.*

> *All praise and thanks to God*
>   *The Father now be given,*
> *The Son, and Him who reigns*
>   *With Them in highest heaven:*
>   *The one eternal God,*
>   *Whom heaven and earth adore;*
>   *For thus it was, is now,*
>   *And shall be evermore.*

5

PAUL GERHARDT

(1607–76)

Give to the winds thy fears;
Hope and be undismayed:
God hears thy sighs and counts thy tears;
God shall lift up thy head.
Through waves and clouds and storms
He gently clears thy way;
Wait thou His time, so shall this night
Soon end in joyous day.

Leave to His sovereign sway
To choose and to command;
So shalt thou wondering own His way,
How wise, how strong His hand.
Far, far above thy thought
His counsel shall appear,
When fully He the work hath wrought
That caused thy needless fear.

(tr. by John Wesley)

PAUL GERHARDT has been called Germany's "gentlest, sweetest singer" and certainly he ranks next to Luther as the most gifted and popular hymn-writer of the Lutheran Church. He reverted to Luther's type of hymn as no one else had done. And yet the hymns of the two men are in some respects very different. Luther's belief in free grace, the work of the atonement and justification by faith, inspired his hymns, whereas it was more the consciousness of the love of God which introduced joyful confidence into the hymns of Gerhardt. He had a firm grasp of the realities of the Christian faith, but he expressed these in very human terms. In Gerhardt's hymns there is a perceptible change from the objective type of hymn, concerning the great realities of the Faith, to a more subjective kind of hymn, though not morbidly so, dwelling more on the feelings and experience of the Christian. Even so, he writes not as a Christian who lays his soul bare but as a representative member of the Church who speaks thoughts and feelings which he shares with his fellow members. In no way can he be charged with an egotistical subjectivity.

Gerhardt had a profoundly spiritual mind and his style is simple and graceful. He is a true poet with several varieties of verse form at his command. From the day of their publication his hymns were popular among all classes. Today a large proportion of his hymns are among those most cherished and most widely used by German-speaking Christians. Those of his hymns which have been translated into English are equally loved and used among English-speaking Christians.

The verses quoted above are taken from one of Gerhardt's best-known hymns. It is said to have been written at a time when he was ordered to leave Prussia, because his views differed from those of the Elector. He left in reduced circumstances, on foot, with his wife and children. One night, after seeking refuge in a village inn, his wife burst into tears. Gerhardt reminded her of the verse in Psalm 37, "Commit thy way unto the Lord," then retired and wrote this hymn, of which there are many more verses than are given in any English hymnbook. The same night two men arrived at the inn, sent by Duke Christian of Merseburg, inviting the poet to settle in that city and offering him a suitable monetary reward. Gerhardt then gave his wife the hymn he had written, saying to her, "See how God provides! Did I not bid you to trust in God and all would be well?" There is some doubt as to the authenticity of the story, but it seems certain that the hymn was written to help his wife at some point of crisis in their lives.

Paul Gerhardt the poet, whom the German people regard so emphatically as their own, was born at Grafenhanichen in Saxony, of which town his father was the burgomaster, or chief magistrate. Not much is known of his early years apart from the fact that he matriculated at the University of Wittenberg in 1628 and that he seems to have remained there until 1642, when he went to Berlin as tutor in the house of an advocate, whose daughter Gerhardt married in 1655.

The outward circumstances of his life were for the most part gloomy. His earlier years were spent amid the horrors of the Thirty Years' War and he did not obtain a settled position in life until he was forty-four, when he became pastor of a church just outside Berlin. Four years later he married. His wife was in every way a helpmeet to him in his many labors and trials. At about the same time he published his hymns which were taken up throughout Germany with great enthusiasm. In 1657 he was called to a pastorate in Berlin, in which city he had often preached, his years of ministry there being the happiest in his life. A faithful pastor and a powerful preacher, he was much loved by the people. He was a compassionate man, and so much concerned about the poor that he took several widowed mothers and their children into his home, supporting them at his own cost.

In 1666 he became involved in a contest between the Elector Frederick (of the Reformed Church) and the Lutheran clergy and he was deposed from office. When he was given this information, he said, "This is only a small Berlin affliction, but I am also willing and ready to seal with my blood the evangelical truth and to offer my neck to the sword." He was reinstated later, but on finding out the conditions of his reinstatement he decided that he could not occupy a false position, and resigned his appointment. He spent several years in Berlin without office and during this period his wife died, after a long illness. Of their five children only one survived childhood.

In the same year that his wife died he was appointed

pastor to a church at Lübben in Saxony. He ministered here as a widower, with his one surviving child, but they were difficult years as the people were rough and unsympathetic, which must have grieved his sensitive spirit. His portrait in the church at Lübben has the inscription in Latin, "A divine sifted in Satan's sieve," probably referring to the unkindness he experienced in Lübben. He died in 1676, repeating one of his own hymns, "Wherefore Should I Grieve and Pine?" His last words—referring to "a Christian man"—were:

> *Him no death has power to kill,*
> *But from many a dreaded ill*
> *Bears his spirit safe away.*

We shall mention Gerhardt's hymns again when we write of John Wesley's translations of them. They combine simplicity with depth and force, and are the heart-utterances of one who had a simple but sublime faith in God. Some of them were translated into other languages as well

Christian Schwartz, German missionary to
India, who was comforted on his deathbed by
a hymn of Gerhardt's sung in Tamil

as English. Schwartz, the first German missionary to India, was comforted on his deathbed by native Christians singing a hymn by Gerhardt in their own Tamil language.

6

METRICAL PSALMS

The Lord's my Shepherd, I'll not want:
He makes me down to lie
In pastures green; He leadeth me
The quiet waters by.

Scottish Psalter, 1650

THERE were two main streams of Christian song in the churches of the Reformation. There was hymnody, following Luther who carried on the tradition established by the Latin hymn, and there was metrical psalmody, after the example set by Calvin who reverted to a still older tradition, going back to primitive days when the Church had only the psalms with which to sing praise to God. These streams ran parallel for many generations; then they converged, and in most churches of the Reformed order they run together today.

Calvin's aim was to return as nearly as possible to primitive usage, and only in the old Hebrew psalms could he find themes of worship to satisfy his requirements. He agreed with Augustine, that there is nothing worthy of being sung to God but what we have received from God. He saw that two things were necessary to fit the psalms for popular use: they must be metricized, and they must be provided with attractive and suitable tunes. Calvin began the task, but with all his gifts he was not a poet. It was Clement Marot who exercised his poetic gifts on the psalms, Calvin recognizing that Marot's work possessed a lyrical grace which he could not reach. In 1543 Marot's *Fifty Psalms* were published at Geneva. Beza completed the task and versified the remaining hundred.

If Calvin was not a poet, neither was he a musician, but he was alive to the power of music to move the heart and to its value as an aid to worship. He was concerned about the kind of tunes the people should sing, as some tunes had been used which were not befitting the worship of God. In Strasbourg Calvin had been impressed by the dignity and strength of some of the German melodies. He brought a musician of "rare capacity and distinction" from Paris, Louis Bourgeois, whom he instructed to prepare music for the new Psalter. "It should be simple and carry

Part of a page from a psalmbook (in French)
printed in Geneva during Calvin's lifetime

weight and majesty suitable for the subject, and be fit to be sung in church." In addition to this assignment Bourgeois organized musical education, training students and children so that their elders also might be instructed. He composed very good tunes—some, like Luther's, being adaptations of popular airs.

The psalms set to music became very popular. A visitor to Geneva in 1557 has left us an account of what he found there. We quote from *The Story of the Church's Song* by Millar Patrick:

> On workdays when the hour for sermon approaches, as soon as the first sound of the bell is heard, all shops are closed, all conversation ceases, all business is broken off and from all sides people go to the nearest meetinghouse. There each draws from his pocket a small book which contains the psalms, and out of full hearts, in the native speech, the congregation sings before and after the sermon.

Soon psalm-singing became the badge of adherence to the Reformation. It became universal among the Huguenots. The popularity of the psalms spread to other lands and they were translated into other languages. Continental Psalters exercised a powerful influence on the shaping of the metrical Psalters of England and Scotland.

Among those who came under the influence of the Reformation was Thomas Sternhold (1500–49), a Gentleman of the Privy Chamber of King Henry VIII. The profane songs of his fellow courtiers and of the common people caused him grief and he asked himself if anything could be done to change the situation. Could the psalms be turned into meter so that the singers might be inclined to sing them to well-known melodies and abandon their obscene songs? He had no choice but to write popular verse and music, as anything more polished would have been useless in such a situation. Sternhold was successful in his humble aim. One day as he was sitting at the organ in his Whitehall chambers, singing some of his own verses, a delicate-looking boy stole into the room and listened with delight. Within a few years that boy was on the throne as Edward VI. Sternhold published thirty-seven of his translations in 1549, dedicating them to the King, but within a few months he died, and his friend John Hopkins, a Suffolk schoolmaster, took up and completed the work.

During the persecutions under Queen Mary many leaders of the Reformation took refuge in Geneva. In 1556 a collection of 51 psalms was published, 44 by Sternhold and Hopkins and 7 by William Whittingham. The next edition added 24 psalms translated by William Kethe, including the world-famous version of the hundredth psalm:

> *All people that on earth do dwell,*
> *Sing to the Lord with cheerful voice;*
> *Him serve with fear, His praise forth tell,*
> *Come ye before Him and rejoice.*

When the exiles returned to England and Wales after the death of Mary they brought the practice of psalm-singing with them. It spread like wildfire. Strype, in his *Annals*, says, "You may sometimes see at St. Paul's Cross, after the service, 6,000 people singing together." Soon "a psalm-singer" became another name for a Protestant.

The complete metrical Psalter, known as the *Old Version*, but more popularly as "Sternhold and Hopkins," was published in 1562. It was bound up with the Bible and continued to be printed as the authorized version of the Psalms in England until the beginning of the 19th century.

To the Puritans the singing of the psalms was the most sacred act of public worship, and it was important to them that the version used should be as good as possible. When the Westminster Assembly of Divines set itself the impossible task of trying to devise a basis for conformity of church organization, belief and worship throughout the kingdom, two rival versions competed for support. The House of Commons ordered that the version of Francis Rous, MP for Truro in the Long Parliament, "and none other," should be used in all churches and chapels. The

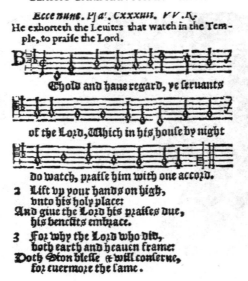

Part of a page of Sternhold and Hopkins Psalmody
as printed in many editions of the Bible after the Reformation

House of Lords favored the rival version of William Barton,
a zealous minister in Leicester. So there was deadlock and
neither version came into use in England, though Rous's
version was accepted in Scotland.

For a time it seemed as if the Lutheran model of
hymnody might become accepted in Scotland, but the influence of Knox arrested that tendency and inclined Scotland to resort to the Genevan example of psalmody as
used by Calvin. Knox had been minister to the congregation of English-speaking refugees in Geneva for two years,
and when he returned to Scotland in 1559 he brought with
him the Anglo-Genevan Psalter. With characteristic independence the Scots revised it thoroughly before using it.
The new version was issued in 1564 and remained the
authorized Scottish Psalter until 1650.

The need for a more modern version became evident in
the 17th century. The union of the crowns of England and
Scotland had taken place, there had been great changes in

Francis Rous

language, and the appearance of the Authorized Version of the Bible in 1611 made a new version of the psalms highly desirable. James I had the hardihood to try to furnish one of his own. Charles I attempted to force the use of this Psalter upon the Scottish people, having it bound up with Laud's liturgy and requiring it to be brought into use. Jenny Geddes gave him the answer when, in St. Giles, she threw a stool at the Dean's head!

The commissioners who represented Scotland when the Westminster Assembly of Divines convened in 1643 were all notable men, including the famous Samuel Rutherford. One of the tasks of the Assembly was to agree on a common book of praise. The Scots recommended the adoption of Rous's version, though again, as in 1557, asserting their right to revise and amend it. Rous's version formed the basis of the Metrical Psalter finally approved and authorized for use in 1650. It is used in Scotland to this day, though Rous, if he were alive, would now have difficulty in identifying it as his own handiwork! Psalm 23 is attributed to him, though only a few lines are as he actually wrote them. This Psalter became very dear to the hearts of

Scottish people. The hills and glens of Scotland must often have echoed to the tunes of the psalms as they were sung by the hunted Covenanters.

A number of the metrical psalms from the 1650 Psalter are to be found in modern hymnbooks, for example:

> *Ye gates, lift up your heads on high;*
> *Ye doors that last for aye,*
> *Be lifted up, that so the King*
> *Of glory enter may!*
> *But who of glory is the King?*
> *The mighty Lord is this,*
> *E'en that same Lord that great in might*
> *And strong in battle is.*

The best-known metrical psalm is, of course, "The Lord's my Shepherd," which is found in almost every modern hymnbook. As we read or sing it we see how close it is to the original words of Psalm 23:

> *Goodness and mercy all my life*
> *Shall surely follow me;*
> *And in God's house for evermore*
> *My dwelling-place shall be.*

7

RICHARD BAXTER

(1615–91)

Lord, it belongs not to my care
Whether I die or live;
To love and serve Thee is my share,
And this Thy grace must give.

If life be long, I will be glad
That I may long obey;
If short, yet why should I be sad
To soar to endless day?

THIS hymn of Richard Baxter's, to which we give special attention, is part of a much longer poem called "The Covenant and Confidence of Faith." Its first two verses—written by Baxter as one stanza—express the contentment of the believer who knows he is in covenant relationship with God. He leaves his life in the hands of his divine Saviour and, desiring only to serve Him, is not anxious whether this shall continue to be on earth or whether he shall be called early to serve Him in heaven.

Christ leads me through no darker rooms
Than He went through before;
And he that to God's kingdom comes
Must enter by this door.

Come, Lord, when grace has made me meet
Thy blessed face to see;
For if Thy work on earth be sweet,
What will Thy glory be?

This section of the hymn refers to the consolation of the believer at the thought of death and of entering upon his eternal inheritance. He finds this consolation in his personal relationship to, and affection for, Christ. Baxter speaks of himself as at the door of eternity. The door here refers to death, but the Christian mind thinks of Christ who said "I am the door," and who has "tasted death for every man." In his *Saints' Everlasting Rest*, Baxter says, "The way is strange to me but not to Christ."

> *Then I shall end my sad complaints*
> *And weary, sinful days;*
> *And join with the triumphant saints*
> *Who sing Jehovah's praise.*

> *My knowledge of that life is small*
> *The eye of faith is dim:*
> *But 'tis enough that Christ knows all,*
> *And I shall be with Him.*

The hymn ends with thoughts of rest, joy and praise, for others as well as for oneself. For Baxter himself the thought of the rest and joy of heaven was very precious because of the bodily affliction, the persecution and imprisonment he knew on earth.

Another of Baxter's hymns still found in many hymn-books is—

> *Ye holy angels bright,*
> *Who wait at God's right hand.*

Parts of this hymn speak to us of the checkered, difficult days in which he lived and labored for Christ—for example:

> *Take what He gives,*
> *And praise Him still*
> *Through good and ill,*
> *Who ever lives.*

Unlike Germany, there were few hymn-writers in the British Isles before Baxter and his contemporaries. Yet there were some lone voices, like that of St. Patrick in the fourth century who wrote what is commonly known as "St. Patrick's Breastplate"

> *I bind unto myself today*
> *The strong Name of the Trinity.*

St. Columba of Iona, who lived in the sixth century, left some relics of verse, and the Venerable Bede wrote and sang hymns to his Saxon harp in the monastery of Jarrow in the eighth century. Much Latin verse was written in the Middle Ages, but nothing in the vernacular. Little more is heard until George Herbert, who wrote his rather quaint verses in the early years of the seventeenth century. Baxter was very fond of Herbert and called him "that heavenly poet of noble extract." Herbert had a fine lyrical sense and wrote good verse, but he never thought of himself as a hymn-writer, or that his verse would ever be used in public as it has been. Had he known this, he might have modified its quaintness. Then, very nearly contemporary with Baxter, we have John Milton, Jeremy Taylor, Henry Vaughan and others.

Richard Baxter was the first British hymn-writer who seems to have felt strongly that hymns should be sung in churches in public worship. He held that hymns had been sung from the beginning and thought it beyond doubt that hymns more suitable to gospel times should now be written and used. His own hymns were definitely intended for congregational singing.

&

Baxter's life is a reflection of the history of England during the seventeenth century. He was born during the reign of James I and died two or three years after the arrival of William and Mary. He witnessed the long struggle for liberty between King and Parliament, the Civil War, the Puritan triumph under Cromwell, the restoration of the monarchy under Charles II, and the orgy of vice which it inaugurated. During his childhood the Pilgrim Fathers founded the states of New England, the Puritan exodus continuing for ten years and more.

Richard Baxter

Richard Baxter was born at Rowton in Shropshire. His father lived rather a "loose" life, and until he was ten he lived in the same house in which he was born, that of his maternal grandparents. From the age of six his education suffered from a series of tutors, some of whom were almost illiterate. Subsequently he went to Wroxeter school until he was nine. Even there he seems to have been given only the rudiments of education, learning no mathematics or science and very little Greek and Latin. Instead of going to Oxford he was placed under the chaplain to the Council at Ludlow, who neglected his pupil, leaving him to read what he would in the library of Ludlow Castle. All through his life Baxter deplored his lack of good academic training.

When he was ten Richard returned to his own home. By that time his father had become a Christian, chiefly through the reading of the Scriptures, and he encouraged his son to do the same. The petty persecutions to which his father was subjected opened Richard's eyes to the true character of the Christian religion. At about the age of fifteen he read several books which were of spiritual benefit to him. "Thus," he says, "without any means but books, God was pleased to resolve me for Himself."

After a short experience as an attendant at Court his strong religious convictions led him to leave a life which was uncongenial to him, in order to follow his own original intention of becoming a minister of the gospel. He placed himself under the tuition of the parish clergyman of Wroxeter, and although his studies were interrupted by illness he pursued them earnestly and passed his examinations. At that time he had no scruples about conformity and was ordained in the Church of England, serving first as an assistant minister at Bridgnorth, then moving to Kidderminster where, with interruptions, he labored for twenty years. He sympathized with the Parliamentarians and was for a time chaplain to one of Cromwell's regiments in the Civil War. In spite of recurring ill health his labors were unremitting in whatever capacity he served. Sometimes he was obliged to "rest" and during one of these periods he wrote his famous book, *The Saints' Everlasting Rest*.

When Baxter went to Kidderminster it was a very immoral place. His preaching was intensely earnest and as practical as it was spiritual. His own prayerful self-denying life bore witness to what he preached. He taught old and young the doctrines of the Faith. He took care also to circulate good books among those who could read. The effects of his labors in Kidderminster were remarkable. The people ceased to be notorious for their impiety and profanity, and became known for their sobriety and godliness. The sounds of praise and prayer were heard in very many households.

Baxter did not marry until after leaving Kidderminster. His wife, Margaret, came from a Shropshire "county" family and had been brought up among the comforts of life. She attended Baxter's church in Kidderminster and for her his sermons were never too long! At first the hero of her girlish worship, he became the pastor of her awakened soul; then she loved and married him and was his devoted helper during nineteen years of married life, happy to share the hardness of his lot.

Although Baxter was a conformist, an Anglican minister, he was very unorthodox and non-Anglican in some of his practices, and his sympathies were increasingly with the Nonconformists. He hated fanaticism and shared the reproach heaped upon all men of moderation in times of stress. "He grew too Puritan for the Bishops and he was too Episcopalian for the Presbyterians." So, inevitably, his position was rather a lonely one and he exposed himself to being misunderstood. He was also a man of independent thought and outspoken opinion. He once went so far as to rebuke Cromwell for assuming supreme power in the state, for while sympathetic with Cromwell and the Parliamentarians he also defended the monarchy. It has been well said that "no saner or more saintly spirit appeared amid the violent partisanship and fierce contentions of the time. He incurred the animosity of both sides by his independence and the steadfastness with which he pleaded for the unpopular grace of toleration."

After nearly twenty years of ministerial labor in Kidderminster he was appointed one of the chaplains to Charles II soon after the Restoration in 1660. He declined a bishopric, asking only to be allowed to return to his flock at Kidderminster. While in London, and before the Act of Uniformity of 1662, which required all ministers of the Established Church to conform in every detail to the Prayer Book, he preached in several parts of London. Three days before the Act came into operation he seceded from the Church of England and unostentatiously retired to Acton.

He remained there while the Conventicle Act was in force, but the eyes of the Royalists were on him and even preaching in his own house led to six months' imprisonment. This imprisonment was pleasant because his wife shared it with him, being then and always, until her death in 1681, a true helpmeet.

On release from prison, following the Declaration of Indulgence, he took out a license as a Nonconformist minister and in 1673 he began to give lectures in London twice a week, while continuing to write books. He later built a chapel in Bloomsbury but was not allowed to use it. Instead he was harassed by threats and fines, and finally he was charged with sedition in his writings and brought to trial before the notorious Judge Jeffreys. Being unable to pay the fine required of him he went again to prison, but by this time his wife had died and he did not have her comfort. However, he was not without human sympathy, as Matthew Henry and other friends sought out this "prisoner of the Lord" and ministered to him. After release from prison he assisted another minister for a few years, then, when he could no longer preach, he still labored with his pen, writing in all about sixty books.

In his old age he lived to see the milder and better days that dawned with the quiet Revolution of 1688 and the accession of William and Mary to the throne. In his intercourse with Cromwell and Charles II he showed himself superior to the undue influence of office or man. By his calm courage in the presence of Judge Jeffreys he proved that he possessed the martyr spirit. As well as being the forerunner of a long line of English hymn-writers, he was an earnest advocate of the missionary cause at a time when few had begun to favor it. His end was calm and triumphant. When someone whispered to him of the good he had done by his books, he faintly answered, "I was but a pen and what praise is due to a pen?" During his last illness another asked him how he was and he answered, "Almost well."

8

JOHN MASON

(c. 1646–94)

I've found the pearl of greatest price,
My heart doth sing for joy;
And sing I must, for Christ is mine,
Christ shall my song employ. . . .

Christ Jesus is my All-in-all,
My comfort and my love;
My life below, and He shall be
My glory-crown above.

VERY little is known of the early days of John Mason, except that he was born in the village of Strixton in Northamptonshire and that he was brought up there. When school days were over he entered Clare Hall, Cambridge, but even his college days seem to have passed without memorable incident.

At last we come to a definite date! In 1668 he was presented to the living* of Stantonbury in Buckinghamshire and in 1674 he became vicar of Water-Stratford in the same county. This village is now, as we suppose it to have been then, a mere hamlet, containing little of interest except its old church. Here John Mason lived and died; here his remarkable ministry was exercised; and here he wrote his *Songs of Praise.*

We can learn what kind of man he was with the help of

---

* The position of vicar or rector with income and/or property.

those who knew him. Richard Baxter, who preceded him by about thirty years, calls him "the glory of the Church of England," and also tells us that "the frame of his ministry was so heavenly . . . , his discourse of spiritual things so weighty, that it charmed all that had any spiritual relish." Mason was "a light in the pulpit and out of it." His grandson tells us that he prayed six times a day, twice alone, twice with his wife and twice with his family. We have, then, a picture of a man of true godliness who lived a life of quiet contemplation and devoted service in uncongenial times. Like Richard Baxter he lived through the days of Charles I, Cromwell, Charles II, James II and William and Mary. He belonged to the generation which saw a Commonwealth, a Restoration and a Revolution. A time of civil war and bloodshed was followed by a short period of peace, leading into a time of license and debauchery in which royalty participated.

In his country parish in Buckinghamshire Mason was far removed from the events of the outside world, and he seems to have taken very little notice of them. He was quietly doing the will of Him whose kingdom cannot be moved. His friendship with Richard Baxter and with Thomas Shepherd, the Nonconformist minister of Braintree in Essex, seems to indicate that he was not out of sympathy with Nonconformity. Thomas Shepherd had seceded from the Church of England and started his work in Braintree in a barn, until a chapel was built for him. With Mason he published a book of poems called *Penitential Cries*.

At the close of Mason's life a strange episode took place. It was connected with the preaching of a sermon on the Ten Virgins, entitled "The Midnight Cry," a sermon proclaiming the close approach of the Second Advent. Mason's thoughts had become concentrated upon the reappearing of the Saviour. His daily communings with the Lord Jesus had made him long to see His face. This longing had grown into hoping, and hoping into something like realization. One night as he lay awake about a month before his death, he turned and, he tells us, saw a vision of Jesus sitting in the room. He then made the mistake of speaking too much to others of his vision, which to him was a premonition of the Second Advent. He was sure that the Lord would come quickly and that He would come to Water-Stratford! People came from all the villages around, either out of curiosity or to witness and share in the Advent. The crowds remained for weeks, filling every available corner in the village. There were scenes of extraordinary excitement. It was the old story of dogmatic assertions about the Lord coming again at a particular time not being realized. Hope slowly died, the crowds dispersed, and the dream of the Second Advent vanished. It is easy for us to smile at vain hopes such as those of John Mason, but we should remember that it was a time of religious as well as political excitement.

Mason's fond hope had gone, the dream had vanished, but the reality of his hope in the Lord remained. His last words were, "I am full of the loving-kindness of the Lord."

The spirit of Mason's book, *Songs of Praise* (1683), may be gathered from words in the preface: "Our blessed Saviour, immediately before He went out to suffer, sang an hymn and His disciples sang with Him. After His ascension into heaven the apostles sang the praises of God and taught others to do so. After them the primitive Christians sang, and so must the Christians of this time." Thus Mason began to sing, and his songs are worth hearing, although only a few of them appear in modern hymnbooks. They have a homespun quality about them; they are not smooth-flowing but have a certain roughness of style. In his forty hymns and songs he gives thanks for our "creation, preservation and all the blessings of this life, but above all for the inestimable love of God . . . for the means of grace and the hope of glory." An example of one of his hymns is:

> *How shall I sing that majesty*
> *Which angels do admire?*
> *Let dust in dust and silence lie;*
> *Sing, sing, ye heavenly choir.*
> *Thousands of thousands stand around*
> *Thy throne, O God most high;*

Ten thousand times ten thousand sound
Thy praise; but who am I? . . .

How great a being, Lord, is Thine,
Which doth all beings keep!
Thy knowledge is the only line
To sound so vast a deep.
Thou art a sea without a shore,
A sun without a sphere;
Thy time is now and evermore,
Thy place is everywhere.

The hymn from which we quoted at the beginning of this chapter is more smooth-flowing and many aspects of truth are expressed in it. There seems to be a polish about it which some of his more "homespun" hymns lack. Its verses not previously quoted run:

Christ is my Prophet, Priest and King;
My Prophet full of light,
My great High Priest before the throne,
My King of heavenly might.

For He indeed is Lord of lords,
And He is King of kings;
He is the Sun of Righteousness,
With healing in His wings.

Christ is my peace; He died for me,
For me He gave His blood;
And, as my wondrous sacrifice,
Offered Himself to God.

It has rightly been said of Mason that "his name is among the honored few who wrote hymns prior to the time when Watts introduced a new era in the history of hymn-writing." His *Songs of Praise* ran through many editions and influenced both Watts and Wesley, who grafted some of his terse lines into their own stanzas.

9

THOMAS KEN

(1637–1711)

MORNING HYMN
Awake, my soul, and with the sun
Thy daily stage of duty run;
Shake off dull sloth, and joyful rise
To pay thy morning sacrifice.

EVENING HYMN
Glory to Thee, my God, this night,
For all the blessings of the light:
Keep me, O keep me, King of kings,
Beneath Thine own almighty wings.

Forgive me, Lord, for Thy dear Son,
The ill that I this day have done;
That with the world, myself and Thee,
I, ere I sleep, at peace may be.

THOMAS KEN was born at Berkhamsted in 1637. His mother died when he was five, his father before he was fourteen, and he grew up under the guardianship of Isaac Walton, author of *The Compleat Angler*, who had married his elder sister Ann. During holidays Walton would take Thomas with him to the banks of the stream where they watched and angled for the spotted trout. His sister educated him at home for a time, teaching him also of spiritual things; then, when he was thirteen, he was sent to Winchester School. At eighteen he went to Hart Hall in Oxford, the present Hertford College. After taking his degree he became a tutor, then a clergyman at the age of twenty-five. For several years he served in small parishes in Essex and the Isle of Wight, then he returned to Winchester as Rector of Woodhay and Prebendary of Winchester.

It was during this period in Winchester that he published *A Manual of Prayers* for the use of the scholars of Winchester College. Reference is made in this book to three hymns for morning, evening and midnight respectively, the scholars being told to "Be sure to sing the morning and evening hymn devoutly, remembering that the psalmist assures you that it is a good thing to tell of the loving-kindness of the Lord in the morning and of His truth in the night season." Probably the hymns were printed as leaflets and fastened to the wall of the dormitory beside the boys' beds. It has been said that the midnight hymn was not used by the scholars because boys sleep well! It seems that this *Manual of Prayers* was useful to George Whitefield in the early days of his college life. Ken himself used to sing the hymns to the accompaniment of the viola or the spinet.

Thomas Ken left Winchester for a time to be chaplain to the Princess Mary of Orange at the Hague, Netherlands. He was dismissed for his faithful remonstrance against a case of immorality at court and returned to Winchester. Strangely, a similar act of faithfulness at Winchester had the reverse effect, as it led to the offer of a bishopric! He refused Nell Gwynne, the mistress of Charles II, the use of his home when Charles came to Winchester, and the easy-going King, either from humor or out of respect for Ken's honesty, not long afterwards appointed him to the bishopric of Bath and Wells. It has been said that on one occasion the King left a social gathering, saying he must go to hear Ken "tell him of his faults." Among many acts of compassion and generosity while a bishop, Ken ministered to the prisoners after an insurrection in favor of the Duke of Monmouth, who fought to take the crown from James, and to those who were sentenced during the "Bloody Assizes," at which Judge Jeffreys inflicted savage sentences on condemned prisoners. The latter was also going from town to

Thomas Ken

town, condemning the misguided country folk and erecting gallows wherever he went. Ken appealed to the King to stop this cruel assize, but instead the King rewarded Jeffreys for his "faithful service."

Ken attended the Duke of Monmouth to the gallows, preaching repentance to him. Previously he had also been one of the bishops at Charles' deathbed. He was one of the seven bishops who refused to read the Declaration of Indulgence (a declaration introduced by James II to favor his Roman Catholic friends), and were imprisoned in the Tower of London by James II for their refusal. At their trial, however, they were triumphantly acquitted. On the accession of William III, after some hesitation, Ken refused to take the necessary oaths, though his attitude as a "nonjuror" was marked by a conciliatory spirit. In 1691 he was deprived of his see. His kind friend Lord Weymouth received Ken into his home at Longleat (Somerset) for his remaining years. He survived all the deprived prelates and after years of suffering died at Longleat in 1711. Those who have visited Longleat, the beautifully situated home of the present Marquess of Bath, the descendant of Lord Weymouth, will realize what a haven it must have been for the persecuted and weary bishop. The library at Longleat, which contains one of the finest collections of books in any private home, is called the "Bishop Ken Library" and is not open to the public. In the grounds, high above the graceful Elizabethan mansion and looking over it and the beautiful valley in which it is situated, is an area called "Heaven's Gate." Local tradition says that it was here that Ken wrote many of his hymns. He was buried in Frome church just as the sun was rising, while those present sang his hymn, "Awake, My Soul, and With the Sun."

The saintliness of Ken's character, with its combination of boldness, gentleness, modesty and love, has been universally recognized. The verdict of Macaulay, with which Ken would doubtless have disagreed, is that he approached "as near as human infirmity permits to the ideal perfection of Christian virtue."

None of Ken's other hymns rank with the three great hymns written at Winchester. In their original forms they were much longer than those found in our hymnbooks today. Extracts from the "Morning Hymn" show the manly godliness, the lively conscience, and the sense of duty of the poet:

> *Thy precious time misspent redeem,*
> *Each present day thy last esteem;*
> *Improve thy talent with due care;*
> *For the great day thyself prepare.*

> *Let all thy converse be sincere;*
> *Thy conscience as the noonday clear;*
> *Think how all-seeing God thy ways*
> *And all thy secret thoughts surveys.*

The "Evening Hymn" shows his spirit of humility and trust:

> *Teach me to live, that I may dread*
> *The grave as little as my bed;*
> *Teach me to die, that so I may*
> *Rise glorious at the judgment day.*
>
> *O may my soul on Thee repose,*
> *And may sweet sleep mine eyelids close,*
> *Sleep that may me more vigorous make*
> *To serve my God when I awake. . . .*
>
> *Praise God, from whom all blessings flow;*
> *Praise Him, all creatures here below;*
> *Praise Him above, ye heavenly host;*
> *Praise Father, Son, and Holy Ghost.*

Montgomery, the hymn-writer, says that this well-known doxology is a masterpiece at once of amplification and compression: amplification on the phrase "Praise God" repeated in each line; and compression by exhibiting God as the object of praise, for all His blessings, by every creature here below and in heaven above. Probably there is no other verse so often sung by Christians of all denominations. William Grimshaw of Haworth used to sing it every morning as soon as he arose. There is a description in Harper's Magazine of its effect as sung at Queen Victoria's Diamond Jubilee Service, in front of St. Paul's Cathedral, where 10,000 people were gathered singing the age-old words. John Wesley gives some beautiful little incidents in his *Journal* which show how this doxology sprang to people's lips in supreme moments of joy.

10

ISAAC WATTS: HIS LIFE

(1674–1748)

L IKE Calvin, Isaac Watts had a powerful mind and dauntless spirit housed in a frail body and, like the famous Frenchman, his output of literary work, among other labors, was prodigious, in spite of physical weakness and much illness.

Isaac's mother was of Huguenot origin, able to trace her descent from the Protestants who fled from France after the notorious Massacre of St. Bartholomew's Day, 1572. His father, a scholastic man who also wrote poetry, kept a boarding school in Southampton when free to do so. He lived in the days of the persecution of Dissenters and would not move one inch towards conformity with Anglicanism. He was imprisoned twice and for two years sought refuge from his persecutors in London where anonymity was not difficult to maintain. Naturally he found it difficult to carry on his school: at one time he became a clothier (a dealer in cloth), and possibly at one time he was a shoemaker. Isaac's mother seems to have encouraged any poetic gift in her eight children, offering monetary reward for any effort they made. Her eldest child, Isaac, seemed to need no reward, his determination to excel being recorded in his earliest lines:

> *I write not for your farthing, but to try*
> *How I your farthing writers may outvie.*

During his childhood his education was carried on for the most part by his father, under whose guidance he be-

Isaac Watts

gan to learn Latin at the age of four! Before he was four-teen he had learned a good deal of Hebrew, Greek and French. Isaac made much progress in classical studies under the skilled tuition of his next tutor, Roger Pinhorne, a Southampton rector who maintained a Free Grammar School. When he was sixteen, serious thought had to be given to Isaac's future studies. He had given promise of outstanding academic ability, and a Southampton doctor offered to defray most of the cost of his support at either Oxford or Cambridge. Both universities required students to conform to the Anglican pattern, whereas Isaac was determined to throw in his lot with the Dissenters. He therefore chose to study at the Nonconformist Academy of Thomas Rowe.

Rowe was also the pastor of a neighboring church, Girdlers' Hall, and it was there that Watts first sought church membership. His time under Thomas Rowe must have benefited him spiritually as well as academically. At the age of twenty, Watts' formal education being complete, he returned to his Southampton home and spent two and a half years in reading, studying, and waiting upon God to know what He would have him to do. Probably the first thoughts of the role he was later to play in transforming one part of Christian worship had come into his mind. It was almost "by accident" that he began hymn-writing. In Southampton he once complained to his father of the lines in poor verse which were all they had to sing. His father suggested that if he were so dissatisfied he should attempt to compose something better. The challenge was accepted and on the following Sunday the young man was ready with the hymn, "Behold the Glories of the Lamb!" It was "lined" out in church at evening service and sung by the people with great delight. They encouraged him to continue his efforts and shortly he had produced over two hundred hymns.

From 1696 to 1702 Watts lived with Sir John Hartopp at Stoke Newington and was tutor to his son. Sir John was a staunch Nonconformist and heavy fines were inflicted on him because of his adherence to his principles. He was a man of deep sympathy with almost every department of literature and science; hence Watts could learn from the father while he taught the son. A deep bond of friendship was established between Sir John and his son's tutor. During the comparative seclusion of this period Watts' principles became firmly grounded, fitting him for the public duties of his long and active life.

Watts preached his first sermon on his twenty-fourth birthday at the Southampton Meeting House and the same year he became assistant to Dr. Isaac Chauncey, the pastor of Mark Lane Church, London, which later moved to Bury Street, not far from the Tower of London. Four years later, when Chauncey resigned his office, Watts was appointed pastor. He remained pastor until his death forty-six years later when he was by far the best-known of all London ministers. Under Watts' ministry the church prospered, and its diminutive preacher—his height was little more than five feet—was thought to be one of the best, if not the best, London preacher of the period. Although oratory was not his particular gift, he preached in clear, forceful language.

In public prayer he used "simple and unadorned language . . . with studied brevity."

In later years Watts' uncertain health made it necessary for him to have an assistant minister, who later became co-pastor with him. In 1712 he had gone on a visit of one week to Sir Thomas Abney at his seat at Theobalds, Herts. This visit led to his permanent residence there, or at Stoke Newington where Sir Thomas had another house. For the remainder of his life (thirty-six years) the poet-preacher found with Sir Thomas and Lady Abney a rural home just suited to his delicate health and to the pursuance of his laborious literary activities. Theobalds had the additional advantage of being within easy reach of his congregation, to whom he preached as often as his health allowed.

Dr. Watts was beloved and useful as a Christian pastor and preacher and his written works had an extensive circulation. He sketched out the plan of *The Rise and Progress of Religion in the Soul,* but growing infirmities prevented him from writing it and he handed the work over to Philip Doddridge, one of his chief friends. Watts took a deep interest in the progress of the book and expressed approval of the manner of its execution.

The Christian character of Watts was of the highest order. He was known for his humility and his generosity. His learning and godliness, his gentleness and largeness of heart, earned him the title of the Melanchthon of his day. He was noted for his tolerance towards those who were not of his own persuasion and enjoyed true Christian friendship and fellowship with Christians of other denominations. It is not necessary to say how zealous he was for the truths of the gospel and the cause of Christ, as this shines out through all that he wrote. He was a friendly person. Although his temperament and poor health required him to live a fairly secluded life he was no recluse, shutting himself off from social contacts. In his seclusion books were his chosen companions, but he maintained contact with the widespread Church of God by means of an extensive correspondence. He carried on a lively correspondence with New England and was much interested in the Awakening linked with the name of Jonathan Edwards.

John and Charles Wesley paid Watts a visit in 1738 and George Whitefield also visited him. In his *Journal* Whitefield speaks of Watts as "my worthy and honored friend Dr. Watts." Watts was the aged Dissenter accustomed to certain set forms of worship and he found it rather difficult to accept the unorthodox methods of the young, roving preacher! Yet to a friend he said, "My opinion is that Whitefield does more good by his wild notes than we do by our set music." At the age of seventy-five, Watts said he was "waiting God's leave to die." Thus he entered his rest. He was buried in the famous Bunhill Fields burying-ground among the sepulchres of such men as John Owen, Thomas Goodwin, John Bunyan and Joseph Hart. We can imagine the joy with which his ransomed soul entered the "land of pure delight where saints immortal reign." Later a memorial tablet was placed in Westminster Abbey, where it can still be seen.

11

ISAAC WATTS:
"PSALMS AND HYMNS
AND SPIRITUAL SONGS"

When I survey the wondrous cross,
On which the Prince of glory died,
My richest gain I count but loss,
And pour contempt on all my pride. . . .

Were the whole realm of nature mine,
That were an offering far too small;
Love so amazing, so divine,
Demands my soul, my life, my all.

I T has been said that Isaac Watts opened the sluice-gates to let the stream of psalmody and hymnody flow freely. As we write about Watts as a hymn-writer we hope to show that this statement is fully justified.

Watts describes the deplorable condition of psalmody in the seventeenth century thus: "To see the dull indifference, the negligent and thoughtless air that sits upon the faces of the whole assembly while the psalm is on their lips, might tempt even a charitable observer to suspect the fervor of inward religion." Yet, strangely, the obstacle to improvement was the determination of these very worshipers to allow no innovation to disturb this unhappy state of affairs. Something like a miracle was needed to produce a change, and genius of an unusual order was needed to work it. The man fitted to perform this miracle was Isaac Watts. His hymns were an assault on the unreasoning immobility of those who presented a stone wall of opposition to any change in the old psalmody. Millar Patrick writes, "Watts saw with the clear intuition of genius what needed to be done and alone he did it." All later hymn-writers, even when they excel him, are his debtors.

In the chapel at Southampton, where the Watts family worshiped, Barton's Psalter was the version in use. Enoch Watts, Isaac's brother, is quoted as saying, "Honest Barton chimes us asleep." There was no better version, so Watts conceived the bold scheme not only of writing a new version of the psalms but of weaving New Testament revelation into them so as to fit them for Christian lips. If psalms were to be metricized, rather than chanted as in the Church of England, Watts claimed the right to treat them freely and to transfuse them with the spirit of the gospel, so that they would be completely suitable for use in Christian worship. He felt that some psalms were unsuitable for use in public worship. In those that were suitable his aim was to see "David converted into a Christian." In 1719 Watts published *The Psalms of David imitated in New Testament language, together with Hymns and Spiritual Songs.* He claimed to be the first "to have brought the royal Author into the common affairs of the Christian life and led the Psalmist of Israel into the Church of Christ."

Sometimes the results of his modernization came very near the grotesque but at best they were indubitably great. We give three examples:

Psalm 100:

> *Before Jehovah's aweful throne,*
> *Ye nations, bow with sacred joy:*
> *Know that the Lord is God alone,*
> *He can create and He destroy.*

Psalm 72:

> *Jesus shall reign where'er the sun*
> *Doth his successive journeys run;*

HYMNS

AND

Spiritual Songs.

In Three BOOKS.

I. Collected from the Scriptures.
II. Compos'd on Divine Subjects.
III. Prepared for the Lord's Supper.

With an ESSAY

Towards the Improvement of Christian Psalmody, by the Use of Evangelical Hymns in Worship, as well as the Psalms of *David*.

By *I. WATTS*.

And they sung a new Song, saying, Thou art worthy, &c. for thou wast slain and hast redeemed us, &c. Rev. 5. 9.
Soliti essent (*i. e. Christiani*) convenire, carmenque Christo quasi Deo dicere. *Plinius in Epist.*

LONDON,
Printed by *J. Humfreys*, for *John Lawrence*, at the Angel in the *Poultrey*. 1707.

Title page of the first edition of Isaac Watts' Hymns, 1707

> *His kingdom stretch from shore to shore,*
> *Till moons shall wax and wane no more.*

and the very majestic hymn based on Psalm 90:

> *Our God, our help in ages past,*
> *Our hope for years to come,*
> *Our shelter from the stormy blast,*
> *And our eternal home.*

We can look with a lenient eye on Watts' failures in our gratitude for the triumphant results of his experiments in renovation.

In examining what Dr. Watts wrote we must always remember that he was hewing his way through unexplored territory and that his successors, not having his rough work to do, could polish and improve. He was hampered also by the fact that he was writing for congregations that were ignorant. His hymns had to be suitable to be announced and sung, line by line, by people many of whom were illiterate. A further limiting factor was that it was necessary for him to confine himself to a few well-known meters. Linguistically, it must be said that he was a son of the seventeenth, rather than of the eighteenth, century. The purging and purifying of the English language came later. Hence we find a contrast between Watts and Charles Wesley. Watts found no meter ready tamed for his use. Wesley found that work done for him. The wonder is not that Watts is sometimes rather rough and grotesque as compared with Wesley, but that Watts achieved as much as he did.

The Scriptures themselves command us to sing and give thanks in the name of Christ. So, argued Watts, if psalms could be made suitable for Christian needs, why could not lyrical expression be given to aspects of Christian thought for which the psalms could not provide? And why should we be forbidden to mention the name of Christ when God's revelation in Christ demands that we should Christianize our singing? Such arguments are unanswerable, but they would have been evaded if Watts had not supported them by supplying convincing examples of what he thought Christian hymns ought to be.

Watts' first hymn, "Behold the Glories of the Lamb!", was written, as we have said, in response to a challenge from his father. After that first attempt he wrote hymns in rapid succession; they were published in 1707; later his psalms and hymns were issued in one volume and passed into very wide use in Independent churches. The time came when, just as people had opposed the introduction of any hymns at all, they resisted the use of any hymns but those of Dr. Watts. As late as the middle of the nineteenth century 60,000 copies of his "Psalms and Hymns" were sold in one year.

Watts was modesty itself in his estimate of his own poetical powers. "I make no pretences," he said, "to the name of poet or polite writer. . . . I am ambitious to be a servant to the churches and a helper to the joy of the meanest Christian." His ambition was abundantly realized and he desired no other reward. Watts set for the long-distant future the example of what a congregational hymn should be. What made his hymns so popular was their faithfulness to Scripture, their consistent objectivity and freedom from introspection, and their exact suitability for giving voice to the thought and emotion of the believer. He showed that for popular use a hymn should have a single theme, organic unity, boldness of attack in the opening lines, and a definite progression of thought leading to a decisive climax. And a hymn should be short. Points such as these justified James Montgomery in saying that Watts was "the real founder of English hymnody."

What were the themes on which Watts delighted to dwell? He loved to write of the greatness, the majesty, the sheer magnificence of God. The "pure adoration" of Deity is found in his hymns. Yet the God who rules on high is not, to Watts, a far-removed abstraction but One who is personal and near.

> *This aweful God is ours,*
> *Our Father and our love.*

Watts also loves to write of the wonders and spaciousness of creation. An example of such a hymn is:

> *I sing the almighty power of God,*
> *That made the mountains rise,*
> *That spread the flowing seas abroad,*
> *And built the lofty skies.*

> *I sing the wisdom that ordained*
> *The sun to rule the day:*
> *The moon shines full at His command,*
> *And all the stars obey.*

Throughout Watts' hymns there is present the glory of Christ as the Son of God and the Son of Man, and as Prophet, Priest and King.

Such a hymn is:

> *Jesus, in Thee our eyes behold*
> *A thousand glories more*
> *Than the rich gems and polished gold*
> *The sons of Aaron wore.*

> *They first their own burnt offerings brought,*
> *To purge themselves from sin:*
> *Thy life was pure; without a spot,*
> *And all Thy nature clean. . . .*

> *But Christ, by His own powerful blood,*
> *Ascends above the skies,*
> *And in the presence of our God*
> *Shows His own sacrifice. . . .*

> *He ever lives to intercede*
> *Before His Father's face;*
> *Give Him, my soul, thy cause to plead,*
> *Nor doubt the Father's grace.*

Another feature of Watts' hymns is the stress placed in many of them upon the atoning work of Christ. What can surpass the stanza:

See from His head, His hands, His feet,
Sorrow and love flow mingled down;
Did e'er such love and sorrow meet,
Or thorns compose so rich a crown?

Another example in this section is:

Not all the blood of beasts,
On Jewish altars slain,
Could give the guilty conscience peace
Or wash away the stain.

But Christ, the heavenly Lamb,
Takes all our sins away;
A sacrifice of nobler name,
And richer blood than they.

Watts sings of almost every aspect of Christian experience:

Give me the wings of faith to rise

I'll praise my Maker while I've breath

Join all the glorious names
Of wisdom, love and power

I'm not ashamed to own my Lord

Two examples of the importance he attaches to the climax of a hymn are:

Where reason fails, with all her powers,
There faith prevails and love adores.

and

Should all the hosts of death,
And powers of hell unknown,
Put their most dreadful forms
Of rage and malice on,
I shall be safe, for Christ displays
Superior power, and guardian grace.

Watts' hymns had a great appeal for William Carey, pioneer missionary to India, who expressed the desire that the following lines should be engraved on his tombstone:

A wretched, poor and helpless worm,
On Thy kind arms I fall.

It is part of the last verse of the hymn, "How Sad Our State by Nature Is!"

There had been notable hymn-writers before Watts, but not one had set so clear and convincing an example. His crowning achievement was, that whereas none before him had succeeded in persuading the Church to accept hymns in its worship, he won an entrance for them. He broke the exclusive domination of the psalms. He vindicated the title of the gospel to a place in the praise of the Christian Church. The sluice gates were wide open; soon the stream was flowing fast.

PHILIP DODDRIDGE

(1702–51)

O God of Bethel! by whose hand
Thy people still are fed;
Who through this weary pilgrimage
Hast all our fathers led. . . .

O spread Thy covering wings around,
Till all our wanderings cease,
And at our Father's loved abode
Our souls arrive in peace.

T HE stream of English hymnody had been set flowing by Isaac Watts. Philip Doddridge was one of his first collaborators, writing many hymns which became tributary to the swelling stream. Doddridge and Watts were contemporaries, though Doddridge, being the younger of the two, was vigorous when Watts' strength was failing. They were kindred spirits and co-operated in some of their work, most notably in the writing of *The Rise and Progress of Religion in the Soul*. Watts wrote the outline of this, but could not do more because of failing health, so Doddridge completed the work and it was later published in his name.

According to the custom of the times, Doddridge wrote his hymns to illustrate and enforce the principal teachings of his sermons. They were sung at the close of the sermon, probably being given out line by line from the pulpit. Although Doddridge was urged to publish his hymns, he seemed rather reluctant to do so and they were collected and published after his death as a supplement to Dr. Watts' hymnbook.

The hymn "Ye Servants of the Lord" deserves special notice, being distinguished for its force, unity and closeness to Scripture:

> *Ye servants of the Lord,*
> *Each in his office wait,*
> *Observant of His heavenly Word,*
> *And watchful at His gate.*
>
> *Let all your lamps be bright,*
> *And trim the golden flame;*
> *Gird up your loins as in His sight,*
> *For holy is His Name. . . .*
>
> *O happy servant he,*
> *In such a posture found!*
> *He shall his Lord with rapture see,*
> *And be with honor crowned.*

Another favorite hymn written by Doddridge, which is excellent for any occasion of personal dedication, is:

> *O happy day, that fixed my choice*
> *On Thee, my Saviour and my God!*
> *Well may this glowing heart rejoice,*
> *And tell its raptures all abroad. . . .*
>
> *High heaven, that heard the solemn vow,*
> *That vow renewed shall daily hear,*
> *Till in life's latest hour I bow,*
> *And bless in death a bond so dear.*

Doddridge's hymns were plainly the progeny of Watts'. They may not have the power and richness of those of Watts, but they excel Watts in simplicity, serenity and tenderness. The hymn

> *Hark, the glad sound! the Saviour comes,*
> *The Saviour promised long;*

Philip Doddridge

Let every heart prepare a throne,
And every voice a song.

is one of the best examples of his style. This hymn is often included among Advent hymns, but it is a close paraphrase of Isaiah 61 as quoted in Luke 4 and was never meant to be just an Advent hymn.

Doddridge is said to have been singularly happy when administering the Lord's Supper, and a hymn he wrote for this occasion is one of his best. It combines feeling, structure and melody:

My God, and is Thy table spread?
And does Thy cup with love o'erflow?
Thither be all Thy children led,
And let them all its sweetness know. . . .

O let Thy table honoured be,
And furnished well with joyful guests;
And may each soul salvation see,
That here its sacred pledges tastes.

Revive Thy dying churches, Lord,
And bid our drooping graces live;
And more, that energy afford
A Saviour's grace alone can give.

Like Watts, Doddridge finds his true pleasure in praising God. Many of his hymns are on the theme of God's providence, as, for example, "O God of Bethel," of which we now quote the remaining verses:

Our vows, our prayers, we now present
Before Thy throne of grace:
God of our fathers, be the God
Of their succeeding race.

Through each perplexing path of life
Our wandering footsteps guide;
Give us each day our daily bread,
And raiment fit provide. . . .

Such blessings from Thy gracious hand
Our humble prayers implore;
And Thou shalt be our chosen God,
And portion evermore.

Doddridge also wrote missionary hymns which antedate by two generations the era of missionary expansion.

James Montgomery, who was born twenty years after the death of Doddridge, says of Doddridge's hymns, "They shine in the beauty of holiness; these offsprings of his mind are . . . lovely and acceptable, not for their human merit but for that fervent, unaffected love to God, His service and His people, which distinguishes them."

જ⁂

Philip Doddridge was born in 1702 in a house in one of the narrow, crowded streets of old London. He was the twentieth and last child of his parents and at birth was thought to be too feeble to live. His grandfather was one of the ministers ejected in 1662 in the reign of Charles II. His father was in business as an oilman. His mother, to whom he owed much, was the daughter of a Lutheran clergyman who had escaped from Prague when Protestants were being persecuted there. In one of the quaintly furnished rooms of their home was a wide open fireplace, displaying an array of Dutch tiles which represented Bible characters and scenes. It was in that charming recess that Philip's mother taught him the Scriptures.

After studying at Kingston Grammar School, at the age of thirteen Philip was placed under the instruction of Rev. Nathaniel Wood at St. Albans. There the orphan—for his parents had already died—found a "friend in need" in Rev. Samuel Clark, a Presbyterian minister. The fact that Doddridge began to keep a diary at the age of fourteen enables us to follow him through both the outward changes and the inward experiences of his spiritual life. At the age of seventeen, when he had given evidence of his godliness and aptitude for the ministry, he went to study in an academy at Kibworth, Leicestershire, run by Rev. John Jennings. He had been offered a university training by the Duchess of Bedford with a view to ordination in the Church of England. By declining this offer and going to Jennings' Academy he associated himself with the Dissenters, as Watts had done before him. The Academy subsequently moved to Hinckley. There Doddridge completed his studies and preached his first sermon at the age of twenty. The blessing of God attended the sermon and two people professed conversion afterwards.

His studies completed, Doddridge accepted the invitation to become the Congregational pastor at Kibworth, the quiet village where his college tutor had ministered in the same capacity. He called the people "a plain, honest, serious, good-natured people," adding, "I heartily love them myself and I meet with undissembled affection on their side." In 1729 the settled work of his life began when, yielding to the advice of Dr. Watts and others, he opened an "academy" at Market Harborough for the training of young men for the ministry. In the following year he became pastor of a church in Northampton. He moved his academy there and carried it on almost to the end of his life. Of the 200 students who received their training at his hands about 120 entered the ministry. The wide range of subjects taught—Hebrew, Greek, Algebra, Trigonometry, Watts' Logic, Philosophy, Divinity—shows the extent of Doddridge's learning. This was recognized by Aberdeen University which presented him with an honorary D.D.

The fame of Doddridge as a divine, together with his wide sympathies and gentle, unaffected goodness, won for him the friendship of others besides Watts, for example, Colonel Gardiner and James Hervey. Doddridge welcomed the work of Wesley and Whitefield and had the privilege of entertaining the latter. We have mentioned his book, *The Rise and Progress of Religion in the Soul*. This book was of

A tune as written by hand about the year 1750

great spiritual service to Wilberforce, whose own book, *A Practical View*, was a direct outcome of it. *The Rise and Progress* . . . was widely circulated, translated into several languages, and regarded by some as the most useful book of the eighteenth century. Doddridge's greatest prose work was *The Family Expositor*, which cost him many years of study. All the moments he could snatch from his numerous occupations were given to it. Doddridge gave strong support to mission work when it was looked upon with comparative indifference.

Doddridge married Mercy Maris of Worcester in 1730. Among rules for the daily conduct of his life he includes the following: "As a husband it shall be my daily care to keep up the spirit of religion with my wife, to recommend her to the Divine blessing, to manifest an obliging, tender disposition, and particularly to avoid anything which has the appearance of selfishness to which, amidst my various cares and labors, I may in some unguarded moments be liable." The strength of attachment on her husband's part received full response in the devotion of his wife. Her letters show this and at the same time indicate that she was a woman of intelligence and good judgment.

Doddridge never enjoyed robust health and died in his fifty-first year. To counteract consumption and to gain the benefit of warmer air he traveled to Lisbon in 1751. On his way there the mild breezes and the new scenery raised his spirits and he said to his wife, "I cannot express to you what a morning I have had. Such delightful and transporting views of the heavenly world is my Father now indulging me with as no words can express." He never returned to his homeland, for soon after his arrival in Lisbon he fell asleep in Jesus.

> *But O when that last conflict's o'er,*
> *And I am chained to earth no more,*
> *With what glad accents shall I rise*
> *To join the music of the skies!*

Soon shall I learn the exalted strains
*   Which echo through the heavenly plains;*
And emulate, with joy unknown,
*   The glowing seraphs round the throne.*

13

JOSEPH HART

(1712–68)

Come, ye sinners, poor and wretched,
Weak and wounded, sick and sore,
Jesus ready stands to save you,
Full of pity joined with power;
He is able,
He is willing; doubt no more! . . .

Come, ye weary, heavy-laden,
Bruised and broken by the fall;
If you tarry till you're better,
You will never come at all:
Not the righteous—
Sinners Jesus came to call.

THESE are two of the six verses of one of the better-known hymns of Joseph Hart. The other four verses are well worth reading.

Joseph Hart came to faith in Christ after many years of spiritual conflict, alternating between despair and hope, lapsing into sin, struggling against it, receiving a measure of enlightenment, then falling again. Before his conversion he looked upon himself as one for whom there remained no more sacrifice for sin, and he thought the lowest place in hell would be his portion. This "gospel" hymn epitomizes much of his bitter, long-lasting experience. He knew what it was to feel "poor and wretched, weak and wounded, sick and sore." He could sympathize with those who were "weary, heavy-laden, bruised and broken by the fall."

He was born in London about 1712. His parents were godly people and it is probable that they attended George Whitefield's ministry. Hart was well educated, although he did not go to the university. His main interest lay in classical studies, to which later he added the knowledge of Hebrew and Greek and in due course became a language teacher. He also edited translations from the classics, adding his own notes.

When he was about twenty-one Hart showed great anxiety about his soul. For about seven years he experienced a restless round of sinning and repenting, trying to amend his life, then falling again. A domestic affliction which came to him seems to have been the means of opening his eyes to his dangerous spiritual state. He longed to know Christ but realized that repentance and faith were the gift of God. Would God give them to him? He filled his mind with doctrine, but his life sank into a worse state of sinfulness, and a spiritual perversion persuaded him that Christ had

The Moravian Chapel, Fetter Lane

given him liberty to sin. For nine to ten years he continued thus, committing "all uncleanness with greediness" and infecting others also. From time to time some spiritual illumination seemed to break in on his darkness. He knew he was not a true Christian but he did not really see the necessity for Christ's death or its infinite value. But now the Spirit of God was working powerfully in him; he had deep exercise of soul which troubled him so much that he dared not close his eyes, even when dog-tired, "lest I should awake in hell." He began to "run backwards and forwards" to places of worship, occasionally receiving some comfort from the Word, but in general "everything served only to condemn me."

At last on Whitsunday 1757—at the age of forty-five—he was delivered from his cruel bondage while listening to a sermon in the Fetter Lane Moravian Chapel on the words, "Because thou hast kept the word of my patience, I also will keep thee from the hour of temptation, which shall come upon all the world, to try them that dwell upon the earth" (Rev. 3:10). On returning home Hart fell on his knees before God, and immediately "such light and comfort flowed into my heart as no words can paint. I cried out, 'What—me, Lord?' His Spirit answered in me, 'Yes, thee.' I threw my soul willingly into my Saviour's hands."

He then wanted to be used in turning souls to God, and soon a door was opened for him. It is said that his first sermon was preached at the Old Meeting House, St. John's Court, Bermondsey. In 1760, at the age of forty-eight, he became minister of Jewin St. Independent Chapel where he remained until his death only eight years later. They were fruitful years, and at his funeral, in the famous Bunhill Fields burial-ground, it is said that "20,000 people came to pay their final respects to the revered writer and pastor"— and, we might add, hymn-writer. He left a widow, who survived him for twenty-two years, and five children.

A strange life! More than twenty years of it was taken up with the secular employment of language teaching. He had a home life in which he fulfilled the role of husband

H Y M N S, &c.

COMPOSED

On · various · Subjects

WITH A

P R E F A C E,

CONTAINING

A BRIEF and SUMMARY ACCOUNT

OF THE

AUTHOR'S EXPERIENCE,

AND

The great Things that God hath done for his Soul.

By J. HART.

O sing unto the Lord a new Song ; for he hath done MARVELLOUS THINGS: *His right Hand, and his holy Arm hath gotten him the Victory.* Psal. xcviii. 1.

LONDON:

Printed by J. EVERINGHAM; and Sold by T. WALLER, in Fleet-street; G. KEITH, in Gracechurch-Street; and D. WILSON and D. DURHAM, opposite Buckingham-street in the Strand. 1759.

[Price Bound 1 s. 6 d.]

Title page of the first edition of Joseph Hart's Hymns, 1759 and father, but his inner life must often have resembled a battlefield, warring forces struggling for his soul. Then there followed the remarkable deliverance of his conversion, though even after this he was often sorely tempted. He had another remarkable experience when the Holy Spirit so revealed the sufferings of Christ to him, and he had such communion with the Lord, that his periods of darkness became fewer. He said of himself, "I confess myself a sinner still, and though I am not much tempted to outward gross acts of iniquity, yet inward corruptions and spiritual wickedness continually harass and perplex my soul and often make me cry out 'O wretched man that I am! Who shall deliver me from the body of this death?'"

Against such a background, and after such a deliverance, his preaching must have been powerful. He knew so well the need of his hearers, as another verse of our hymn illustrates:

> Let not conscience make you linger,
> Nor of fitness fondly dream;
> All the fitness He requireth
> Is to feel your need of Him:
> This He gives you;
> 'Tis the Spirit's rising beam.

The hymns of Joseph Hart are little known at the present day, except in certain Strict Baptist churches, probably being too "experiential" for modern Christians. Hart's hymns have a spiritual quality all their own, as will be realized by all who care to turn to a hymnbook and read them. His hymns are evangelical and his experience-oriented language is suited to those who have also experienced severe conflict and conviction of sin. He stresses the need of the sinner and of the believer to "feel" at every stage of their experience, but this emphasis never causes him to forsake the objective gospel. This point can be illustrated by a few verses from his hymn on the Holy Spirit:

> Come, Holy Spirit, come,
> Let Thy bright beams arise;

Dispel the sorrow from our minds,
  The darkness from our eyes. . . .

Revive our drooping faith,
  Our doubts and fears remove,
And kindle in our breasts the flame
  Of never-dying love. . . .

Convince us of our sin,
  Then lead to Jesus' blood;
And to our wondering view reveal
  The secret love of God.

Hart had a true poetic gift, but he rarely allowed himself to use poetic language. His style is unequaled for power and terseness of expression. He dwells much on the sufferings and vicarious sacrifice of Christ and on His priestly office, presenting Him as the one who is able to save to the uttermost all that come to God by Him. He handles most aspects of Christian truth as an able minister of Christ, gifted with a poetic talent.

Most Christians know—and most hymnbooks contain—the two verses:

How good is the God we adore,
  Our faithful, unchangeable Friend!
His love is as great as His power,
  And knows neither measure nor end!

'Tis Jesus, the First and the Last,
  Whose Spirit shall guide us safe home;
We'll praise Him for all that is past,
  And trust Him for all that's to come.

But how many know that these triumphant words were written by Joseph Hart?

14

NICOLAUS LUDWIG VON ZINZENDORF

(1700–60)

Jesus, Thy blood and righteousness
My beauty are, my glorious dress;
Midst flaming worlds, in these arrayed
With joy shall I lift up my head. . . .

This spotless robe the same appears
When ruined nature sinks in years;
No age can change its glorious hue,
The robe of Christ is ever new. . . .

O let the dead now hear Thy voice!
Now bid Thy banished ones rejoice!
Their beauty this, their glorious dress,
Jesus the Lord our Righteousness.

(tr. by John Wesley)

NICOLAUS Ludwig von Zinzendorf, the founder of Herrnhut and chief man among the United Moravian Brethren, was born in Dresden in 1700, the son of Count Zinzendorf who held high office under the Elector of Saxony. The Count died when Nicolaus was six weeks old and, as his mother remarried, his education was entrusted to his maternal grandmother. She was a learned lady, linked with Pietism, a religious movement which began in Germany at the end of the seventeenth century.

Even as a child Zinzendorf gathered children to pray with him, and when at the age of eleven he went to study at Halle under A. H. Francke, the celebrated Pietist, he formed himself and his young companions into a religious order. In 1716 his uncle, General Zinzendorf, who was his guardian, sent him to Wittenberg University where Lutheran orthodoxy was preferred to Pietism. He was to study law, but the change of place and purpose did not turn him from religious pursuits or from his resolve to be a Christian minister.

A period of travel followed and at twenty-one he entered upon his official duties as a judge and member of the Council in the Electorate of Saxony. His mind was still devoted to Christian work and in 1722 he bought the estate of Berthelsdorf, rebuilt the mansion, and appointed J. A. Rothe, an earnest Christian and a good hymn-writer, as pastor. In the same year he married Erdmuth Dorothy, a woman of talent and godliness, a real helpmeet for him. They had twelve children, several dying in infancy. On marriage he transferred his property to his wife so that, unhindered, he might give himself wholly to the service of Christ.

Shortly afterwards he heard of the sufferings the Moravian Brethren were enduring under the Austrian government and expressed his readiness to receive the persecuted refugees on his estate. (The Moravians were the followers of John Huss in Moravia, descendants of the faithful few who had never yielded to Greek or Roman Churches.) In 1722 Christian David, a carpenter and a converted Roman Catholic, felled the first tree and with a few companions began to build their dwelling near Berthelsdorf. The settlement was called Herrnhut, i.e., "Under the protection of the Lord," the word hut meaning protection and pasture. To this settlement, which grew by the arrival of fresh immigrants, Zinzendorf gave much of his property and his time and energies. He bore with them in their strifes, saved them from division, and defended them from misrepresentation and persecution. In 1731 he resigned his public du-

Nicolaus Ludwig von Zinzendorf

ties in order to devote himself entirely to its spiritual interests. In order to obtain the requisite qualification to act as assistant pastor he went to two theological colleges. Later he went on an evangelical mission to Denmark, Holland, Prussia and England, but his later years were devoted without reservation to the spiritual good of Herrnhut. As he drew near to death he was filled with joy as he saw the love that prevailed among the brethren and the success which had attended their labors in the world. His last words were, "I am going to the Saviour. If He does not wish to employ me any longer here below, I am quite ready to go to Him, for I have nothing else to keep me here."

Although one of the worthiest of men, Zinzendorf had to bear the misrepresentation of friends as well as the opposition of enemies. He was continually spoken against. To the men of sects, Zinzendorf, owing to his charity and readiness to receive truth from every quarter, seemed to be a latitudinarian. To men of expediency his simplicity of life and freedom from worldliness seemed strange and unreasonable. To his honor it must be said that, having devoted his life to a great spiritual enterprise, he was singularly free from personal ostentation and self-assertion.

Zinzendorf's prose works were numerous, but our interest lies in the hymns which he wrote. He was writing hymns all his life, as a child and in old age, amid the excitement of Paris and in the quietness of Berthelsdorf. Some of his best hymns were written on his voyage to America in 1741, although "Jesus, Thy Blood and Righteousness" was written during his return journey from the island of St. Thomas in the West Indies. There was a period between 1740 and 1750 when his hymns gave expression to compassion and gratitude for the sufferings of Christ rather than to the Scriptural view of the meaning and value of the Atonement. Later he realized that he had been sidetracked and he suppressed these hymns.

Zinzendorf wrote about 2,000 hymns in all, many extemporaneously. He says, "After the discourse I generally announce another hymn appropriate to the subject. When I cannot find one I compose one. I say, in the Saviour's name, what comes into my mind."

In his *Dictionary of Hymnology* Julian says,

> The keynote of Zinzendorf's hymns and of his religious character was a deep and earnest personal devotion to and fellowship with the crucified Saviour. This is seen even in his worst pieces where it is his perverted fervor that leads him into objectionable familiarity with sacred things. If his self-restraint had been equal to his imaginative and productive powers he would have ranked as one of the greatest German hymn-writers. Many of his hymns are worthy of note and are distinguished by a certain noble simplicity, true sweetness, lyric grace, unshaken faith in the reconciling grace of Christ, entire self-consecration, willingness to spend and be spent in the Master's service, and fervent brotherly love.

Hymns by Zinzendorf which are still found in our

hymnbooks include:

> *Jesus, still lead on,*
>   *Till our rest be won;*
> *And although the way be cheerless*
>   *We will follow, calm and fearless;*
> *Guide us by Thy hand*
>   *To our fatherland.*
>
> *If the way be drear,*
>   *If the foe be near,*
> *Let not faithless fears o'ertake us,*
>   *Let not faith and hope forsake us;*
> *For through many a foe,*
>   *To our home we go.*

This hymn used to be taught to the children in almost every religious German household.

Then there is a hymn more typical of Zinzendorf:

> *I thirst, Thou wounded Lamb of God,*
>   *To wash me in Thy cleansing blood;*
> *To dwell within Thy wounds; then pain*
>   *Is sweet, and life or death is gain.*
>
> *Take my poor heart, and let it be*
>   *Forever closed to all but Thee;*
> *Seal Thou my breast, and let me wear*
>   *That pledge of love forever there.*
>
>   *(tr. by John Wesley)*

As Charles Simeon, the well-known Anglican minister of Cambridge, was waiting in a churchyard, he read on a tombstone a verse from the hymn, "Jesus, Thy Blood and Righteousness":

> *When from the dust of death I rise*
>   *To claim my mansion in the skies,*
> *E'en then shall this be all my plea,*
>   *Jesus hath lived, hath died for me.*

He looked around for someone to whom it might be made a blessing, and seeing a young woman reading inscriptions on gravestones he called her attention to it, saying, "When you can say the same from your heart you will be happy indeed." The young woman was in trouble and much distressed. Simeon visited her home and had the joy of helping her. A year later he visited her again and found her living a consistent Christian life. This hymn has an abiding place in the hearts of Christians, many being comforted by it on their deathbeds. It was a favorite of Rowland Hill's and was sung at his funeral.

Herrnhut

In one way the important thing for us about these hymns of Zinzendorf's is not their literary merit, but the fact that they were the songs in which the congregation at Herrnhut sang themselves hoarse for the love of Christ. The visits of the Wesleys to the village of Herrnhut were very important to them. They were not in any sense disciples of Zinzendorf, but it was when they heard the hymns of Herrnhut that they found the answer to one of their own problems. By 1738, the year of their conversion, it had been troubling the two brothers for ten years or more. How was this zeal for the gospel to come to life among English people at large? They were helped to find the answer when they heard the people of Herrnhut singing their Moravian hymns.

15

JOHN WESLEY:
HIS LIFE
(1703–91)

JOHN WESLEY once told a Methodist friend that his experience might always be found in the following lines:

> *O Thou who camest from above,*
> *The pure celestial fire to impart,*
> *Kindle a flame of sacred love*
> *On the mean altar of my heart.*
>
> *There let it for Thy glory burn*
> *With inextinguishable blaze;*
> *And trembling to its source return,*
> *In humble prayer and fervent praise.*

It is also said that some of his preachers said to him, "Mr. Wesley, you often ask us about our current experience; we should like to be favored with yours." He replied, "Very well, I will tell you," and he gave his reply in the form of the third verse of the same hymn, written by his brother:

> *Jesus, confirm my heart's desire*
> *To work and speak and think for Thee;*
> *Still let me guard the holy fire,*
> *And still stir up Thy gift in me.*

"That is my experience," said Mr. Wesley, "Can any Christian give better?"

John Wesley, age 63

The thought of fire seems to have remained with Wesley all his life since, as a child, he was rescued by neighbors through an upper window when the Epworth rectory went up in flames. His mother called him "a brand plucked from the burning." She made vows on his behalf, saying "I do intend to be more specially careful of the soul of this child," and she was sure he had a special work to do. Samuel Wesley, John's father, was rector of Epworth in Lincolnshire. His father and grandfather had both been ejected from the Established Church in 1662 after the passing of the Act of Uniformity. John's mother, Susanna, was the daughter of an eminent Nonconformist divine, Samuel Annesley. She had nineteen children in twenty years. Her husband was never out of debt; the family often lacked the bare necessities of life, and it became her responsibility to look after the souls as well as the bodies of her numerous offspring. She was a remarkable woman, and in manhood as well as in childhood, John often deferred to her judgment in important matters.

Life was real and earnest in the Epworth rectory, and its disciplines were good preparation for the later Methodism of John and Charles. Susanna made herself responsible for the education of her sons until they went away to school, after which she pursued them with earnest letters. John was sent to Charterhouse in London and went from there to Christ Church, a college of Oxford University where he graduated. He then became a fellow of Lincoln College, Oxford, and became M.A. in 1726. Shortly afterward he was ordained and went to be curate to his father, but after two years he was summoned back to Oxford to assist in college tuition. He found established there a little band of "Oxford Methodists," nicknamed "The Holy Club," which included his brother Charles. It was largely in derision that they were called "Methodists." They followed a strenuous and consistent routine, including early rising, Bible reading and academic study, regular communion, the observance of fasts and church festivals, and visitation of the sick and those in prison. They read devotional classics together and shared Christian fellowship, meeting in one another's rooms but mainly in John's study, still to be seen in the inner quadrangle of Lincoln College.

The Rector of Epworth was aging, but John did not care for his older brother Samuel's suggestion that it was his duty to go to his father's help. On his father's death he went to London to present the Rector of Epworth's *Commentary on the Book of Job* to the Queen. While there he met some of the trustees of the colony of Georgia who were looking for someone to preach the gospel to the settlers and the Indians. Dr. Burton, an Oxford friend of Wesley's, introduced him to General Oglethorpe, the Governor of the colony, as a man eminently qualified for the work. Wesley hesitated on account of his mother, now a widow, but Susanna's noble reply was that if she had twenty sons she would be glad to see them all employed in this way.

From a distance Georgia looked like a paradise free from

Susanna Wesley

earthly entanglements, whereas in England the enemy kept coming in like a flood in spite of rules, short sleep, scant food or no food at all. John thought that in Georgia he would find the unspoiled children of nature and the "noble savage" of eighteenth-century tradition, and that there he could hope to direct all to heaven by his rules and his Holy Club methods. The prospect might have been pleasant but the reality was very unpleasant. He found a world of rape, murder and sin. There was no open door for work among the Indians, so he labored in Savannah amidst inconveniences and dangers, enduring all trials that he might preach the gospel (so far as he knew it) and do good to all who would receive it. His work was interrupted by an unhappy love affair which precipitated his return to England. During the return voyage he became conscious of a great change in his religious feelings. He says,

It is upwards of two years since I left my native country in order to teach the Georgian Indians the nature of Christianity, but what have I learned in the meantime? Why, what I least of all suspected, that I, who went to America to convert others, was never converted myself. . . . Being ignorant of the righteousness of Christ I sought to establish my own righteousness.

He arrived in England to find that Whitefield, under whom the religious movement soon known as Methodism had made great progress, had sailed for Georgia the day before. On his journey from Deal to London he was still under conviction of sin and concerned about a lack of assurance of forgiveness. Wesley had been favorably impressed by a company of Moravians on his outward journey and he met Moravians in London, Peter Böhler in particular.

One memorable night (May 24th, 1738) he went to a meeting in Aldersgate Street where someone was reading Luther's *Preface to the Epistle to the Romans*. There,

About a quarter before nine, while he was describing the change which God works in the heart through faith in Christ, I felt my heart strangely warmed. I felt I did trust in Christ, Christ alone, for salvation; and an assurance was given me that He had taken away my sins, even mine, and saved me from the law of sin and death.

From that moment, says Julian,

his future course was sealed, and for more than half a century he labored, through evil report and good report, to spread the everlasting gospel, traveling more miles, preaching more sermons, publishing more books and making more converts than any one man of his day or perhaps of any day, and dying at last, in harness, at the patriarchal age of 88.

But we cannot confine the life of Wesley to a nutshell so we will return to events subsequent to his conversion.

Three weeks after his conversion Wesley determined to retire for a short time to Germany, hoping that further contact with the Moravians would be a means, under God, of establishing his soul. So he went to Herrnhut, the Moravian headquarters, and saw for himself how the community there conducted itself. He met Zinzendorf at that time, though not actually at Herrnhut. Wesley now became concerned that new converts needed fellowship and teaching which they could not obtain in the Church of England. Did the warmth of fellowship at Herrnhut and the enthusistic singing of hymns which he witnessed there give an impetus to his own formation of "societies" which before long were springing up all over England?

On his return to England Wesley found that Whitefield had returned from Georgia and they soon became intimately associated. From this time the history of Wesley became merged in that of Methodism. He remained firmly Anglican, but being refused the use of Anglican pulpits he followed Whitefield's method of open-air preaching and shortly gave his sanction to lay preaching. In 1740 he broke with Moravians on doctrinal points, and before the year ended, for similar reasons, he had also broken with Whitefield, the result being two permanently distinct Methodist bodies. But the two men renewed and maintained their personal friendship until Whitefield's death in 1770.

Wesley's whole life as a Methodist evangelist can be described as "in journeyings often." He rode forty, fifty, even sixty miles a day, reading as he rode and sometimes preaching five times a day. Towards the end of his life he exchanged horseback for a chaise and so was not hindered by the most severe weather. His *Journals* are filled with graphic accounts of his preaching, and sometimes of his persecutions. On one occasion he was dragged by the hair through the streets of Walsall, his life being imperiled.

We have been looking at Wesley as a public figure, but what was he like as a man? In his earlier years as a preacher, angry men often abused his person and denounced his work. Amidst all their hot-tempered misrepresentations, the hotter they became the cooler he remained, neither losing his temper nor answering his accusers passionately. He ignored much that others considered the necessities of life; he had a work to do and he was not to be deflected from it. Wesley was always kind, always concerned about the health of others. He was especially solicitous of the well-being of his helpers. He knew them by their Christian names, and advised them in matters of the heart as well as on what they should read. He gave financial help when they needed it. He listened to their complaints about the difficulties of the work and advised them on the spiritual welfare of their societies. So behind his apparent austerities we find the most human and lovable of men.

Wesley preached his last sermon in the open air at Winchelsea in October 1790 from the text "The kingdom of God is at hand: repent ye, and believe the gospel." His last sermon indoors was preached at Leatherhead in February 1791. A few days later he became very ill, though he rallied again. As he sat in his chair in his home on City Road, London, he said, "I have no other plea than this:

> I the chief of sinners am,
> But Jesus died for me."

Sometimes when he gathered strength he would break out into singing. His "swan song" was the last verse he had given out in City Road Chapel, the exultant stanza:

> I'll praise my Maker while I've breath,
> And when my voice is lost in death,
> Praise shall employ my nobler powers.

Then his trembling voice failed. Later he gave composed directions about his funeral, and after lying silent a little he whispered with kindling face, "The best of all is, God is with us." Then lifting his hand as though to wave it, he cried, like a soldier exulting in the moment of victory, "The best of all is, God is with us." All through the night broken words of praise fell from his lips, "The Lord is with us, the God of Jacob is our refuge," "I'll praise . . . I'll praise. . . ."

The following morning, while a group of faithful com-

panions stood around his bed, Wesley whispered, "Farewell," and his spirit passed away. Joseph Bradford at that
moment was repeating the words, "Lift up your heads, O
ye gates; and be ye lift up, ye everlasting doors." Then
those in the room broke into singing:

Waiting to receive thy spirit
Lo! the Saviour stands above,
Shows the purchase of His merit,
Reaches out the crown of love.

Wesley's body was laid to rest in his own chapel graveyard on City Road, London.

16

JOHN WESLEY:
TRANSLATOR OF HYMNS

Thou hidden love of God, whose height,
Whose depth unfathomed, no man knows,
I see from far Thy beauteous light,
And inly sigh for Thy repose;
My heart is pained, nor can it be
At rest, till it finds rest in Thee.

Is there a thing beneath the sun
That strives with Thee my heart to share?
Ah! tear it thence, and reign alone,
And govern every motion there:
Then shall my heart from earth be free,
When it has found its all in Thee.

Gerhard Tersteegen 1697-1769,
(tr. by John Wesley)

JOHN WESLEY's father was something of a poet and five of his children inherited the poetic gift. The household at Epworth was a musical one also and sang together in the home at a time when this practice was not common. Samuel Wesley was disappointed that his parishioners preferred the "scandalous doggerel" of Sternhold and Hopkins to the new version of the Psalms by Tate and Brady.

When John Wesley went to Georgia in 1735 he took with

him to study on the voyage Watts' hymns, Austin's hymns, and manuscript hymns by his father and his older brother Samuel. Even better inspiration awaited him on board in the form of twenty-six Moravian emigrants with their bishop. They sang hymns in all weathers and never more fervently than in the heart of a storm. John was so moved by what he heard that on the third day of the long voyage he began to study German and was soon able to join the emigrants in worship. The hymns which Wesley now heard were a revelation to him; there was spiritual richness and depth in them such as he had not found before, and the fervor with which they were sung was in striking contrast with the dull and lifeless drawl of the psalmody he knew at home. He was powerfully moved. Before the voyage was over he was steeped in the contents of the Moravian hymnbook and had already begun the work of translating the hymns into English verse.

John Wesley's mission to Georgia was spiritually a failure but it had one notable result. Wesley introduced hymns into America. In 1737, at Charleston in the Carolinas, he issued a collection of Psalms and Hymns two years before the first edition of Watts' hymns was published in America. He received no credit at all for his enterprise; instead he was severely castigated. He was arraigned before a grand jury at Charleston for altering authorized psalms and for introducing unauthorized compositions into church services.

Wesley had an instinct for gauging the public mind, which was an element in his success, and he saw that hymns might be utilized not only for raising the standard of devotion but also for instructing and establishing the faith of disciples. He intended hymns to be a kind of creed in verse. They were to be "a body of experimental and practical divinity."* It is not easy to ascertain what part he actually took in writing hymns. He produced some original compositions which are not unworthy to stand beside his brother's, but it is for his translations of German hymns

* That is, a collection of hymns designed to teach personally experienced and practical theology.

that he has achieved fame. He was not content merely to convey in more or less singable verse the sense of the original; he reproduced it in a form which has all the freshness of an original hymn.

Oliver Wendell Holmes once said to a friend that most hymns were mere cabinet work, not poetry, but there was one supreme hymn, "Thou Hidden Love of God"; to which his friend replied, "That is the supreme hymn." Tersteegen's original was reborn in Wesley's soul before he gave it its perfect expression. The fourth verse runs:

> *Each moment draw from earth away*
> *My heart, that lowly waits Thy call;*
> *Speak to my inmost soul and say,*
> *"I am thy Saviour God, thy All!"*
> *To feel Thy power, to hear Thy voice,*
> *To taste Thy love, be all my choice.*

Gerhard Tersteegen

Tersteegen, a German hymn-writer, was born in 1697 and when school days were over was apprenticed to his elder brother, a shopkeeper. During this time he was converted, and after serving his apprenticeship he resolved to devote himself entirely to the service of God. He went to live alone in a small cottage and for some years supported himself by weaving silk ribbons. He was very happy in his solitude, with opportunities for uninterrupted meditation and communion with God, until spiritual darkness fell upon him. He remained in this state for five years, having "no sensible impression of the love of God and sometimes doubting whether there were a God at all," until during a journey to a neighboring city he "received such an internal manifestation of the goodness of God and the suffering of the Saviour that all doubts and troubles vanished in a moment." Henceforward he had peace and joy and an intense power of realizing the unseen which, combined with his own experience, gave him a wonderful ability to touch and strengthen other hearts. To a large extent he spent the rest of his life giving such help to others. For a period

John Wesley, age 85

Tersteegen worked ten hours a day at his loom, devoting two hours daily to private prayer and the rest of the time to writing doctrinal works and addressing private meetings of friends. This last-named occupation, which he began reluctantly, soon became his principal one. He soon had to give up weaving altogether and devote himself entirely to an informal but real ministry. He also set up a dispensary in his home, at first compounding the medicines himself.

From his thirtieth to his sixtieth year his life was spent in incessant exertion for the good of others. Frequently there were between twenty and thirty people waiting to see him. He held meetings in the ground floor of his house which, were he to use every room, could accommodate about 400 people—who came there from many European countries. He had no opportunity for rest, and to his quiet temperament this lack of solitude was most uncongenial, but he accepted it as his appointed task, saying, "I love more to be with the Father, but I am glad to be with the children!"

Tersteegen never joined any sect, though many, especially the Moravians, made advances to him. He was a mystic of the purest type. In his later years he was singularly free from extravagances or intolerance. In the preface to his poems he says,

> In that sweet name of Jesus, Immanuel, God with us, the tender and overflowing love of God has made for itself a new way into the very depths of our hearts and has come unspeakably close to us poor fallen children of Adam! Since, then, the kingdom of God is so near at hand . . . we may enter at once by this new and living Way into the sanctuary of eternal communion with God. We have but to let this Divine love lead us out from the cheating pleasures of this world . . . and to give our heart and will captive to this Love that it may be our All in All. . . . Behold, this is the kernel of the whole matter.

A mystic Tersteegen may have been, but an evangelical mystic.

Johann Rothe

Another of John Wesley's translations is that of a hymn by Johann Rothe:

> *Now I have found the ground wherein*
> *Sure my soul's anchor may remain—*
> *The wounds of Jesus, for my sin*
> *Before the world's foundation slain;*
> *Whose mercy shall unshaken stay,*
> *When heaven and earth are fled away.*
>
> *Father, Thine everlasting grace*
> *Our scanty thought surpasses far,*
> *Thy heart still melts with tenderness,*
> *Thine arms of love still open are,*
> *Returning sinners to receive*
> *That mercy they may taste and live.*

Rothe was born in Silesia in 1688, and after studying theology at Leipzig University was licensed as a preacher. Zinzendorf heard him preach in 1722, liked his preaching, and invited him to the vacant pastorate at Berthelsdorf, his home and community. Rothe took a great interest in the Moravian community which formed part of Zinzendorf's estate. When Rothe had to report to higher ecclesiastical authorities regarding the doctrinal views of the Moravians, Zinzendorf showed resentment and Rothe was pleased to accept another call. Rothe's hymns were characterized by tenderness of feeling and depth of Christian experience. The hymn we quoted is a powerful and beautiful one and has found wide acceptance, proving a comfort and blessing to many. It was doubtless suggested by Hebrews 6:19, "Which hope we have as an anchor of the soul. . . ."

> *Fixed on this ground will I remain,*
> *Though my heart fail and flesh decay;*
> *This anchor shall my soul sustain,*
> *When earth's foundations melt away:*
> *Mercy's full power I then shall prove,*
> *Loved with an everlasting love.*

Paul Gerhardt

We have given a separate chapter to Paul Gerhardt, including mention of his hymn, "Give to the Winds Thy Fears," which Wesley translated. Two other hymns of Gerhardt's, also translated by Wesley, are:

> *Commit thou all thy griefs*
> *And ways into His hands,*
> *To His sure truth and tender care,*
> *Who heaven and earth commands.*

> *Who points the clouds their course,*
> *Whom winds and seas obey,*
> *He shall direct thy wandering feet,*
> *He shall prepare thy way. . . .*

> *Put thou thy trust in God,*
> *In duty's path go on;*

Walk in His strength with faith and hope,
So shall thy work be done.

and

Jesus, Thy boundless love to me
No thought can reach, no tongue declare;

of which the last verse reads:

In suffering, be Thy love my peace:
In weakness, be Thy love my power;
And when the storms of life shall cease,
Jesus, in that tremendous hour
In death, as life, be Thou my Guide,
And save me, who for me hast died.

Nicolaus Ludwig von Zinzendorf

We have already written of Zinzendorf's hymn "Jesus, Thy Blood and Righteousness." Wesley also translated two other hymns written by him in conjunction with Anna Nitschmann, before she became his second wife, and her brother Johann. They are:

O Lord, enlarge our scanty thought,
To know the wonders Thou hast wrought.

and

I thirst, Thou wounded Lamb of God
To wash me in Thy cleansing blood.

Ernst Lange

A hymn by Ernst Lange, translated by Wesley, is worthy of mention:

O God, Thou bottomless abyss!
Thee to perfection who can know?
O height immense! What words suffice
Thy countless attributes to show?

Lange lived in Danzig, and after visiting the Netherlands he allied himself with the Mennonites and Pietists. His hymns were mostly written at a time when pestilence visited Danzig, and he published a collection of them as a thank-offering for preservation during this trying time. It contained 61 hymns, one for each year of his life.

Johann Scheffler

Yet another writer was Johann Scheffler who wrote the hymn (translated by Wesley) commencing:

> *Thee will I love, my strength, my tower,*
> *Thee will I love, my joy, my crown,*
> *Thee will I love with all my power,*
> *In all Thy works, and Thee alone;*
> *Thee will I love, till the pure fire*
> *Fill my whole soul with chaste desire.*

Scheffler, though brought up a Lutheran, leaned towards mysticism and finally was received into the Roman Catholic Church. It has been said that his hymns are "the work of a true poet, almost perfect in style and beauty of rhythm, concise and profound! They were the fruits of mysticism but of mysticism kept in bounds by deep reverence and by a true and fervent love to the Saviour." Scheffler holds a high place in the ranks of German sacred poets.

There are translations of hymns by other German hymn-writers, but those we have given will suffice to show what a debt the Christian church owes to those Moravians who sang through Atlantic storms and whose hymns so fired Wesley's heart that he translated them, passing them down to us to strengthen and comfort our hearts.

17

CHARLES WESLEY:
HIS LIFE
(1708–88)

T HE premature arrival of Susanna Wesley's eighteenth child threw the household at the Epworth rectory into confusion. To use the words of his earliest biographer,

> Charles Wesley was born December 18, 1708, old style, several weeks before his time. He appeared dead rather than alive when he was born. He did not cry, nor open his eyes, and was kept wrapt in soft wool until the time when he should have been born according to the course of nature, and then he opened his eyes and cried. Not a very propitious start to life!

The story of John Wesley's rescue from the burning Epworth rectory is well-known, but Charles, who was seventeen months old at the time, was also mercifully preserved. He owed his rescue to a maid who carried him out of the burning building in her arms. As we have already seen in our chapter on John Wesley, Susanna Wesley brought up, disciplined and taught her own children, with little help from her literary, burdened husband. Charles was in her schoolroom until Samuel, the eldest son, knowing his father's straitened circumstances, made himself responsible for Charles' maintenance and education. Samuel was seventeen years older than Charles and when Charles went to Westminster School at the age of nine, Samuel was already ordained and was an usher in the school. Charles became captain of the school and in 1726 gained a "studentship" at Christ Church, Oxford.

After the novelty of the first year, he settled down with great diligence to his work. It was while his brother John was away from Oxford, helping their father at Epworth, that, with others, he began to lead a disciplined life. Charles himself said:

> Diligence led me into serious thinking. I went to the weekly sacrament and persuaded two or three others to accompany me, and to observe the method of study prescribed by the statutes of the University. This gave me the harmless name of Methodist.

In those days Oxford was not exactly a hive of industry, and Charles' newly-found discipline was a modest and conscientious move towards the University's true function. It is even more significant that in this revealing comment regarding "the harmless name of Methodist," we find the germ of Methodism. Now all was changed for Charles and, like a seedling, the little group began to grow. They had a single-minded and undramatic application to their immediate duty, and when this attitude was later linked to active evangelism Methodism was born. When John returned to Oxford he became the natural leader of this "Holy Club" and also, through natural circumstances, his influence over Charles takes the place of that of Samuel who until then had been his mentor and guide.

When John Wesley went to Georgia, Charles accompanied him, having been invited by General Oglethorpe, the Governor of the colony, to be his secretary, even though he lacked secretarial qualifications. He was ordained, somewhat reluctantly, before he went to Georgia. The second day after his arrival in Georgia he was astonished to find Oglethorpe at loggerheads with him, and inclined to treat him with a roughness which augured ill for the future. Later, says Charles, "the hurricane of his passion drove me away." The explanation for Oglethorpe's behavior may lie in the fact that the General was very hard-pressed and harassed, the colony being on a war footing. Charles looked wistfully back to life in Oxford. There was no "noble savage" in Georgia, no field ripe for harvest—only rough living, office chores and angry women. Presently the General and his secretary were reconciled, but Charles had already resolved to return to England. He traveled via Boston where he was delayed by illness. The subsequent voyage from there to England was made wretched for him by further illness and storms.

Up to this time Charles does not appear to have been in possession of what he afterwards saw to be vital godliness. The reading of Luther's *Commentary on Galatians* was of great spiritual help to him, as also was his association with Count Zinzendorf and Peter Böhler who both met him when they visited London. Like John, he had been impressed by a group of Moravians who shared their outward voyage to Georgia. Charles also speaks of the benefit he received from a Mr. Bray whom he describes as "a poor, innocent mechanic who knows nothing but Christ." Charles found a haven in Mr. Bray's house when he was again ill.

Epworth Rectory

"I longed to find Christ," he says, "that I might show Him to all mankind." He was already actively commending Christ from his sickbed and others were being converted. Bray's sister, a Mrs. Turner, who had been converted under her brother's guidance, longed to help Charles. Overcoming her shyness, she told him about her conversion and he was impressed by her simple testimony. On Whitsunday 1738 Charles prayed for the gift of the Comforter and afterwards heard a voice which said, "In the name of Jesus of Nazareth, arise and believe, and thou shalt be healed of thine infirmities." Later he learned that Mrs. Turner had spoken the words. "Christ," she said, "commanded me to say them and I could not forbear." This proved to be the turning point in the spiritual experience of Charles Wesley. The voice of the woman was as the voice of God. He found, and felt, while she was speaking, the assurance that he sought. Charles took his Bible and opened it at words singularly prophetic, "He hath put a new song in my mouth, even praise unto our God." That night he recorded in his *Journal*, "I now found myself at peace with God. . . . I saw that by faith I stood."

His next concern was for his brother John. If only John could receive the same assurance! Within three days the miracle was repeated. "Towards ten my brother was brought in triumph by a troop of our friends and declared, 'I believe.'" They sang a hymn together with much joy and parted with prayer. The two brothers lost no time in communicating their experiences to their acquaintances; some responded, but most were cynical. About a year after his conversion Charles became curate to his friend the vicar of Islington, but the opposition of the churchwardens, because Charles was unlicensed, was so great that he resigned the appointment. From that time his work was identified with that of his brother and both became indefatigable itinerant and field preachers.

London was a very sordid place when the work of Methodism began there. The two brothers often had to preach "against a background of persecution, fighting, swearing, drunkenness—some drunk with religion, others with gin." Their congregations were mostly composed of those who swarmed out of their hovels and tenements eager for sensation and ripe for excitement, just like the crowds which gathered at Tyburn to watch criminals being hanged. We can understand Charles' reluctance to face them. It required a lot of courage. No other men in England cared more deeply for the classes of society for whom no man seemed to care, or went to such lengths to reach them. Charles found the work in Bristol more congenial than that in London, even when it was among the colliers in the wild mining area of Kingswood. The work there had been begun by George Whitefield and had met with great success. Schools were started there, a chapel was built, and there was also a preachers' settlement. Charles preached regularly, and successfully, both at Kingswood and at other places in Bristol but, unlike John, even when successful he was very easily cast down and depressed.

We next find Charles back in London taking over his brother's work at "the Foundery," where he found that many of his old friends were deserting to the Moravians. During this period he found a stalwart ally in Howel Harris and despite doctrinal differences they remained lifelong friends. The popular conception of the division of labor between the two brothers is that John was the preacher and Charles the hymn-writer. This is not altogether correct. Charles was a great preacher, second only to his brother and George Whitefield. When John speaks of the evangelistic work he says, "My brother and I," and when he speaks of the hymns it is still, "My brother and I."

The years passed with the two brothers traveling and preaching all over the country. In 1749 Charles married Sarah Gwynne. He found her in that part of South Wales where the rugged mountains run down to the green Breconshire valleys. Her father, Marmaduke Gwynne, was Squire of Garth, near Builth Wells, a zealous magistrate and devout churchman. His mansion, Garth House, can still be seen overlooking the winding river. Their marriage seems to have been a very happy one. His wife accompanied him on his evangelistic journeys, which were as frequent as ever until the year 1756 when he largely ceased to itinerate and devoted himself to the care of the Societies in London and Bristol. In 1771 he moved his headquarters from Bristol to London. Besides attending to the Societies he devoted himself, as he had done in the early days after his conversion, to the spiritual care of the prisoners in Newgate. He was concerned for the malefactors under sentence of death, often spending the night before their execution in their cells with them.

In the 1780's Charles began to feel that his lifework was ending and his death approaching. Only a few days before he died he dictated to his wife the last lines he composed:

> *In age and feebleness extreme,*
> *Who shall a helpless worm redeem?*
> *Jesus, my only hope Thou art,*
> *Strength of my failing flesh and heart.*
> *O could I catch a smile from Thee*
> *And drop into eternity!*

Charles Wesley died in London on March 20, 1788, and was buried in Marylebone churchyard. His brother was deeply grieved because he would not consent to be interred in the burial ground of City Road Chapel, but Charles said, "I have lived and I die in the Church of England and I will be buried in the yard of my parish church." He had a large family and was survived by four of them. Three sons all became distinguished in the musical world and the one daughter inherited some of her father's poetic genius.

18

CHARLES WESLEY:
HYMN-WRITER

O Love divine, how sweet Thou art!
When shall I find my willing heart
All taken up by Thee?
I thirst, I faint, I die to prove
The greatness of redeeming love,
The love of Christ to me.

JOHN WESLEY had realized the great potential of the use of hymns in the work of evangelization and of spiritual instruction. As we said when writing of him, he intended hymns to be a kind of creed in verse. They were to be "a body of experimental and practical divinity."* It was largely Charles Wesley who provided such hymns for the gathering stream of Methodism and for the whole body of Christian churches in the following centuries.

In 1779 John Wesley produced a collection of hymns under the title, *A Collection of Hymns for the Use of the People called Methodists* (which was in use until 1904). It is a devotional treasury and John Wesley's preface ends with the words, "When Poetry thus keeps its place, as the handmaid of Piety, it shall attain, not a poor perishable wreath, but a crown that fadeth not away." A large proportion of the hymns in this book were written by Charles, and after the

---

* See footnote, page 104.

Charles Wesley

Bible, this collection of hymns served as the devotional classic of the Methodists. In the preface already mentioned, John Wesley particularly asks editors of hymns never to attempt to improve those written by his brother Charles, for, he says, "None of them is able to mend either the sense or the verse." Bernard Lord Manning, in his book *The Hymns of Wesley and Watts*, says, "This little book—some 750 hymns—is . . . a work of supreme devotional art by a religious genius." The hymns express the characteristics and mood of the Revival. Up to that time there had been little hymn-singing in Anglican churches. Abortive attempts had been made to introduce them, but most churches, including that at Epworth in which Charles was brought up, used the rather bleak metrical psalms of Sternhold and Hopkins or the rather livelier version of Tate and Brady. In some churches, mainly Dissenting ones, the hymns of Watts had gained acceptance. He had opened the way, but in the providence of God it was left to Charles Wesley to write hymns which were to be used not only by Methodists but by Anglicans and Dissenters, as their rather cold formality in worship yielded to the stimulus of the Revival.

Charles Wesley had the gift of expressing sublime truths in simple language. Just occasionally one can see the fingerprints of the classical scholar, but usually it is the method of plain speech which he employs. We find an example of this in his hymn for a New Year's watch-night service:

> *Come, let us anew*
> *Our journey pursue,*
> *Roll round with the year*
> *And never stand still till the Master appear.* . . .
>
> *Our life is a dream;*
> *Our time as a stream*
> *Glides swiftly away,*
> *And the fugitive moment refuses to stay.*

The hymns of Charles Wesley are charged with doctrine. We never move far from the doctrines of the Holy Trinity, of the incarnation, and of the resurrection. Hear him on the incarnation:

> *Let earth and heaven combine,*
> *Angels and men agree,*
> *To praise in songs divine*
> *The incarnate Deity,*
> *Our God contracted to a span*
> *Incomprehensibly made man.*

For Wesley the important things are the great objective truths about God—the Father, the Son and the Holy Ghost—and the definite impact of faith in these doctrines on his own life and that of others. To quote Manning again, "There is the solid structure of historic doctrine, there is the thrill of present experience, but there is, too, the glory of a mystic sunlight coming directly from another world.

This transfigures history and experience. This puts past and present into the timeless, eternal NOW."

This mystical quality is illustrated in the hymn "Thou Shepherd of Israel and Mine," in which Charles Wesley is at the height of his genius:

> Thou Shepherd of Israel and mine,
>   The joy and desire of my heart,
> For closer communion I pine,
>   I long to reside where Thou art:
> The pasture I languish to find
>   Where all, who their Shepherd obey,
> Are fed, on Thy bosom reclined,
>   And screened from the heat of the day. . . .
>
> 'Tis there, with the lambs of Thy flock,
>   There only, I covet to rest,
> To lie at the foot of the rock,
>   Or rise to be hid in Thy breast:
> 'Tis there I would always abide,
>   And never a moment depart,
> Concealed in the cleft of Thy side,
>   Eternally held in Thy heart.

What poignant longing is expressed in the last verse! The last line is perfect in expression—"Eternally held in Thy heart!"

Two other examples of his mystical, experience-oriented hymns are:

> Thou hidden source of calm repose,
>   Thou all-sufficient love divine,
> My help and refuge from my foes,
>   Secure I am, if Thou art mine:
> And lo! from sin and grief and shame,
>   I hide me, Jesus, in Thy Name.

and again,

> O Jesus, full of truth and grace,
>   More full of grace than I of sin . . .

> *Thou knowest the way to bring me back*
> *My fallen spirit to restore:*
> *O for Thy truth and mercy's sake,*
> *Forgive, and bid me sin no more;*
> *The ruins of my soul repair,*
> *And make my heart a house of prayer.*

Contraposition (that is, contrast or opposition of ideas) was a favorite device of Charles Wesley, as in "Jesus, Lover of My Soul," particularly in the lines:

> *Just and holy is Thy Name,*
> *I am all unrighteousness;*
> *False and full of sin I am,*
> *Thou art full of truth and grace.*

In both the first two lines and the second two lines we have two persons in contrast, the holy Saviour and the sinful speaker. Another example is found in the hymn we have just quoted:

> *O Jesus, full of truth and grace,*
> *More full of grace than I of sin . . .*

and in the lines:

Garth House

> *Kindle a flame of sacred love*
> *On the mean altar of my heart.*

"Jesus, Lover of My Soul," a hymn which has enjoyed such a wide usefulness and popularity, was written while Charles Wesley was staying at Garth House, his wife's old home. The story is that he wrote it during a threatened storm when a bird flew in at the open window for refuge.

It was four years after his conversion that Wesley composed one of his finest hymns, "Wrestling Jacob." Watts said it was worth all the verses he himself had written. With unerring genius Charles makes use of the story of Jacob, adapting it to his own experience of conversion.

> *Come, O Thou Traveler unknown,*
> *Whom still I hold, but cannot see!*
> *My company before is gone,*
> *And I am left alone with Thee;*
> *With Thee all night I mean to stay,*
> *And wrestle till the break of day. . . .*
>
> *I know Thee, Saviour, who Thou art,*
> *Jesus, the feeble sinner's Friend;*
> *Nor wilt Thou with the night depart,*
> *But stay and love me to the end;*
> *Thy mercies never shall remove:*
> *Thy nature and Thy Name is Love.*

Another conversion hymn, hardly less dramatic than "Wrestling Jacob," is:

> *And can it be that I should gain*
> *An interest in the Saviour's blood?*
> *Died He for me, who caused His pain?*
> *For me, who Him to death pursued?*
> *Amazing love! how can it be*
> *That Thou, my God, shouldst die for me? . . .*
>
> *No condemnation now I dread;*
> *Jesus, and all in Him is mine!*
> *Alive in Him, my living Head,*
> *And clothed in righteousness divine,*

Bold I approach the eternal throne,
And claim the crown, through Christ my own.

Peter Böhler, Wesley's Moravian friend, said, "If I had a thousand tongues I'd praise Christ with them all." Charles took up this theme for his hymn written for the anniversary of his conversion:

O for a thousand tongues to sing
My dear Redeemer's praise,
The glories of my God and King,
The triumphs of His grace!

My gracious Master and my God,
Assist me to proclaim,
To spread through all the earth abroad
The honors of Thy Name.

How abundantly the prayer uttered in the last verse was answered!

Charles was constantly composing hymns. Where John used his *Journal* to set down his activities, Charles recorded his experience in verse. Julian names him "the great hymn-writer of all ages." A more modern writer says, "We are left with an impression of light, happiness, soaring vitality, as of a strong man rejoicing in his strength. It is an exhilarating experience even to read Wesley's hymns."

Many of his hymns have dynamic openings:

Christ, whose glory fills the skies

Soldiers of Christ, arise

Rejoice, the Lord is King

Jesus, the Name high over all

O for a heart to praise my God

A charge to keep I have

Forth in Thy Name, O Lord, I go

Then again, Charles Wesley wrote some of the greatest festival hymns of Christendom:

Peter Böhler

Hark! the Herald Angels Sing
Christ, the Lord, Is Risen Today
God Is Gone Up on High
and
Hail the Day that Sees Him Rise
with its splendid second verse:

There the glorious triumph waits;
Lift your heads, eternal gates!
Christ hath vanquished death and sin;
Take the King of glory in.

We can almost hear the sound of trumpets and the roll of drums.

The early Methodists attached great importance to the observance of the Lord's Supper, and Charles Wesley's communion hymns reveal his comprehension of apostolic truth. We give just one example:

Jesus, we thus obey
  Thy last and kindest word;
Here in Thine own appointed way
  We come to meet our Lord. . . .

Thus we remember Thee,
  And take this bread and wine
As Thine own dying legacy,
  And our redemption's sign. . . .

Now let our souls be fed
  With manna from above,
And over us Thy banner spread
  Of everlasting love.

"O Love Divine, How Sweet Thou Art!", the hymn quoted at the opening of the chapter, is one of Wesley's best hymns. For its delight in heartfelt, spiritual blessedness, and warmth of expression of desire after the love of God, it may be compared with the best productions of Bernard of Clairvaux:

Stronger His love than death or hell;
Its riches are unsearchable;
  The first-born sons of light
Desire in vain its depths to see;
They cannot reach the mystery,
  The length, and breadth, and height.

We never for a moment think of Charles Wesley as a writer who sat down to compose hymns, but we feel that he was compelled by a delightful necessity to give expression to the thoughts and words that burned within him. This agrees with what is known of the history of his hymn-writing. Some of his hymns were written on cards as he rode on horseback, and sometimes he would hurry home and call for pen and ink lest the moment of inspiration should pass. Truly he says of himself:

My heart is full of Christ, and longs
  Its glorious matter to declare!
Of Him I make my loftier songs,

> *I cannot from His praise forbear:*
> *My ready tongue makes haste to sing*
> *The glories of my heavenly King.*

A quality which strikes us is the faithful, moving, but unsentimental record of every phase of religious feeling. Souls depressed, elated, energetic, full of doubt, serene in faith, can find in Charles Wesley's hymns, as nowhere else but in the book of Psalms, the appropriate words in which to pour out prayer and praise to God.

One of the most touching of Wesley's hymns, and said by John Wesley to be the sweetest he ever wrote, is:

> *Come, let us join our friends above*
> *That have obtained the prize,*
> *And on the eagle wings of love*
> *To joys celestial rise. . . .*
>
> *One family we dwell in Him,*
> *One church, above, beneath,*
> *Though now divided by the stream,*
> *The narrow stream of death:*
>
> *One army of the living God,*
> *To His command we bow;*
> *Part of His host have crossed the flood,*
> *And part are crossing now.*

There is a touching story about the hymn which opens,

> *Depth of mercy! Can there be*
> *Mercy still reserved for me?*

An actress in a provincial town, overhearing this hymn being given out by one of a small company assembled in a cottage for worship, was so struck by it that she went into the cottage and joined in the worship. She obtained the book containing the words and by reading it her heart was changed. This led her finally to abandon the stage. On one occasion, being prevailed upon to act a familiar part, she could only utter the words of the hymn, to the astonishment of the audience! She afterwards led a Christian life and married a Christian minister.

It is clear that Charles Wesley has enriched the whole church by his hymns. If the succession of hymn-writers can be compared to a long range of hills, Wesley is like a towering peak among them. His hymns will not be forgotten while the world stands. Among the 6,000 which he composed some are mediocre, but at his best he is unsurpassed. As David was the sweet Psalmist of Israel, Charles Wesley is undoubtedly the hymnist of the English-speaking race.

19

JOHN CENNICK

(1718–55)

Jesus, my all, to heaven is gone,
  He whom I fix my hopes upon:
His track I see, and I'll pursue
  The narrow way till Him I view.

The way the holy prophets went,
  The way that leads from banishment,
The King's highway of holiness,
  I'll go, for all His paths are peace.

J OHN CENNICK was born in Reading, Berkshire, in 1718. His Quaker grandparents had been persecuted and imprisoned for their faith, but his parents brought up John in the Church of England, "thrusting an outward conformity to piety on him." One event which much impressed him as a boy was the death of his mother's aunt. The vigorous assurance of salvation which she gave on her deathbed had a lasting effect on him, bringing him to realize his own need of Christ.

Cennick says that as a boy he was "fond of play, of fine clothes and of praise. . . . My natural temper was obstinate and my lips full of lies." Above all he delighted in reading and seeing plays. When he was about sixteen years old God began to work in his life and he records his experience, saying, "As I was walking hastily on Cheapside, London, the hand of the Lord touched me. I felt at once an

uncommon fear and dejection, and though all my days
had been bitter through the fear of going to hell, yet I
knew not any weight before like this." His autobiography
tells how, for two long years, he continued under this terrible sense of guilt, with an intense longing for salvation
and peace. He tried to pray but he could not. He read the
Bible but it condemned him. He fought with fears and evil
desires; he tried fasting, running, eating acorns, leaves of
trees and grass. But amid all his striving he "saw no help"
and experienced neither peace nor comfort. And then, in
the awful realization of his own failure, he was given to
see something of the truth that Jesus had accomplished
salvation for him on the cross. This assurance was a ray of
light piercing the darkness of his soul. He went into a
church to pray, still feeling destitute, then suddenly he
was overwhelmed with joy. "I believed there was mercy
for me. . . . I heard the voice of Jesus saying, 'I am thy
salvation.'"

Cennick's hymn, "Jesus, My All" (partly quoted above),
is to a large extent autobiographical, as the remaining
verses show:

> *The more I strove against sin's power*
> *I sinned and stumbled but the more;*
> *Till late I heard my Saviour say,*
> *"Come hither, soul, I am the Way!"*
>
> *Lo! glad I come; and Thou, blest Lamb,*
> *Shalt take me to Thee as I am!*
> *Nothing but sin have I to give;*
> *Nothing but love shall I receive.*

The last verse of the hymn could be termed prophetical,
describing, as it does, his occupation for the rest of his
short life:

> *Now will I tell to sinners round*
> *What a dear Saviour I have found!*
> *I'll point to Thy redeeming blood,*
> *And say, "Behold the way to God!"*

John Cennick

Thus a life of Christian joy began for Cennick. He daily grew in grace, but he was alone and longed for Christian company. At this time Whitefield's *Journal* fell into his hands. Hearing that he was in London, Cennick walked all night to get there—he was by this time a land surveyor in Reading—and called on him at 8 a.m. "Our conversation was sweet and I stayed with him for several days." It was on the basis of this budding relationship that Whitefield asked him to undertake work in the school for coal miners' children which he was opening at Kingswood, Bristol. "The thing seemed to be of God," said Cennick, "and I was obedient." So, as Whitefield went for the second time to Georgia, Cennick went to Bristol, only to find that the building of the school in which he was to teach had not even begun. He found also a large assembly of people in the open air who were disappointed because the expected preacher had not arrived. He was persuaded to address them and he did so with success. The following day he preached again, and then almost every day, sometimes twice a day.

Thereafter his preaching ministry continued with great power and blessing until his death.

Cennick became one of Whitefield's closest friends, and for some time his chief assistant, taking pastoral charge of Whitefield's Tabernacle in London and the general oversight of Whitefieldian Methodism while Whitefield went to America. He was highly esteemed and at first the work continued harmoniously; then problems arose and Cennick was not gifted to deal with discord and division. He had been at his best under Whitefield's leadership but was ill at ease trying to fill his place. Moreover, he had for some time enjoyed close relations with several leading Moravians and he longed to join them. Finally, he wrote to Whitefield informing him of this decision and he made the move. Howel Harris then took charge at the Tabernacle, where Cennick was still beloved. The affection between himself and Harris and Whitefield remained as warm as ever.

Cennick visited the headquarters of the Moravian Movement in Germany and then responded to a pressing invitation to preach in Dublin. Before two months had passed he was preaching daily to crowds so great that those who wished to hear him had to be there two or three hours before time. On Sundays huge congregations gathered and Cennick had to creep over the heads of people to reach his pulpit through a window! He finally handed this work over to an excellent young preacher while he himself moved on to an itinerant ministry in Northern Ireland. He ranged over seven counties, preaching in barns, fields and houses. He was beaten by hoodlums, attacked by mobs, set upon by dogs. He often addressed thousands in the open air in heavy rain. He condemned sin in every form and was utterly uncompromising in his preaching of the gospel, but people saw in him a Christianity that was beautiful and real (he was patient, kind and tender), and he won affection and esteem. He and his wife lived in poverty, yet they were often overflowing with the joy of the Lord.

In his early thirties Cennick's many sufferings and ceaseless labor began to take their toll. From 1750 he was unwell much of the time, yet continued to preach twenty times a week. Leaving Ireland he set out for Wales, but on reaching England he went instead to London, arriving in a dying state at the Moravian meetinghouse in Fetter Lane. On July 4, 1755, "he quietly breathed his soul into the arms of Jesus." He was thirty-six years of age. Cennick was one of the greatest preachers of the eighteenth-century revival, and a poet of no mean ability. Several of his hymns are still widely used.

In his *Life of George Whitefield*, Arnold Dallimore writes:

> John Cennick loved the Lord and served Him with gladness. For His sake he calmly endured suffering and reproach. Jesus, the Lamb of God, filled all his thought and captivated all his affection. His life has been sadly overlooked but we are refreshed by the memory of that simple, inoffensive and mighty man of God, dear, good and gracious John Cennick.

Cennick wrote many of his hymns while at Kingswood, one of the best-known being:

> *Children of the heavenly King,*
> *As ye journey, sweetly sing;*
> *Sing your Saviour's worthy praise,*
> *Glorious in His works and ways.*

One of the characteristics of Cennick's hymns is their simplicity, as seen in the following two hymns:

> *Be with me, Lord, where'er I go;*
> *Teach me what Thou wouldst have me do;*
> *Suggest whate'er I think or say;*
> *Direct me in the narrow way. . . .*

> *Assist and teach me how to pray;*
> *Incline my nature to obey;*
> *What Thou abhorrest let me flee,*
> *And only love what pleases Thee.*

and again,

> *Ere I sleep, for every favor*
> *This day showed*
> *By my God*
> *I will bless my Saviour. . . .*

> *So, whene'er in death I slumber,*
> *Let me rise*
> *With the wise,*
> *Counted in their number.*

Cennick is also the author of two well-known graces for before and after eating: "Be present at our table, Lord, . . ." and "We thank Thee, Lord, for this our food. . . ." These two graces are printed on John Wesley's large family teapot, still preserved in Methodist premises on City Road, London.

20

ANNE STEELE

(1717–78)

Father, whate'er of earthly bliss
Thy sovereign will denies,
Accepted at Thy throne of grace
Let this petition rise:

Give me a calm, a thankful heart,
From every murmur free;
The blessings of Thy grace impart,
And let me live to Thee.

ANNE STEELE was born in the village of Broughton
in Hampshire, midway between Salisbury and
Winchester, in 1717. For several generations her
family had borne its Christian witness in this small farming community. They engaged in business also, her father
being a timber merchant as well as the Baptist minister.
Doubtless, during the generations, they had come to be
held in high esteem for their integrity in business as well
as for their Christian faith.

Anne seems to have been a quiet, self-effacing person.
As far as outward circumstances were concerned, "along
the cool sequestered vale of life" she kept the noiseless
tenor of her way, to quote Gray's well-known elegy. She
did not often leave home, but this was not unusual in days
when traveling was slow and difficult, if not hazardous. In
those days of slow communication Broughton must have

seemed far away from world events, news of which might be long in arrival. It must have seemed remote even from an important British celebration such as the coronation of George III in 1760. Anne wrote hymns suitable for these important occasions, but those which have survived in use draw their inspiration from the peaceful country scenes around her.

Although outwardly her life moved in this quiet, somewhat insulated groove, there was much in her life which caused suffering and grief. Her first experience of sorrow must have been the death of her mother when she was quite a child, but because she had a good stepmother this does not seem to have been a lasting sorrow. She was baptized on confession of her faith at the age of fourteen or fifteen and became a member of her father's church.

A few years later she fell from a horse and injured her hip. She seems to have suffered from the effects of this injury all her life and this probably further decreased her mobility, keeping her at home when possibly she might have been able to venture further afield.

The occasion of the writing of the hymn "Father, Whate'er of Earthly Bliss" seems to have been that of the drowning, while swimming, of her fiancé just a short time before they were to be married. The sentiments of the hymn seem to confirm the validity of this. The three verses of the hymn are actually part of a longer hymn which begins, "When I survey life's varied scene."

> *When I survey life's varied scene*
> *Amid the darkest hours,*
> *Sweet rays of comfort shine between,*
> *And thorns are mixed with flowers.*
>
> *Lord, teach me to adore the hand*
> *Whence all my comforts flow,*
> *And let me in this desert land*
> *A glimpse of Canaan know.*

Anne Steele is not to be compared with Watts, Wesley and others (incidentally she does seem to have been influenced by Watts), but she stands high in the lower rank of hymn-writers and is in the foremost rank of women hymn-writers. The last verse of our hymn gives a clue to her character as a Christian and as a hymnist:

> *Let the sweet hope that Thou art mine*
> *My path through life attend,*
> *Thy presence through my journey shine,*
> *And crown my journey's end.*

Her language was often that of hope rather than of assurance. Some short quotations from her hymns will illustrate this:

> *My God, my Father, blissful Name,*
> *O may I call Thee mine?*

> *And may I hope that love extends*
> *Its sacred power to me?*

> *When sins and fears prevailing rise*
> *And fainting hope almost expires.*

Birthplace of Anne Steele, Broughton, Hants

But from time to time her assurance breaks through and we have such a verse as:

> On Thee alone my hope relies,
> Beneath Thy cross I fall,
> My Lord, my Life, my Sacrifice,
> My Saviour and my All.

This surely was the true expression of her faith. But she seems on the whole to shrink from too certain an expression of her very real faith, and this tends to make her seem rather subjective and introspective. She does sing the praises of redeeming love and grace, as in the quotation above, though usually in a subdued way. She always desires to submit her will to the sovereignty of God, in which she has a very firm belief, and through all the spiritual conflict which can be traced in her hymns there is a deep-seated, though quietly expressed, joy.

Her hymns are truly "heart breathings." They consistently show an earnest desire after the Lord and a looking away to things unseen. They have a sweetness and fragrance all their own, and these qualities, together with her truly poetic expression, ensure for them an enduring place in hymnology. As might be expected, she shrank from publicity and only agreed to have her hymns published under the pen name of Theodosia, so those in her village community may not have known they had a poetess and hymn-writer in their midst.

How surprised and alarmed Anne Steele would have been had she known that her hymns would find a place in most hymnbooks more than 200 years after her death and that she would have considerable mention in the *Dictionary of National Biography*!

It is said that she never really recovered from her father's death in 1769. She herself passed peacefully to be with her Saviour in 1778. Though her hymns so often spoke of hope rather than assurance, there was no lack of assurance when she reached the end of her earthly pilgrimage. This ended with the assertion, "I know that my Redeemer liveth."

So our gentle, self-effacing hymn-writer made her contribution to divine worship much further afield than her own native village. We close with a verse very typically from Anne Steele's pen and heart:

> *Yes, Lord, I own Thy sovereign hand,*
> *Thou Just and Wise and Kind:*
> *Be every anxious thought suppressed*
> *And all my soul resigned.*

21

WILLIAM WILLIAMS
(PANTYCELYN)
(1717–91)

Guide me, O Thou great Jehovah,
Pilgrim through this barren land;
I am weak, but Thou art mighty,
Hold me with Thy powerful hand;
Bread of heaven,
Feed me till I want no more.

I F there is any subject on which Welshmen, looking across the centuries, are agreed, it is that William Williams, Pantycelyn, is "the Sweet Singer of Wales," "the poet laureate" of the religious revival of the eighteenth century, one "who impressed the stamp of his genius forever on Welsh literature." "While a Welsh heart responds to its God in its own tongue, the hymns of William Williams will live." His Welsh hymns number nearly one thousand, but it is not widely known that he wrote some 123 hymns in English, the best known of which is quoted at the head of this chapter. A few of the English hymns are translations from the Welsh. In addition he wrote several elegies and two larger works in Welsh: *A View of the Kingdom of Christ* and *The Life and Death of Theomemphus*. This latter work was written to help "the seeker after God," and "is conceived in the spirit of Bunyan's *Pilgrim's Progress*."

William Williams was born at Cefn-coed, near Llandovery, Carmarthenshire, in 1717. His father, John Williams, who was sixty-one at the time of his son's birth, was a ruling elder of the Independent Church at Cefnarthen, which built its chapel when seventeenth-century persecutions of Nonconformists ended in 1688. Its history in the 1730's was marked by a cleavage between Calvinists and others holding looser doctrine, the result being that John Williams and fellow-Calvinists seceded and formed the Independent Church of Clunypentan. It does not appear, however, that John Williams' son was deeply moved by religious convictions in his early youth, for it was not until he was twenty years of age that he experienced conversion, and that with great suddenness. His parents intended that he should become a doctor of medicine, and to educate him for this purpose they sent him to an Academy situated near Hay, which, though located in Breconshire, is within a stone's throw, as it were, of Radnorshire and Herefordshire. But Hay is some thirty miles, as the crow flies, from Pantycelyn, so the youth must have lodged during term in or near the Academy.

We mention geography at this point because Williams' conversion resulted from his nearness to Talgarth, which lies midway between Hay and Brecon. But Talgarth was the home area of Howel Harris, the pioneer of Methodism in Wales, and it happened on a never-to-be-forgotten occasion that Williams was passing through Talgarth when he was attracted by a voice that, in the outcome, was evidently "from heaven." Harris was preaching the gospel from a spot in Talgarth churchyard. The medical student was caught up in the crowd of hearers; the arrow of conviction wounded his heart; the gospel's healing balm was applied by a greater than Harris; Scripture truth entered the youth's heart with convincing power; and before many days had passed the medical student had become convinced that he was called to become a physician of men's souls.

Later, Williams wrote an elegy in which he mentions a few of the circumstances linked with his conversion. It was the first time he had set eyes on the preacher, although Harris had been engaging in open-air preaching for about

William Williams (Pantycelyn)

two years. Standing in front of the church porch, on the morning of what would probably be a Sunday, Harris exhorted his hearers to give heed to what the Bible revealed of the future: of the Second Coming of Christ, and of a Judgment to come. For the youth of twenty, it proved to be the turning-point in his life, a true Damascus-road experience. "Lord, what wilt Thou have me to do?" was the cry that came from his innermost being. Shortly he asked for the advice of leading Methodists—Harris, Daniel Rowland of Llangeitho, and others—as to what step he should take, and as a consequence he applied for ordination in the Anglican ministry. In 1740 he was ordained by the Bishop of St. David's, and appointed to the curacy of Llanwrtyd and Llanddewi Abergwesyn, in the northern part of Breconshire and a mere twelve or fifteen miles northeast of Pantycelyn.

But Williams soon let it be known that he had no wish to be tied down to a ministry in two thinly-peopled parishes. He preferred to itinerate and to preach where he could find people willing to listen to the gospel. In this respect he and Howel Harris were decidedly of one mind. Complaints from his parishioners reached the Bishop and it soon became clear that the curate could not proceed to full ordination in the Established Church. This was also the period when George Whitefield paid occasional visits to South Wales, and it seems to have been due, in part, to his influence that Williams was encouraged to go into highways and byways with the gospel instead of enduring the comparative sterility of his mountain parishes. It was also during this period that Harris could write, "Hell trembles when Williams comes, and souls are daily taken by Brother Williams in the gospel net."

An important development took place in 1743. Leading Methodists, Williams among them, met at Watford, near Caerphilly, to confer on their common activities, and to form a Calvinistic Methodist Association. They agreed to continue in membership of the Established Church, but to organize their extramural activities—to use a modern expression—as seemed best to themselves, for encouragement within the Church they received but little. It was not until 1811 that the final breach came about, and by that time Williams had been dead twenty years. In 1744 he resigned his curacy and was requested by the Association to become assistant to Daniel Rowland in his itinerant ministry. In other words, he received a roving commission, and this precisely fitted his own wishes.

Williams' father had died in 1742 and his mother Dorothy had inherited from a brother the farm known as Pantycelyn, near Llandovery, so that the family felt no financial strain. Shortly before the half-century ended Williams married Mary Francis who, for some time, had been lady-companion to Mrs. Griffith Jones, wife of the vicar of Llanddowror who had established the famous Circulating School system which brought the basic elements of education, linked with Scripture truth, to many in remote country districts who would never otherwise have learned to read the Word. With his wife's portion Williams was able to buy more land in the Pantycelyn area, and there he remained until his death in 1791.

Maybe "remained" is scarcely the appropriate word, for every year he traveled extensively in the principality and must have been absent from home as often as he was present, and perhaps more often. Preaching was the joy of his life, the writing of hymns his meat and drink. "He sang Wales into piety" was the verdict of an English writer; he was, in fact, the Charles Wesley of Wales.

A very interesting letter is that which he wrote to Thomas Charles of Bala, pioneer in North Wales Methodism, on the first of January 1791, only ten days before he died. After giving his learned friend details of a ten-week illness which had terminated his away-from-home activities, he proceeds to say three things which merit attention:

1. I have acquired more knowledge of myself and of the goodness of God during these weeks than during the forty previous years.

2. The Bible, which I used to read in great measure for the edification of others, I now apply entirely to myself, as the only book by which I shall be tried in the great Judgment; and although I have hundreds of books, not one of them suits my taste like the Bible.

3. I have come to see that true religion consists of three parts:

a) true light respecting the plan of salvation, God's eternal covenant with His Son to pay the debt of believing sinners, all the truths of the new covenant by which He becomes all in all in creation, in all-embracing providence and in redemption.

b) the keeping of a close and intimate fellowship with God in all our dealings with the world and in all our religious practices and ordinances.

c) life and conduct such as would reveal to the ungodly that there is a great difference between us and them. The Christian is forgiving, humble, thoughtful, truthful, honest, and seeks to do good to all, so that the scripture may be fulfilled, "Let your light so shine before men, that they may see your good works and glorify your Father which is in heaven."

At one point in the letter he says,

Think how disappointing it is for a man who traveled nearly 3,000 miles every year for over fifty years now not to be traveling more than forty feet a day—from the fireside to bed; but this is how my God wishes to deal with me, and it is well.

ॐ

It remains to mention the hymns for which William Williams is justly famed. According to tradition, at an early Association meeting, Howel Harris challenged his fellow-workers in the gospel to apply themselves to the writing of some hymns (as specimens) by the next Association meeting. Thomas Charles later explained that Harris' desire was to ascertain "whether the Lord had given the gift of poetry to one of them." In the sequel it was unanimously agreed that the gift had certainly been conferred upon Williams of Pantycelyn. In fact, both in quantity and quality, Williams outstripped all others of his time, and to him the church and nation soon owed an incalculable debt.

Williams' hymns cover the whole range of Christian experience, from deepest despair to the heights of full assurance. There was a lively sympathy between his mind and the varying phases of nature. He wrote hymns about the dawn and the sunset, about the cornfields, the mountains, the quiet havens of the sea, a summer evening, a winter's night, and a clear morning after a night of storm. We give but one typical example:

> While the stormy winds are blowing,
> From the north so bleak and dull,
> Saviour, keep my soul defended
> From the fear of coming ill.

Change the winter
Into balmy days and still.

The most famous of Williams' hymns found in English hymnbooks is, beyond all question, "Guide Me, O Thou Great Jehovah," the first verse of which we quoted at the head of this chapter. It is actually a part of a Welsh hymn of which an English translation was published in 1771 by Peter Williams; but the author himself, using Peter Williams' effort as his starting point, produced the wording much as we know it today. It has, in fact, long been one of the most popular of English hymns. Its images are basic to life—land, bread, fountain, stream, cloudy pillar. But Wales, its rivers and streams, gives place to Canaan and to Jordan before the hymn closes. The prayer for divine guidance during pilgrimage concludes with "songs of praises." It was in the year 1772 that Williams published these verses as a leaflet headed, *A Favourite Hymn, sung by Lady Huntingdon's young Collegians, printed by the desire of many Christian friends. Lord, give it Thy blessing.* (The reference to "Collegians" points to the establishment by the Countess and her friends of the Trefecca College, near Talgarth, for ministerial students, in 1768.)

> *When I tread the verge of Jordan,*
> *Bid my anxious fears subside;*
> *Death of death and hell's destruction,*
> *Land me safe on Canaan's side;*
> *Songs of praises*
> *I will ever give to Thee.*

The second most popular of Williams' English hymns is:

> *O'er the gloomy hills of darkness*
> *Look, my soul, be still and gaze;*
> *All the promises do travail*
> *With a glorious day of grace:*
> *Blessed jubilee!*
> *Let thy glorious morning dawn.*

The clear implication is that its author was, at the time of writing, in a mountainous terrain with very forbidding features, whereas beyond lay a much more pleasing scene and prospect. Naturally we desire to learn the area in Wales to which Williams refers. One tentative answer is that he was staying at Llwyn-gwair in Pembrokeshire, where the prominent Methodist family of Bowen resided. Mr. Bowen requested a poem including mention of the Prescelly Mountains, and "O'er the Gloomy Hills of Darkness" was the outcome. A different explanation runs as follows: Williams was visiting eastern Glamorganshire and making his way to a farm near Port Talbot where his sister lived. While he was crossing Pen-rhys in the Rhondda in bad weather, the mountains ahead presented the forbidding sight which is usual when they are shrouded in mist and rain. As he pressed ahead he was pondering over a request by the Countess of Huntingdon for a missionary hymn for her use; hence the imagery with which this particular hymn opens. By the time he had reached his destination, the hymn was complete. The two explanations may serve to remind us that contradictory stories about the origin of popular hymns are not of rare occurrence. Where truth actually lies, who can say?

We have already mentioned that some of Williams' hymns were issued and sold on loose sheets of paper. Reference to this practice is made in a letter to Miss Sally Jones who later became the wife of Thomas Charles. It is dated February 25, 1776:

> I have sent you a small bundle with William Evans containing 5 doz., 13 in each doz., of peny hymns on the new metre called Haleluia. Pray sell em for me—you may send them to be sold with some of yr. exorters. . . . Pardon me that the peny hymns are so little, it was for want of proper paper, but at the same time tho the paper is small yet 9 hymns for a peny is not very dear to such as love to sing hymns.

The majority of Williams' hymns were published in five quite substantial volumes (some of them published in parts) between 1744 and 1772, but pamphlets rather than volumes were published from time to time, especially towards the end of his life. But, whether found in book or pamphlet, the influence of the hymns was both deep and nationwide.

22

JOHN BERRIDGE

(1716–93)

To Christ for help I fly,
The Friend of sinners lost,
A refuge sweet and sure and nigh,
And there is all my trust.

No help in self I find,
And yet have sought it well;
The native treasure of my mind
Is sin and death and hell. . . .

And when the hour is near
That flesh and heart will fail,
Do Thou in all Thy grace appear,
And bid my faith prevail.

I N an epitaph for his own tombstone this somewhat eccentric clergyman gave some autobiographical facts. It reads as follows:

Here lie the remains of John Berridge, Late Vicar of Everton and an itinerant servant of Jesus Christ, who loved his Master and His work; and after running on His errands for many years was caught up to wait on Him above. Reader, art thou born again? (No salvation without a new birth.) I was born in sin February 1716; remained ignorant of my fallen state till 1730; lived proudly on faith and works for

salvation till 1754; was admitted to Everton Vicarage 1755; fled to Jesus for refuge 1755; fell asleep in
Jesus January 22, 1793.

His whole life is epitomized here, but the outline needs
filling in a little!

John Berridge was born in Kingston, Nottinghamshire.
His father was a wealthy farmer and he meant his son to
follow in his footsteps. John was a particular favorite of an
aunt in Nottingham and he spent the first fourteen years of
his life with her although of his school days nothing is
known. At this time John knew nothing of scriptural religion, probably having received no instruction either at
home or at school. Then a remarkable thing happened. As
he was returning home from school one day a youth invited him into his house and asked him if he might read to
him from the Bible. John went in and his friend read a
portion of Scripture. The invitation was renewed several
times and, although John felt a secret dislike to the pro-
ceedings, his desire to maintain a reputation for piety kept
him from refusing the invitation. One day he was returning from a fair when his young friend again called him for
Bible reading, and on this occasion proposed prayer also.
John consented and they both prayed.

When John was fourteen he became convinced of his
sinfulness, and it was at about this time that he left school
and returned home with the intention of taking up his
father's business. This plan soon fell to the ground, for he
proved so stupid in agricultural matters that his father
said to him, "John, I find you cannot form any idea of the
price of cattle and I shall have to send you to college to be
a light to the Gentiles." Although he said this, John was
kept in suspense for a year or two as his father was not
going to let his son forsake oxen and sheep to go to college
without a hard struggle to keep him. But the son's distaste
for his father's calling was deep and insuperable, while his
religious impressions continued and even deepened by
conversation with a tailor in Kingston, so that at last old
Mr. Berridge had the good sense to consent to John going

to Cambridge. He entered Clare College, Cambridge, in 1734 when he was eighteen.

Berridge found university life congenial, he studied diligently, sometimes for fifteen hours a day, and attained considerable distinction. After graduating M.A. he became a Fellow of his College. He had studied Classics, Mathematics, Philosophy, Logic and Metaphysics and had read the works of most of the eminent divines. His academic attainments had won for him the respect of university men, while his talent for conversation and his ready humor made his society desirable. Sadly, as he rose socially, he sank spiritually. He was influenced by Deists, turned from the Scriptures and gave up private prayer for ten years or more.

In 1749 it pleased God to awaken his conscience again and, having been ordained some years before, he accepted the curacy of Stapleford near Cambridge. Although he had renounced his errors he had not fully received the gospel, and his labors there for six years met with no real success. He became Vicar of Everton in 1755 but met with no more success than at Stapleford. At length he received the truth himself and so could make it known to others. For as he sat one morning, musing on a text of Scripture, the following words darted into his mind like a voice from heaven, "Cease from thine own works; only believe." At once the scales seemed to fall from his eyes and he saw "the rock on which he had been splitting" for many years—that is, by endeavoring to blend the law and the gospel and to unite Christ's righteousness with his own. There and then he began to think on the words "faith" and "believe" and instantly resolved to preach Jesus Christ and salvation by faith. God very soon began to bless this new kind of ministry and he determined in future to know nothing but Jesus Christ and Him crucified. He was deeply humbled that he should have spent so many years preaching error, and burned all his old sermons, shedding tears of joy over their destruction. The neighborhood was aroused by this time and his church soon became crowded with hearers. Men and women became convinced of their sin and were converted.

John Berridge

John Berridge, whether converted or unconverted, was not a man to do anything by halves, and he now threw himself wholeheartedly and strenuously into his Master's service. He became the friend of John Wesley and Whitefield and, following their example, he began to preach outside his own parish, thus provoking the opposition of the bishops. He preached in houses and barns and in the open air throughout Bedfordshire. Soon he was preaching in the counties round about, ten or twelve times a week. Like Latimer, Rowland Hill and some other popular preachers, he knew both how to attract or enliven his hearers by humorous turns of expression and how to touch their hearts by pathetic allusions or appeals. He was much opposed in his preaching. One man confessed after service on Sunday at Everton that he had only come to confuse the preacher, but that God had made Mr. Berridge the means of convincing him that he was a lost sinner. On another occasion, when he was preaching in the open air, two men hid themselves under the table on which he was standing, with the intention of upsetting it, but the power of the Word of God made their hearts relent. Others confessed they had filled their pockets with stones to throw at him while preaching, but such had been the effect of his preaching that they had gradually emptied their pockets and they now asked him to pray for them.

Berridge never married. In this connection there is a somewhat amusing story. After preaching on one occasion at Whitefield's Tabernacle in London he was visited in his home by a lady. She came down from London in her carriage "to solicit his hand in marriage," assuring him that the Lord had revealed to her that she was to become his wife. He was not a little surprised and after pausing for a few moments replied, "Madam, if the Lord has revealed it to you that you are to be my wife, surely He would also have revealed it to me that I was designed to be your husband; but as no such revelation has been made to me, I cannot comply with your wishes."

Age and infirmities caused Berridge to be almost blind and deaf before he died. He said:

> My ears are so dull they are not fit for converse and my eyes are so weak I can read but little and write less. Old Adam whispers in my ear (and he can make me hear with a whisper), "What will you do if you become deaf and blind?" I tell him I must think more and pray more and thank the Lord for the ears and eyes enjoyed for seventy years and for the prospect of a better pair of eyes and ears when these are gone.

Berridge died at the age of seventy-six in great confidence and peace of mind.

Of all the evangelical leaders of the eighteenth century Berridge was undoubtedly the most quaint and eccentric, but with all his peculiarities he was a man of rare gifts and deeply taught by the Holy Spirit. He was a mighty instrument for good in the orbit in which he moved. He published a volume of poems called *Zion's Song's*, but it must be admitted that many of his hymns too are quaint. Bishop Ryle in his *Christian Leaders of the Eighteenth Century* says,

"The hymns I must leave alone. The Vicar of Everton was no more a poet than Cicero or Julius Caesar; and although the doctrine of his hymns is very sound, the poetry of them is very poor, while the ideas they present are sometimes painfully ludicrous." Even so, some of his hymns have survived until the present day and can be found in recently produced hymnbooks. One of them is on the subject of marriage:

> *Thou who at Cana didst appear,*
> *To bless a marriage feast,*
> *Vouchsafe Thy gracious presence here;*
> *Be Thou with us as Guest. . . .*
>
> *Through life their every step attend*
> *With tokens of Thy love,*
> *And having reached their journey's end,*
> *Complete their bliss above.*

Another hymn which seems fairly poetic begins:

> *The means of grace are in my hand,*
> *The blessing is at God's command.*

One of the later verses reads:

> *Prepare my heart to love Thee well,*
> *And love Thy truth which doth excel,*
> *And love Thy children dear;*
> *Instruct me how to live by faith,*
> *And feel the virtue of Thy death,*
> *And find Thy presence near.*

A verse which does not appear in hymnbooks was pasted on to Berridge's clock!

> *Here my master bids me stand,*
> *And mark the time with faithful hand;*
> *What is his will is my delight,*
> *To tell the hours by day, by night.*
> *Master, be wise and learn of me,*
> *To serve thy God, as I serve thee.*

And so we leave the quaint but lovable Vicar of Everton. There were few greater, better, holier and more useful ministers in the eighteen century than old John Berridge.

23

THOMAS OLIVERS

(1725–99)

The God of Abraham praise,
Who reigns enthroned above,
Ancient of everlasting days,
And God of love.
Jehovah! Great I AM!
By earth and heaven confessed;
I bow and bless the sacred Name
Forever blest. . . .

The God of Abraham praise,
Whose all-sufficient grace
Shall guide me all my happy days
In all my ways.
He is my faithful Friend,
He is my gracious God;
And He shall save me to the end
Through Jesus' blood.

THOMAS OLIVERS was born at a village called Tregynon in Montgomeryshire, Wales, in 1725. His father died when he was four, and a few months later his mother died of a broken heart. Thomas was then looked after by an uncle until he too died, leaving Thomas a small fortune. He was finally brought up by a farmer, Mr. Tudor, at Forden, also in Montgomeryshire. Thomas was sent to school, where, to use his own words, "I re-

Thomas Olivers

ceived such learning as was thought necessary." And "as to religion I was taught to say my prayers morning and evening, to repeat my Catechism, to sing psalms and to go to church twice a Sunday."

He fell into evil ways when very young, lying a great deal and taking the name of God in vain. There was a man in the parish who was notorious for cursing, swearing and horrid blasphemies. Thomas imitated him and says that he was "so apt a scholar that before I was fifteen I vied with my infernal instructor." He was reckoned to be the worst boy known in those parts during the space of twenty or thirty years.

At eighteen Olivers was apprenticed to a shoemaker but by that time he had become so idle that he did not really learn his trade. Finally his conduct became so bad that he had to leave the neighborhood. He went first to Shrewsbury, then to Wrexham and Bristol. One evening he met a crowd of people going to hear George Whitefield preach. He decided that he too would go the following evening, but he arrived too late; however, being determined to hear him, he went on the third evening nearly three hours before time. The sermon was on the text, "Is not this a brand plucked from the burning?" Olivers tells us,

> When the sermon began, I was certainly a dreadful
> enemy to God and to all that is good, and one of
> the most profligate and abandoned young men liv-
> ing: but by the time it ended I was become a new
> creature. I was deeply convinced of the great good-
> ness of God towards me all my life, particularly in
> that He had given His Son to die for me. I had also
> a far clearer view of all my sins, particularly my
> base ingratitude towards Him. These discoveries
> quite broke my heart and caused showers of tears
> to trickle down my cheeks. I was likewise filled
> with an utter abhorrence of my evil ways and was
> very much ashamed that I had ever walked in them.
> And as my heart was thus turned from all evil, so it
> was powerfully inclined to all that is good. It is not
> easy to express what strong desires I had for God
> and His service, and what resolutions I had to seek
> and serve Him in the future, in consequence of
> which I broke off all my evil practices and forsook
> all my wicked and foolish companions without de-
> lay, and gave myself up to God and His service
> with my whole heart. O what reason have I to say,
> "Is not this a brand plucked from the burning?"

The other people in his lodgings saw that something
remarkable had happened to him and were surprised that
he wept so much. They thought that he had lost a near
relation or that he had been disappointed in love. At last
the great change in his life showed them that it was a
concern for salvation which so deeply affected him. He
then told them what had happened, and though they were
not interested in religion they all rejoiced at the obvious
change they saw in him. After his conversion Olivers spent
several weeks doing little else than going to services and
praying. At that time he spent so many hours on his knees
that he developed a limp when walking. It is not surprising that he should have a great love for George Whitefield,
the instrument used by God for his wonderful deliverance

and conversion. After a few months he went to live at Bradford in Wiltshire (now called Bradford-on-Avon). He soon found where preaching took place and for two years he did not miss a single sermon, however early or late the time of it. Because he did not belong to the Methodist "Society" he could only attend public meetings. He longed to join the Society, and when he was asked if he would like to do so, he says, "My heart leaped for joy and I told them I should be exceedingly glad to join. I was so elevated that I felt as if I could literally fly away to heaven."

In the course of time Olivers thought that he was called to preach and was advised to begin to do so. Sometimes he was tempted to believe that he was running before he was sent—until, taking a New Testament, his eyes fell on the words, "He that putteth his hand to the plough and looketh back is not fit for the kingdom of God." So he took courage and continued preaching until serious illness prevented him for a time. After paying all the debts he had incurred in earlier years in various parts of the country, he set up his own business in Bradford. He had not really settled in it before John Wesley asked him to give it up and to go to Cornwall as one of his traveling preachers. Subsequently he preached not only in Cornwall but in many parts of England and Ireland. Most of his journeyings were on horseback and for twenty-five years he had one horse on which he rode 100,000 miles. Like most preachers in those days he was not without his share of opposition and violence. Later he took charge of Wesley's printing, but he had to leave this work after some years because "his literary accuracy and scholarship were found inadequate."

Olivers died suddenly in London in 1799 and was buried in the same vault as John Wesley in the City Road Chapel graveyard. His soul had gone to join "The whole triumphant host" who

Give thanks to God on high;
"Hail, Father, Son and Holy Ghost!"
They ever cry.

Hail, Abraham's God and mine!
I join the heavenly lays;
All might and majesty are Thine,
And endless praise.

Olivers' educational advantages were small; yet he wrote several excellent hymns, of which only one—"The God of Abraham Praise"—remains in general use. It was written in London in 1770 and is said by Olivers to be a free rendering of the Hebrew Yigdal or Doxology which rehearses in metrical form the thirteen articles of the Hebrew creed. It seems that Olivers visited the Great Synagogue in Aldgate and heard a celebrated air sung by a Signor Leoni. He was so captivated by the tune that he resolved to write a hymn to suit the air. Both hymn and tune were received with such enthusiasm by Methodists that eight editions were needed in two years.

The hymn was a source of great consolation to Henry Martyn when, in 1805, with mingled feelings of regret and hope, he was saying goodbye to England and setting out on his important missionary career. Martyn himself wrote,

> I was much engaged at intervals in learning the hymn, "The God of Abraham Praise." As often as I could use the language of it with any truth my heart was a little at ease. There was something particularly solemn and affecting to me in this hymn. . . . The truth of the sentiments I knew well enough. But, alas! I felt that the state of mind expressed in it was above mine at the time and I felt loath to leave all on earth.

In a Methodist magazine of earlier days many instances are quoted of the usefulness of the hymn. We give but one of them. A Methodist minister after "a short but glorious career" was laid low by illness. Shortly before he died he exclaimed with triumphant faith, "Christ is mine, heaven is mine," and repeated the lines:

He by Himself hath sworn—
I on His oath depend;

> *I shall, on eagles' wings upborne,*
> *To heaven ascend.*

Montgomery says, "There is not in our language a lyric of more majestic style, more elevated thought or more glorious imagery."

Although Olivers gave the hymn "as decided a Christian character as I could," when we read its verses we see a great deal of Old Testament language in it: "Ancient of everlasting days," "Jehovah! Great I AM," "My shield and tower," "on eagles' wings upborne." Intermingled with the Old Testament imagery we have the New Testament content, the assurance that "He shall save me to the end through Jesus' blood" and the looking forward to the time when

> *I shall behold His face,*
> *I shall His power adore,*
> *And sing the wonders of His grace*
> *Forevermore.*

24

MICHAEL BRUCE

(1746–67)

Where high the heavenly temple stands,
The house of God not made with hands,
A great High Priest our nature wears,
The Saviour of mankind appears.

He who for men their surety stood,
And poured on earth His precious blood,
Pursues in heaven His mighty plan,
The Saviour and the Friend of man.

THE name of Bruce is very familiar to all Scotsmen, and to many others, being usually associated with Bannockburn. But how many have heard of Michael Bruce, who has been aptly described as "Loch Leven's gentle poet" and whose name, had he lived longer than his brief twenty-one years, might have been as well known as those of his near-contemporaries, Watts, Charles Wesley, Doddridge, Cowper and Newton?

Michael Bruce, the fifth of eight children of Alexander Bruce, was born at Kinnesswood, Kinross-shire. "A short distance up a narrow, rugged lane named 'The Loan on the Hill,' passing through the quaint village, you come to the humble cottage where Michael Bruce was born. The village rests at the foot of the Lomond Hills, near the north-eastern shore of Loch Leven." His father, a master weaver and a self-educated man, was an elder of the seceding church associated with the name of Ebenezer Erskine, who was for many years minister in the nearby village of Portmoak. The secession had taken place because Ralph and Ebenezer Erskine, with others, had felt inhibited from protesting effectively against abuses in the Church of Scotland, particularly patronage. This meant that ministers were presented to churches by patrons instead of being elected by the congregations, as the seceders demanded.

It has been said of Alexander Bruce that "poetry, history and especially theology were so much his delight that they often robbed the loom of the attentions due to it!" But he was adept at the wheel and soon made up for any lost time. Like many who came under the influence of Ebenezer Erskine he was an exemplary Christian, as also was his wife. We are told that she possessed as much piety as her husband, though not as much discretion! David Pearson, who lived with the Bruce family for three years and became a close friend of Michael's, wrote of Alexander Bruce that "he was excellent at his business and taught a number of

Ebenezer Erskine

apprentices who revered him as a parent, teacher, master and friend." His shrewd mind quickly discerned the mental ability of his fifth child and it must have been with a feeling of satisfaction that he took him to the parish school for the first time, having already taught him to read simple Bible stories. To the surprise of his teacher, Michael took the Bible to school as his lesson book—children usually brought the Shorter Catechism from which to learn to read. The enthusiastic teacher was "greatly taken" with Michael, who soon held foremost place in classes, without exciting the jealousy of his two rivals who were the schoolmaster's own son and William Arnot, "the young laird of Portmoak," who was his friend. In the summer months Michael made himself useful as a "wee herd loon" (shepherd boy, in English!).

He displayed remarkable intelligence and ability for learning, which made him "the prodigy of the school." At one bound he came into "the front rank of poetic genius." When still a boy he had found peace with God and rest and satisfaction for his soul in Christ. He truly expressed his feelings when he sang:

> O happy is the man who hears
> Instruction's warning voice,
> And who celestial Wisdom makes
> His early only choice.

Dr. Mackelvie, the minister of the church of which the Bruces were members, tells us that Michael's conversation was generally about spiritual things and that he had obvious enjoyment when any new thought connected with theology was suggested to him. When at any time his father was away from home at the usual time for family prayer, Michael, by the common consent of the household, led the devotions. Following the bent of his mind, and gratifying a long-cherished wish of his father's, Michael decided to study for the ministry and at the age of eleven joined a class of senior pupils in order to prepare for college. The death of William Arnot, his intimate school friend, had the effect of drawing Michael into close friendship with his father, David Arnot, who treated Michael as his own son.

He gave him free access to his well-filled library, giving him also guidance as to what he should read and generally helping forward his education.

In 1762, Bruce enrolled as a student in the Greek class at Edinburgh—though he learned a wide variety of subjects besides Greek—being helped financially by a legacy his father had received and by David Arnot's unfailing kindness. He made many friends at the university, acquired an admirable prose style and contributed some poems to the Literary Society. Leaving the university in 1765 he became schoolmaster at Gairney Bridge in Kinross-shire. He had twenty-eight pupils, each of them paying two shillings a quarter, and free board with those parents who could afford to give it. Bruce next entered the Theological Hall at Kinross conducted by a Professor Swanston, but his delicacy of health showed itself during his first session at the Hall and Professor Swanston advised him to refrain from study altogether for a time. In 1766 he went to teach at Forest Mill near Tillicoultry in Clackmannanshire. The school was "low-ceiled, earthen-floored, chilly and musty; outside were dreary spaces of moor; society was uncongenial; children dense, stupid and backward." It was a melancholy period for Bruce and probably hastened the tuberculosis which had already taken hold of him. He left the school and walked the twenty miles back to the kindly influences of home and friendship. He was tenderly cared for at home but his life on earth was drawing to a close. He had no hope of recovery. He wrote his "Elegy on Spring"— his last spring—of which we quote the first and last verses:

Now spring returns; but not to me returns
The vernal joy my better years have known;
Dim in my breast life's dying taper burns,
And all the joys of life with health are flown. . . .

There let me sleep, forgotten in the clay,
When death shall shut these weary, aching eyes;
Rest in the hope of an eternal day
Till the long night's gone, and the last morn arise.

For Bruce the bitterness of death had long been over. He had learned that to those who rest in Christ, death is a glorious, happy exchange. In his last illness one of his fellow-students called on him and observed that he was glad to find him so cheerful. "And why," said he, "should not a man be cheerful on the verge of heaven?" Soon after this Bruce "imperceptibly fell asleep, aged twenty-one years and three months." His Bible was found on his pillow marked at Jeremiah 22:10—"Weep not for the dead, neither bemoan him." He was buried in the "kirkyard" at Portmoak which slopes towards Loch Leven.

It is not easy to say precisely when Bruce began to write poetry, but it is possible to date the origin of his paraphrases on scriptural subjects. In 1764 he attended a singing class for teaching psalmody to the younger people in the church. It was reckoned a sin to use the metrical version of the psalms for the purpose of practice and Bruce was asked to write a number of hymns as a substitute. The hymn we quoted at the beginning was probably written about 1764 for this class and in 1781 it was included, with others by Bruce, in *Translations and Paraphrases in Verse of Several Passages of Sacred Scripture* as a rendering of Hebrews 4:14–16. "Where High the Heavenly Temple Stands" is a good example of the type of hymn which Bruce wrote. His hymns are

> admirable for their faithfulness to the passages of Scripture they render, for their poetic imagery and for their style which is dignified without being pretentious. Here and there they reveal a pensive tendency, resembling what is found in the author's letters, suggestive of high purposes disappointed by life's early decay.

His hymns have been a source of comfort and refreshment to many in trying circumstances. The remaining verses of the hymn quoted at the beginning are surely in the category of "a source of comfort":

Though now ascended up on high,
  He bends on earth a brother's eye;
Partaker of the human name,
  He knows the frailty of our frame.

Our fellow-sufferer yet retains
  A fellow-feeling of our pains,
And still remembers in the skies
  His tears, His agonies and cries.

In every pang that rends the heart,
  The Man of Sorrows had a part;
He sympathizes with our grief,
  And to the sufferer sends relief.

With boldness, therefore, at the throne
  Let us make all our sorrows known;
And ask the aid of heavenly power
  To help us in the evil hour.

Bruce's paraphrases are among the best known of Scottish paraphrases. Another example is:

Behold, the mountain of the Lord
  In latter days shall rise
On mountain tops above the hills,
  And draw the wondering eyes.

To this the joyful nations round,
  All tribes and tongues, shall flow;
Up to the hill of God, they'll say,
  And to His house we'll go. . . .

No strife shall rage, nor hostile feuds
  Disturb those peaceful years;
To ploughshares men shall beat their swords,
  To pruning hooks their spears.

Come then, O come from every land,
  To worship at His shrine;
And, walking in the light of God,
  With holy beauties shine.

This is a paraphrase of Isaiah 2, verses 1–5 and Micah 4, verses 1–5.

Another hymn of Bruce's still found in modern hymnbooks is:

> *Almighty Father of mankind,*
> *On Thee my hopes remain;*
> *And when the day of trouble comes,*
> *I shall not trust in vain. . . .*
>
> *Therefore in life I'll trust to Thee,*
> *In death I will adore,*
> *And after death I'll sing Thy praise,*
> *When time shall be no more.*

If ever you are near Loch Leven it would be well worth turning aside to the churchyard at Portmoak and finding there the monument to Michael Bruce erected by Dr. Mackelvie, the minister of his church, out of the profits of his edition of Michael Bruce's poems.

25

SAMUEL MEDLEY

(1738–99)

Awake, my soul, in joyful lays,
And sing thy great Redeemer's praise;
He justly claims a song from thee:
His lovingkindness, O how free!

He saw me ruined by the Fall,
Yet loved me, notwithstanding all;
He saved me from my lost estate:
His lovingkindness, O how great!

SAMUEL MEDLEY was born at Cheshunt, Herts, England, in 1738, the son of Guy Medley who had been tutor to the Duke of Montague and later kept a school at Cheshunt. Even so, Medley was educated by his mother's father, William Tonge, and at the age of fourteen he was apprenticed to an oilman in the city of London. This occupation not being to his liking, he claimed the privilege, granted in that time of war, of finishing his apprenticeship in the navy, which he joined in 1755. In this way he had an opportunity to see much of the world; but alas! the profanity which characterized him at this time probably had more outlet in the navy than in civil life. Later in life he often mentioned the awful lengths to which he was permitted to go, and how much he was under the dominion of his corruptions, being "utterly averse to every serious reflection that might occasionally intrude upon his mind. Possessing considerable classical learning, a ready wit and an unbounded flow of spirits, he was at once the life of the giddy circle in which he was daily associated." His volatile turn of mind was his greatest snare.

In a naval action between the French and English in 1759, off Cape Lagos (Portugal), he received a severe leg wound which daily grew worse until the surgeon told him that because of the danger of gangrene the only means of saving his life would be to amputate the leg. The surgeon said he would make a final decision the following morning. This was sad news to Medley. He called to mind the prayers of his father and grandfather on his behalf, and considering his case to be desperate, "it occurred to his mind that prayer to God must be his last resource." He prayed very fervently for the restoration of his limb and the preservation of his life. He remembered that he had a Bible which someone, perhaps his father, had put in his chest and, though he had never opened it before, like many others when sick, he began to read it avidly. When the surgeon examined the wound next morning he exclaimed that the change was little short of a miracle. Medley set this down as an answer to prayer and began to think there was something in religion after all. This thought wore off, however, as the wound healed.

On the return of the fleet to England Medley was taken to his grandfather's house. Mr. Tonge had trained him as a child and now he gladly took him into his house in London to care for him in his time of need. He took every opportunity to wean his grandson from the love of the world and to lead him to pursue a better life.

One Sunday evening Mr. Tonge remained at home for the express purpose of reading a sermon to his grandson, an unwilling listener. The sermon was by Isaac Watts on Isaiah 42, verses 6–7. The seventh verse, "To open blind eyes, to bring out the prisoners from the prison . . . ," was felt by the hearer to describe himself. He saw his sinful condition and cried to God for mercy. Soon he was sufficiently recovered to go out and hear the preaching of

Samuel Medley

George Whitefield, Andrew Gifford and others, and he "soon received the comforts of the gospel, by a believing view of the fullness and sufficiency of the atonement of the Lord Jesus."

Medley gave up thoughts of returning to the navy, despite the offer of promotion. At this time he became acquainted with Andrew Gifford, assistant librarian at the British Museum and also pastor of a Particular Baptist church in Holborn. He joined this church in 1760. About the same time he married and moved the school he had opened near Seven Dials, London, to King Street, Soho, where it proved successful. In 1766 Dr. Gifford questioned him on the subject of the ministry. Soon afterwards he was heard by the church, called by them to the work of preaching, and the following year accepted a call to a church in Watford, Herts. Four years later he had a further call to a Baptist Church on Byrom Street, Liverpool, beginning his ministry there early in 1772. His career as a preacher in Liverpool was one of remarkable and increasing popularity and soon a much larger building had to be erected for him. Having been at sea himself, he understood the seafaring men who frequented his church and did a valuable work among them.

Every year Medley visited London, preaching at Rowland Hill's Surrey Chapel and at Tottenham Court Road Chapel, opened during Whitefield's lifetime. It was on one of these journeys that his final illness came upon him. His mind was at first depressed by his affliction, but he regained his composure and spent his remaining days in telling of the blessings of the gospel. Among his last words were, "I am now a poor shattered bark just about to gain the blissful harbor, and oh! how sweet will be the port after the storm! But a point or two, and I shall be at my heavenly Father's house." Or, to express the thoughts in the last two verses of the hymn we have already quoted:

> *Soon shall I pass the gloomy vale,*
> *Soon all my mortal powers must fail;*
> *O may my last expiring breath*
> *His lovingkindness sing in death!*
>
> *Then let me mount and soar away*
> *To the bright world of endless day,*
> *And sing with rapture and surprise*
> *His lovingkindness in the skies.*

Medley's hymns were originally printed as single sheets or in the *Gospel Magazine* and other publications. Later they were collected into small volumes, the first being published in 1785. More hymns were added in later editions. A modest preface disclaims merit on the part of the author and expresses his desire to comfort Christians and to glorify Christ. Julian says of Medley's hymns that they "have been popular in his own denomination, particularly among the more Calvinistic churches. Their charm consists less in their poetry than in the warmth and occasional pathos with which they give expression to Christian experience." In most of them also there is a refrain in the last line of each verse, as for example in the hymn first quoted, where God's "lovingkindness" is said to be free, great, strong, good, unchanging, a comfort in death, and a source of joy in heaven.

It has been said that the general scope of Medley's ministry was "to humble the pride of man, exalt the grace of God in his salvation, and promote real holiness in heart and life," and there is no doubt that his ministry both in preaching and hymn-writing achieved these ends. We close with verses from another hymn which both exalts Christ and answers to the experience of believers' hearts:

I know that my Redeemer lives;
What joy this blest assurance gives!
He lives, He lives, who once was dead:
He lives, my everlasting Head. . . .

He lives to bless me with His love,
And still He pleads for me above;
He lives to raise me from the grave,
And me eternally to save.

He lives, my kind, wise, constant Friend,
Who still will keep me to the end:
He lives, and while He lives I'll sing,
Jesus, my Prophet, Priest and King.

He lives my mansion to prepare;
And He will bring me safely there;
He lives, all glory to His Name!
Jesus unchangeably the same!

26

JOHN NEWTON

(1725–1807)

In evil long I took delight,
  Unawed by shame or fear,
Till a new object struck my sight,
  And stopped my wild career.
I saw One hanging on a tree,
  In agonies and blood,
Who fixed His languid eyes on me,
  As near His cross I stood.

Sure never till my latest breath
  Can I forget that look;
It seemed to charge me with His death,
  Though not a word He spoke.

My conscience felt, and owned the guilt,
  And plunged me in despair;
I saw my sins His blood had spilt,
  And helped to nail Him there.

Alas! I knew not what I did;
  But now my tears are vain;
Where shall my trembling soul be hid?
  For I the Lord have slain.

A second look He gave, which said,
  "I freely all forgive;
This blood is for thy ransom paid,
  I die, that thou may'st live."

Thus, while His death my sin displays
In all its blackest hue,
(Such is the mystery of grace)
It seals my pardon too.

With pleasing grief and mournful joy
My spirit now is filled,
That I should such a life destroy,
Yet live by Him I killed.

JOHN NEWTON's hymn, quoted above (and rarely found in hymnbooks), is one of the best of all autobiographical hymns, including as it does both the objective and the subjective aspects of the salvation that is to be found in Christ and in Christ alone. An editor of former days gave the title *Out of the Depths* to Newton's autobiography. His life before conversion was one of outstanding interest and his service for God after conversion was also outstanding.

Calvin has been described as "the man God mastered." John Newton also was such a man. His description of himself as a "wretch" bent upon a "wild career" is strictly true, because as a young man he was an uncontrolled profligate. Before his conversion he was so bent on evil that the Lord in "mastering" him had to deal with him as a man might seek to tame a wild beast. Chastisement followed chastisement, and he knew suffering and distress almost indescribable before he was brought to the end of himself and his headstrong character was mastered by One stronger than he.

John Newton was born in London in 1725. His father, a seafaring man, was for many years master of a ship in the Mediterranean trade. He was a severe father but he had married a gentle, godly woman of dissenting convictions, and John being her only child she was able to devote all her attention to him. He could read when he was four and his mind was stored with Scripture and with Dr. Watts'

Shorter Catechism. His mother hoped that he might enter the ministry, but she died when he was seven and was not privileged to see that the seed she had sown in his young heart and mind bore fruit after many days.

John went to school for about two years, then when he was only eleven his father took him to the Mediterranean in his own ship. Before he was fifteen he had made several voyages and after some restless years he agreed to his father's proposal that he should go to the West Indies. Before he went something happened which was to influence his whole future career. Some distant relatives of his mother's invited him to visit them in Kent before he went abroad. He did so and fell in love with their elder daughter, Mary Catlett, who was then only fourteen years old. Long afterwards he said, "I was impressed with an affection for her which never abated or lost its influence over me. None of the scenes of misery and wretchedness I afterwards experienced ever banished her for an hour from my waking thoughts for the seven following years."

He displeased his father greatly by staying three weeks instead of three days with the Catletts and so missing his ship to the West Indies. His life of profligacy had begun; he deserted from the ship on which he finally sailed; he was publicly flogged and degraded from the rank of midshipman. Only the thought of Mary Catlett saved him from drowning himself in despair. At length he arrived in Africa, not the West Indies, and determined to stay there. As he wandered about, utterly destitute, he was glad to enter into the service of a slave trader on Plantain Island which lies just off the coast of Sierra Leone. Here he passed through a time of terrible hardship, wretchedness and degradation. The slave trader was absent for a time and his black mistress treated Newton with the utmost cruelty, even when he was almost dying of fever. When he began to recover he was nearly starved to death and in his own *Narrative* he tells how hunger compelled him to go out at night to prowl about for food, pulling up roots and eating them raw. Sometimes the poor slaves in their chains pitied

John Newton

him and secretly gave him some of their scanty food. When his master returned, his life became even more wretched.

One day a strange ship came in sight. It was that of a Mr. Manesty of Liverpool who had been asked by Newton's father to try to find his son. Although Mr. Manesty rescued him, his troubles were not over, for the ship was almost wrecked in a storm. During some hours of solemn reflection Newton reviewed his whole life, especially his scoffing at Scripture, his vicious conduct, the dangers he had been in and the wonderful deliverances he had experienced. The ship outrode the storm and the awakened sinner was saved to serve God in the world.

Before his father left to take up an appointment with the Hudson Bay Company he had given consent to his son's marriage, and when Newton was twenty-five he married Mary Catlett whom he had loved, and continued to love, with unfailing constancy. Until 1754 we find Newton actively engaged in what he did not then regard as an unlawful occupation—the slave trade—though later he did his utmost to expose its cruelties. At the end of 1754, as he was about to set out on a voyage, he was seized with an apoplectic fit. This was the Lord's means of delivering him from slave trading. For eight years he was tide-surveyor at Liverpool, during which time his Christian life was making progress. He read a great deal and at this time he providentially met a man who proved to be a counselor and guide to him:

> He not only improved my understanding but inflamed my heart. He encouraged me to open my mouth in prayer and to venture to speak for God. I was delivered from a fear which had long troubled me, the fear of relapsing into my former apostasy. But now I began to understand the security of the covenant of grace and to expect to be preserved, not by my own power and holiness but by the mighty power and promise of God, through faith in an unchangeable Saviour.

Newton now began to study the Scriptures in Hebrew and Greek, and after a year spent in this routine of duty and study he seems to have had his first thoughts of entering the ministry. The informal addresses he had been giving at private meetings had been well received and he was urged by his friends to seek to become an Anglican clergyman. With Mrs. Newton he visited Yorkshire, where he had heard of remarkable revivals; he spoke with several evangelical ministers and returned greatly refreshed in spirit and with his desire to enter the ministry confirmed. After five more years in secular duties the curacy of Olney in County Bucks was offered to, and accepted by, him.

He went to Olney in 1764 when he was thirty-nine and remained there nearly sixteen years. He succeeded the Rev. Moses Browne, a faithful evangelical minister whose preaching had prepared the people of Olney for Newton's ministry. The services in church were well attended, cottage meetings were started in surrounding hamlets, and meetings were held in a room of what was known as "the Great House," a mansion belonging to, but not often used by, the evangelical Earl of Dartmouth. We shall say more about the Great House when we deal later with the *Olney*

Hymns which were written by Newton and the poet William Cowper.

The living* at Olney was a poor one, Newton's salary being little more than $60 a year, but a generous friend, John Thornton, allowed him $200 a year which enabled Newton and William Cowper, his friend and helper, to give help to the struggling poor when they visited their homes. There were nearly always visitors at the vicarage, for Thornton had said, "Be hospitable and keep an open house for such as are worthy of entertainment." Newton's friendship with Cowper is the most remarkable feature of his life in Olney. There are people even now who say that Newton's austere views of religion were the cause of Cowper's later insanity. This statement is quite groundless as Cowper's malady was constitutional and had first showed itself in early days when he had no thought of religion. Largely due to his friendship with John Newton the years Cowper spent in Olney were the happiest and most useful years of his life. He very much needed "a companion of kindred spirit and equal understanding," and the warmth of affection which accompanied Newton's masculine nature made him the gentle counselor whom Cowper needed. For his part Newton reckoned Cowper's friendship among his "principal blessings."

In 1770 Newton's friend John Thornton offered him the living* of St. Mary Woolnoth in London. There he became well-known and extremely useful in the Lord's service, not only through his preaching but in conversation and in correspondence. Several of his printed works consist of letters, one being entitled *Cardiphonia* or "heart breathings." During his twenty-eight years at St. Mary Woolnoth Newton applied himself to his ministerial and pastoral work. Sometimes he was accused by Calvinists of being an Arminian and by Arminians of being a Calvinist. He was courteous and tolerant towards all who differed from him and was greatly respected and loved. By the wish of

---

* The position of vicar or rector with income and/or property.

Charles Wesley he was one of the eight ministers who
were pallbearers at his funeral.

By nature Newton had great warmth of heart as well as
energy of mind. He was always self-abasing and humble
on account of his former wickedness of life and his pre-
sumptuous rejection of the gospel. He knew that God had
forgiven him but he could not forgive himself. With his
humility was mingled perpetual admiration of the mercy
and grace of God towards such a sinner as himself. He had
a complete resignation to the will of God and a constant
sense of the presence and providence of God in every event

John Newton's study at Olney

of his life. He had great sympathy and kindness of heart and literally wept with those who wept and rejoiced with those who rejoiced. The law of love was in his heart and the language of it on his lips.

After the death of Mrs. Newton in 1790 he suffered a succession of trials and afflictions. His sight was feeble, his strength decreased, and the niece who looked after him had to be taken to a mental hospital. He continued his own ministerial work without remission. "I cannot stop," he said. "What! should the old African blasphemer stop while he can speak!" At the last public service he conducted, a collection was taken up for the benefit of the sufferers from the Battle of Trafalgar. His faculties were so far gone that he had to be reminded of the subject of the sermon. Finally he could preach no more and during the year 1807 he was mostly confined to the house, then to his room, where he enjoyed the visits of friends.

Richard Cecil preached his funeral sermon in which he described Newton as "gradually sinking as the setting sun, shedding to the last those declining rays which gilded and gladdened the dark valley. In the latter conversations I had with him he expressed an unshaken faith in eternal realities and when he could scarcely utter words he remained a firm witness to the truth he had preached."

27

WILLIAM COWPER

(1731–1800)

God moves in a mysterious way
His wonders to perform;
He plants His footsteps in the sea,
And rides upon the storm.

Deep in unfathomable mines
Of never-failing skill
He treasures up His bright designs,
And works His sovereign will.

Ye fearful saints, fresh courage take;
The clouds ye so much dread
Are big with mercy, and shall break
In blessings on your head.

THE first six years of Cowper's life were spent in his father's rectory at Great Berkhamsted, Herts, where he was born in 1731. He retained a lifelong devotion for his mother though she died when he was six, leaving a child temperamentally unsuited to face the battle of life. Though so young he was sent to boarding school where he faced loneliness, insecurity, and bullying which must have left a scar on his nervous system. At about the age of nine he went to Westminster School. His father, though a minister, had not taught the gospel to his sons and William learned nothing of true religion at Westminster. He later regretted that he learned Latin and Greek at the expense of much more important knowledge.

Cowper's father decided what career he was to follow. "I was bred to the law," Cowper wrote, "a profession to which I never had much inclination." In 1752, at the age of twenty-one, he had proceeded far enough in his profession to take rooms in the Temple,* where he remained for twelve years. Soon after he was established in his new quarters he tells us, "I was struck with such a dejection of spirit as none but they who have felt the same can have the least conception of." In his desperation he turned to religious duties, but when the depression passed he concluded that all that was needed to prevent its return was "a continual circle of diversion," in which he proceeded to engage.

As the years passed, life became more and more futile; his father and stepmother died, then his closest friend was drowned. Only one more shock was needed to bring about his collapse and this came in 1763. Although now in his early thirties he had made little professional progress and his future was uncertain. A relative, seeing his insecurity, and having the right to do so, offered him the vacant position of Clerk of the Journals of the House of Lords. It would have been a lucrative position, but to qualify for the post Cowper had to be publicly examined at the bar of the House of Lords. It would have been a simple procedure, but to Cowper this examination became an insurmountable problem and he was seized by despair. Before the dread morning of his trial arrived he sought more than once to end his life. After the failure of these attempts he grew worse and settled into a condition of madness. His brother John, who was a minister and a don at Cambridge, tried in vain to help. Rev. Martin Madan brought a gleam of hope by showing him "how faith receives Christ's righteousness for our justification," though for the moment the lesson did not avail. Cowper was then entrusted to the care of Dr. Nathaniel Cotton, an evangelical who kept a home for the insane at St. Albans. After a few months there the never-to-be-forgotten day came.

---

* The area of London which houses the legal profession.

I flung myself into a chair near the window and, seeing a Bible there, ventured once more to apply to it for comfort and instruction. The first verse I saw was the 25th of the 3rd of Romans, "Whom God hath set forth to be a propitiation through faith in his blood, to declare his righteousness for the remission of sins that are past, through the forbearance of God." Immediately I received strength to believe it and the full beams of the Sun of Righteousness shone upon me. I saw the sufficiency of the atonement He had made—my pardon was sealed in His blood. . . . I could only look up to heaven in silent fear, overwhelmed with love and wonder.

His testimony is surely found in his hymn, "Hark, My Soul! It Is the Lord":

> *I delivered thee when bound*
> *And, when bleeding, healed thy wound;*
> *Sought thee wandering, set thee right,*
> *Turned thy darkness into light.*

After eighteen months Cowper was able to leave Dr. Cotton's and, in order to be near his brother John in Cambridge, he took lodgings in Huntingdon, feeling that he never wanted to see London again. He soon met problems; he was not the man to live alone; there were housekeeping difficulties and he spent a year's income in four months! He met no like-minded Christian and complained, "I felt like a traveler in the midst of an inhospitable desert, without a friend to comfort." Unknown to him his solitariness had already been noticed and almost immediately the whole course of his life was changed. A young man, William Unwin, approached Cowper and they found themselves of one mind in the gospel. The next Sunday Cowper had dinner with Unwin's parents and very shortly he was welcomed to the home as a permanent "lodger." Rev. Morley Unwin was a rector in Norfolk but, as was possible in those days, he chose to live quietly in Huntingdon. The light of the home was Mary Unwin, a bright, well-read

William Cowper

woman, strong both in character and in evangelical belief and practice. She was much younger than her husband and only eight years older than Cowper, who was extremely happy with his new and congenial way of life. Month followed month in harmonious routine until Morley Unwin, when riding to take a service, was thrown from his horse. He died of a fractured skull.

Mrs. Unwin did not wish to stay in Huntingdon and the question as to where they should go was decided by the arrival of a visitor, "a little, odd-looking man of the Methodistical order." The curate of Olney, John Newton, at the suggestion of a mutual friend, had called to extend his sympathy. Within weeks the matter was settled. The parish of John Newton must be their home and Mrs. Unwin, her daughter and Cowper moved to Olney in September 1767.

Newton, then age forty-two, and Cowper, age thirty-five, were to spend the next twelve years together, forming one of the most delightful friendships recorded in Church history. They spent a great deal of time together. Newton says of Cowper, "I can hardly form an idea of a closer walk with God than he uniformly maintained."

In the stagecoach days of 200 years ago, Olney, with its lace-making industry, was a thriving place. It was "a large and necessitous parish" which kept Newton so busy that he needed a helper. This helper Cowper now became. He cared for the poor, visited the sick and dying, and was always present at the meetings for prayer in "the Great House." As to public prayer, Newton says of his friend, "He spoke with self-abasement and humiliation of spirit, yet with a freedom and fervency as if he saw the Lord whom he addressed face to face."

From time to time there had been reminders of Cowper's earlier mental disorder, and a depression would sometimes trouble his spirit. Newton would note in his diary, "Mr. Cowper down in the depths." In 1771 there were indications of an increase of gloom and at that time, out of concern to arrest the tendency, Newton proposed that they should start hymn-writing. Although the signs of persistent melancholy were distressing to Newton and Mrs. Unwin, they gave little evidence of the storm which broke in 1773. His previous derangement returned with full force. We draw a veil over the period except to say that for eleven months he and Mrs. Unwin stayed at the vicarage, where Newton and his wife Mary gave themselves unstintingly to help him.

When the storm subsided Newton wrote, "Some little incident made him smile, the first time, it seems, for sixteen months." Many suggestions have been made as to why Cowper collapsed again, but the ultimate cause of Cowper's illness is shrouded in mystery. The awareness that God knew and appreciated the burdens under which his reason reeled was probably the inspiration for "God Moves in a Mysterious Way," the last hymn which Cowper contributed to the Olney hymns as the storm closed about him. The tempest had subsided but the tragedy was not over. Cowper was slowly nursed back to sanity by the inexhaustible courage and care of Mary Unwin. Every art was used to reawaken his interest in life—the garden, the tame hares which amused him, carpentry, painting, long walks, and taking up seriously the writing of poetry. Yet spiritually there seemed little or no recovery. Newton's six years of pleasure with his friend were succeeded by six years in which, he says, "I walked with him through the valley of the shadow of death." His friend's restoration was no nearer when Newton left Olney for London in 1780.

Cowper never recovered. An attempt to improve his condition came about when he and Mrs. Unwin left the old, damp home at Olney for a more attractive residence in a nearby village, but within weeks he suffered another bout of insanity and for six months his condition was as desperate as ever.

In the last decade of his life he suffered the great trial of the physical and mental breakdown of his faithful friend, Mary Unwin. A relative of Cowper's moved them to Norfolk, but neither sea nor fresh rural scenes could break Cowper's gloom. Mrs. Unwin died in 1796. He lingered until April 1800, when he slipped so quietly from this life that those around his bedside did not observe the moment of his departure. His remains were laid to rest beside those of Mrs. Unwin in the church of East Dereham while his spirit at last entered upon the work for which it had years before so keenly longed:

> Then in a nobler, sweeter song,
> I'll sing Thy power to save,
> When this poor, lisping, stammering tongue
> Lies silent in the grave.

Newton, seventy-five years old, took his friend's funeral service, preaching from Ecclesiastes 2:2–3. He said, "What a glorious surprise must it be to find himself released from all his chains in a moment and in the presence of the Lord whom he loved and whom he served."

28

THE OLNEY HYMNS
(1779)

Amazing grace—how sweet the sound—
That saved a wretch like me!
I once was lost, but now am found;
Was blind, but now I see.

'Twas grace that taught my heart to fear,
And grace my fears relieved;
How precious did that grace appear
The hour I first believed!

Through many dangers, toils and snares
I have already come;
'Tis grace has brought me safe thus far,
And grace will lead me home.

When we've been there ten thousand years,
Bright shining as the sun,
We've no less days to sing God's praise
Than when we'd first begun.

John Newton

IT was in 1767 that two residents of the small town of
Olney in Bucks became friends. This friendship gave
rise to a collection of Christian verse which was to
enrich all the churches of the English-speaking world.
When the *Olney Hymns* were published in 1779, 268 were

by John Newton and 68 by his companion William Cowper. They wrote on a common theme but the two men differed as much in their backgrounds as they did in their appearance. The short-statured Newton, with his cheerful face, was a compelling character. There was only a six-year difference between them (Newton being the elder), but Newton had sailed the high seas and reached depths of profligacy before Cowper had lifted his shy, sensitive face from the pages of the Greek and Roman classics at Westminster School. Had it not been for the gospel, their paths would not have remotely approached the one to the other.

The *Olney Hymns* was an unpretentious book, intended primarily for the country people who attended the weeknight meeting which Newton had started in 1765 and which was so well attended that it had to move from the small church room to a larger room in "the Great House," a little-used country residence of the evangelical patron of the parish, Lord Dartmouth. The hymns were "for the use of plain people," it having been agreed by the two men that "perspicuity, simplicity and ease should chiefly be attended to, and the imagery of poetry, if admitted at all, should be indulged very sparingly and with great judgment."

The hymns were avowedly Calvinistic. Newton explains in his preface that certain "gracious persons" thought that he should "for their sake studiously avoid every expression which they could not approve." But he complains that they do not care to impose such a restraint upon themselves and pleads for an equal liberty. He continues, "The views I have received of the doctrines of grace are essential to my peace. I could not live comfortably for a day, or an hour, without them."

How few of the people, Christian and non-Christian, who today sing the hymn "Amazing Grace" know of its humble origin! Probably at the present day it is the best known of the Olney Hymns written by Newton, and certainly autobiographical.

Let us look in more detail at some of the hymns, starting with those by Newton. His hymns seem to show some of the many facets of his character. For example, the following lines show how the robustness of his character is reflected in the strength of his faith:

> *Glorious things of thee are spoken,*
> *Zion, city of our God!*
> *He, whose Word cannot be broken,*
> *Formed thee for His own abode.*
>
> *On the Rock of Ages founded,*
> *What can shake thy sure repose?*
> *With salvation's walls surrounded,*
> *Thou may'st smile at all thy foes.*

Newton's exterior may have been robust but he was a gentle, kindly man who loved intensely the One who had saved him from his former wretched life. So he could write such a hymn as

> *How sweet the Name of Jesus sounds*
> *In a believer's ear!*
> *It soothes his sorrows, heals his wounds,*
> *And drives away his fear. . . .*

Olney Vicarage

Dear name! the Rock on which I build,
My Shield and Hiding-place,
My never-failing treasury filled
With boundless stores of grace.

and

One there is above all others,
Well deserves the name of Friend;
His is love beyond a brother's,
Costly, free and knows no end:
They who once His kindness prove,
Find it everlasting love.

Newton was also a man who, because of his wild early life, experienced conflict and remorse, and dreaded the removal of the conscious presence of his Saviour. So we have the hymn:

Begone unbelief;
My Saviour is near,
And for my relief
Will surely appear:
By prayer let me wrestle,
And He will perform;
With Christ in the vessel,
I smile at the storm. . . .

His love in time past
Forbids me to think
He'll leave me at last
In troubles to sink;
Each sweet Ebenezer
I have in review
Confirms His good pleasure
To help me quite through.

and

Why should I fear the darkest hour,
Or tremble at the tempter's power?
Jesus vouchsafes to be my tower. . . .

Against me earth and hell combine;
But on my side is power divine;
Jesus is all, and He is mine.

Other hymns of Newton's are:

Approach, My Soul, the Mercy Seat
Come, My Soul, Thy Suit Prepare
Great Shepherd of Thy People, Hear
Let Us Love and Sing and Wonder
Rejoice, Believer in the Lord

and a hymn doubtless based on his own experience after conversion:

I asked the Lord that I might grow
In faith and love and every grace,
Might more of His salvation know,
And seek more earnestly His face.

'Twas He who taught me thus to pray,
And He, I trust, has answered prayer;
But it has been in such a way
As almost drove me to despair. . . .

"Lord, why is this?" I trembling cried,
"Wilt Thou pursue Thy worm to death?"
"'Tis in this way," the Lord replied,
"I answer prayer for grace and faith.

"These inward trials I employ,
From self and pride to set thee free,
And break thy schemes of earthly joy,
That thou mayest seek thy all in Me."

Newton probably observed in his friend a return of the mental weakness which had earlier asserted itself, and he hoped that engaging him in congenial literary work of a Christian nature might serve to ward off a mental breakdown.

My part of the work would have been smaller than it is . . . if the wise, mysterious providence of God

A page from Olney Hymns (1779)

had not seen fit to cross my wishes. We had not proceeded far upon our proposed plan before my dear friend was prevented by a long and afflicting indisposition from affording me any further assistance. My grief and disappointment was great.

Yet if Cowper's contribution to the Olney Hymns was thus limited, it must be agreed, as Newton himself conceded, that Cowper had the greater poetic gift of the two. As with Newton, his hymns reflect his own personality and experience. A hymn which surely does this is:

> Sometimes a light surprises
> The Christian while he sings;
> It is the Lord who rises
> With healing in His wings:
> When comforts are declining,
> He grants the soul again
> A season of clear shining,
> To cheer it after rain.

as also does:

> What various hindrances we meet
> In coming to the mercy-seat;
> Yet who, that knows the worth of prayer,
> But wishes to be often there!

> Prayer makes the darkened cloud withdraw,
> Prayer climbs the ladder Jacob saw,
> Gives exercise to faith and love,
> Brings every blessing from above.

Although there is a timidity and wistful longing in Cowper's hymns he undoubtedly knew the full assurance of faith. Otherwise how could he have written such a hymn as:

> There is a fountain filled with blood
> Drawn from Immanuel's veins;
> And sinners plunged beneath that flood
> Lose all their guilty stains. . . .

> *E'er since by faith I saw the stream*
> *Thy flowing wounds supply,*
> *Redeeming love has been my theme,*
> *And shall be till I die.*

The wistful longing returns in the hymn:

> *Hark, my soul! it is the Lord;*
> *'Tis thy Saviour, hear His word;*
> *Jesus speaks, and speaks to thee:*
> *"Say, poor sinner, lov'st thou Me? . . ."*

> *Lord, it is my chief complaint*
> *That my love is weak and faint;*
> *Yet I love Thee and adore;*
> *O for grace to love Thee more!*

Another hymn of Cowper's probably hints at a shadow of impending darkness of mind:

> *O for a closer walk with God,*
> *A calm and heavenly frame,*
> *A light to shine upon the road*
> *That leads me to the Lamb!*

> *Where is the blessedness I knew*
> *When first I saw the Lord?*
> *Where is the soul-refreshing view*
> *Of Jesus and His Word?*

> *What peaceful hours I once enjoyed!*
> *How sweet their memory still!*
> *But they have left an aching void*
> *The world can never fill.*

Other hymns of special note by Cowper include:

> *The Spirit Breathes Upon the Word*
>
> *Jesus, Where'er Thy People Meet*
>
> *Heal Us Immanuel; Hear Our Prayer*

In a long "Introductory Essay" on the hymns in an edition published in 1829, James Montgomery wrote,

This volume of OLNEY HYMNS ought to be forever dear to the Christian public, as an unprecedented memorial in respect of its authors, of the power of divine grace which called one of them from the negro-slave market on the coast of Africa to be a shining light in the church of God at home, and raised the head of the other, when he was a companion of lunatics, to make him (by a most mysterious dispensation of gifts) a poet of the highest intellectuality and in his song an unshaken, uncompromising confessor of the purest doctrine of the gospel, even when he himself had lost sight of its consolations.

We close with a benediction written by Newton for the close of worship:

> *May the grace of Christ our Saviour,*
> *And the Father's boundless love,*
> *With the Holy Spirit's favor,*
> *Rest upon us from above.*
>
> *Thus may we abide in union*
> *With each other and the Lord,*
> *And possess, in sweet communion,*
> *Joys which earth cannot afford.*

29

AUGUSTUS M. TOPLADY

(1740–78)

Rock of Ages, cleft for me,
Let me hide myself in Thee;
Let the water and the blood
From Thy riven side which flowed,
Be of sin the double cure,
Cleanse me from its guilt and power.

THE hymns of Isaac Watts and Charles Wesley stand apart in a class of their own, but Toplady takes his place with the other great English hymn-writers of the eighteenth century, Doddridge, Cowper, Newton and others. The hymn-writers who followed Watts were often cast in his mold, but Toplady's style was distinctively his own and is characterized among other things by the power of his opening lines:

Rock of Ages, cleft for me,
Let me hide myself in Thee.

A debtor to mercy alone,
Of covenant mercy I sing.

A sovereign Protector I have,
Unseen, yet forever at hand.

Object of my first desire,
Jesus crucified for me.

Compared with Christ, in all beside
No comeliness I see.

Furthermore, Toplady was an outspoken Calvinist and there is much doctrinal content in his hymns. For example, in "A Debtor to Mercy Alone" he proclaims the great doctrines of imputed righteousness and final perseverance:

A debtor to mercy alone,
Of covenant mercy I sing:
Nor fear, with Thy righteousness on,
My person and offerings to bring;
The terrors of law and of God
With me can have nothing to do;
My Saviour's obedience and blood
Hide all my transgressions from view. . . .

My name from the palms of His hands
Eternity will not erase;
Impressed on His heart it remains,
In marks of indelible grace;
Yes, I to the end shall endure,
As sure as the earnest is given;
More happy, but not more secure,
The glorified spirits in heaven.

The same theme of imputed righteousness, combined with that of the atonement, occupies the whole of his hymn, "Fountain of Never-ceasing Grace":

In Him we have a righteousness,
By God Himself approved,
Our rock, our sure foundation this,
Which never can be moved.
Our ransom by His death He paid,
For all His people given,
The law He perfectly obeyed,
That they might enter heaven.

In one of his letters Toplady writes of our Saviour, "To those who believe He is preciousness"—a reference to 1 Peter 2:7. This idea is expounded in the beautiful hymn,

Augustus M. Toplady

"Happiness, Thou Lovely Name," which in many hymn-books starts with the third verse:

Object of my first desire,
Jesus crucifed for me;
All to happiness aspire,
Only to be found in Thee:
Thee to praise and Thee to know,
Constitute my bliss below;
Thee to see, and Thee to love,
Constitute my bliss above.

Before we write of Toplady's masterpiece, "Rock of Ages," we will give some account of his life. He was born at Farnham in Surrey in 1740. His father, a major in the army, died of yellow fever at the siege of Cartagena in South America, a few months after the birth of his son. Toplady retained a deep and lasting sense of indebtedness to his mother who showed him much love and planned his education wisely. He went first to Westminster School, starting there as William Cowper would be leaving. Later, when providential circumstances took his mother to Ireland, he entered Trinity College, Dublin, graduating in 1760.

Toplady was "born again" in Ireland, under remarkable circumstances, of which he himself writes, "Strange that I, who had so long sat under the means of grace in England, should be brought near to God in an obscure part of Ireland, amidst a handful of people met together in a barn, and by the ministry of one who could hardly spell his name." He said later that although he was "awakened" in 1755, he was not led into a full and clear view of the doctrines of grace till 1758 when, through the great goodness of God, "my Arminian prejudices received an effectual shock in reading Dr. Manton's sermons on John 17."

Memorial tablet in Broad Hembury Church

Toplady's first living* after being ordained into the Church of England was at Blagdon in Somerset. He was there for two years, but in that short time he endeared himself to the inhabitants, as seems to have been the case also in two other places where he labored for a short time before becoming vicar of Broad Hembury (near Cullompton in Devon) in 1768. It was here that many of his hymns were written, but the moist air of Devonshire was thought to be injurious to his lungs, and though retaining his living in Broad Hembury, and visiting there occasionally, from 1775 he lived in London as advised by his doctor.

Thomas Wright, who wrote a biography of Toplady, likens him to a "caged lion" in Broad Hembury. He had already begun to exercise considerable influence, despite the fact that for six years he had been confined to hamlets and small villages. Before moving to London he had preached there frequently. Besides being a magnetic preacher, he was a man of many parts, with great intellectual ability and a highly developed critical faculty. He stoutly maintained Calvinistic doctrine, in opposition to the Wesleys, and he "sometimes indulged in the severe and scurrilous language that was tolerated in controversy in those times. But though the controversialists differed in doctrine they were alike in the sweetness and spirituality of their songs."

After Toplady moved to London he went to hear Whitefield as often as he could, but it was to William Romaine, whose chapel was close to where his mother now lived, that he owed his greatest debt. The following year friends and admirers obtained for him the use of the French Huguenot Chapel, on Orange Street, Leicester Fields (now Square). With fast-failing health he ministered there to overflowing congregations of 1200–1500 people for just over two years, "preaching with the solemnity of a voice from the tomb and the joy of one on the very verge of heaven."

The closing days of Toplady's life were triumphant and

---

* The position of vicar or rector with income and/or property.

happy. When his doctor told him that his pulse was growing weaker, he replied, "Why, that is a good sign that my death is fast approaching and, blessed be God, I can add that my heart beats every day stronger and stronger for glory." When close to the end, bursting into tears as he spoke, he said, "It will not be long before God takes me, for no mortal man can live after the glories God has manifested to my soul." He had requested that the funeral should be as private as possible and that there should be no funeral sermon, but thousands gathered and Rowland Hill felt impelled to address the multitude.

The hymn "Rock of Ages" is based on the marginal reading of Isaiah 26:4, "For in the Lord Jehovah is the Rock of Ages." The thought of the Lord as a Rock had fascinated Toplady as far back as his Trinity College days. In the neighborhood of Blagdon, where Toplady first ministered, there is a walk to Burrington Gorge, one of the awe-inspiring ravines for which the Mendips are famous. Near the ravine there is a huge cleft rock, known locally as "The Rock of Ages." The story runs that one day Toplady was overtaken by a storm and that, while sheltering in this cleft rock, his imagination began to work and expressed itself some years later in the hymn which will always be associated with his name. It is unlikely that the story is true, but it is certain that thoughts of Christ as a cleft and sheltering Rock had taken hold of Toplady's mind. Years ago the writer herself stood in this cleft rock, feeling very small as she looked up to its summit which is as high as the roof of a house. The cleft rock is a striking illustration of the truth expressed in the hymn, even though it may not have provided the inspiration for it.

> While I draw this fleeting breath,
>   When my eyelids close in death,
> When I soar through tracts unknown,
>   See Thee on Thy judgment throne;
> Rock of Ages, cleft for me,
>   Let me hide myself in Thee.

In an unpublished sermon of Toplady's there is another interesting allusion to the Rock of Ages. Toplady says that the Lord is a Rock in three ways: as a Foundation to support (Matt. 7:25; 16:16–18), a Shelter to screen (Isaiah 32:2), and a Fortress to protect (Song of Solomon 2:14). In another unpublished manuscript Toplady says, "The finest sight in the world is a stately ship, lying at anchor by moonlight in the mouth of the harbor, waiting for high water to carry it into the haven. Such is the dying Christian at anchor, safely reposed in Christ, the Rock of Ages." The complete hymn was printed in the *Gospel Magazine* of 1776 when Toplady was for a short time its editor.

Toplady's many works in poetry and prose have all been surpassed by this one hymn. How it would have rejoiced his heart to know that Christians all over the world sing:

> *Not the labors of my hands*
> *Can fulfill Thy law's demands:*
> *Could my zeal no respite know,*
> *Could my tears for ever flow,*
> *All for sin could not atone:*
> *Thou must save and Thou alone.*

It has been said that this one hymn has given him a deeper place in millions of human hearts, from generation to generation, than almost any other British hymn-writer. J. C. Ryle, the godly bishop of Liverpool in the late nineteenth century, says, "Of all English hymn-writers none perhaps has succeeded so thoroughly in combining truth, poetry, life, warmth, fire, depth, solemnity and unction as Toplady has."

30

JOHN RYLAND

(1753–1825)

O Lord, I would delight in Thee,
And on Thy care depend;
To Thee in every trouble flee,
My best, my only Friend.

When all created streams are dried,
Thy fullness is the same;
May I with this be satisfied,
And glory in Thy Name!

No good in creatures can be found
But may be found in Thee;
I must have all things and abound,
While God is God to me.

I N the eighteenth century few names were more honored in the Baptist denomination than that of Ryland, not least the John Ryland of whom we write, "J.R. Jun" as he used to sign himself. His father was John Collett Ryland, pastor of the Baptist Church at Warwick at the time of John's birth. The elder Ryland was a fine scholar and taught his son Hebrew at the age of five and Greek before he was nine. From his godly mother he received, as Doddridge had done, scriptural instruction from the Dutch tiles which adorned their fireplace.

When about fourteen years of age "J.R. Jun" experienced a great spiritual change and, in company with some friends

John Collett Ryland, the hymn-writer's father

from his father's school, he made a profession of conversion to Christ, was baptized in the river Nen, near Northampton, when he was still only fourteen, and was received into membership of his father's church. Subsequently he increased his own knowledge while assisting in his father's school in Northampton, to which town they had moved in 1759. After a time, and with the approval of the church at Northampton, he helped his father in the ministry. In 1781 he was ordained and appointed co-pastor, and when his father moved to London in 1786 he succeeded him as sole pastor. He preached in many parts around Northampton and by pen as well as voice contended earnestly for the faith.

In December 1793, Ryland left Northampton to become president of the Baptist College in Bristol and pastor of Broadmead Chapel, retaining these twofold duties until his death. In his late sixties his constant labors began to wear down his constitution. Each year found him weaker, until on May 25, 1825, after uttering the words "No more pain," his spirit departed peacefully to be with Christ.

John Ryland's earliest literary productions were poetical. Between the age of twenty and the year of his death he composed 99 hymns. One of them, "Lord, Teach a Little Child to Pray," was composed at the request of Andrew Fuller for his daughter who was dying at the age of six. This hymn was often repeated to her and she told her father that she used to pray over it. The hymn runs:

> Lord, teach a little child to pray,
> Thy grace to me impart;
> And grant Thy Holy Spirit may
> Renew my youthful heart.
>
> A sinful creature I was born,
> And from my birth have strayed;
> I must be wretched and forlorn
> Without Thy mercy's aid.
>
> But Christ can all my sins forgive,
> And wash away their stain:
> Can fit my soul with Him to live,
> And in His kingdom reign. . . .
>
> For all who early seek His face
> Shall surely taste His love;
> Jesus shall guide them by His grace
> To dwell with Him above.

Regarding the hymn we quoted at the beginning, "O Lord, I Would Delight in Thee," in the original manuscript the interesting note is given, "I recollect deeper feelings of mind in composing this hymn than perhaps I felt in making any other." The hymn does seem to come straight from the experience of the writer's heart. The last three verses read:

> O that I had a stronger faith,
> To look within the veil,
> To rest on what my Saviour saith,
> Whose word can never fail!
>
> He that has made my heaven secure
> Will here all good provide;

While Christ is rich, can I be poor?
What can I want beside?

O Lord, I cast my care on Thee,
I triumph and adore;
Henceforth my great concern shall be
To love and please Thee more.

Two other hymns by Ryland are:

Thou Son of God and Son of Man,
Beloved, adored Immanuel;
Who didst, before all time began,
In glory with Thy Father dwell:

and

Let us sing of King Messiah,
King of righteousness and peace;
Hail Him, all His happy subjects,
Never let His praises cease:
Ever hail Him;
Never let His praises cease. . . .

Majesty combined with meekness,
Righteousness and peace unite
To ensure Thy blessed conquests;
On, great Prince, assert Thy right:
Ride triumphant
All around the conquered globe.

The last verse of this hymn leads us on to mention Ryland's great interest in, and involvement with, missionary work, particularly of the Baptist Missionary Society, of which he was one of the founding members.

It has been said that "the gospel was rediscovered as a thing of music"—the revival associated with the Wesleys had awakened Christian song, whose outburst Watts had anticipated—"then came the yearning to proclaim it to mankind." William Carey could not have won men to take an interest in missions had they not first recaptured Christian joy. John Ryland had the privilege of baptizing Carey one Sunday morning in 1783 in the same river Nen in which he himself had been immersed about fifteen years earlier.

When Carey became a pastor he was admitted to the Ministers' Fraternal of the Northampton Association. The elder Ryland insisted that he and other new members should offer themes for discussion. Carey proposed that they should consider "Whether the command given to the apostles to teach all nations was not binding on all succeeding ministers to the end of the world," whereupon Ryland, it is said, disapproved the theme with a rough "Young man, sit down, sit down. You're an enthusiast. When God pleases to convert the heathen, He'll do it without consulting you or me." The younger Ryland later pronounced the outburst apocryphal, but Thomas Wright of Olney, the chief authority on the elder Ryland, regards it as completely typical of "the vehement gruff Calvinist."

Carey pressed the Northamptonshire Baptists to take action. He besought them on Christ's behalf to become His

House in Kettering in which
the Baptist Missionary Society was formed

world ambassadors and to dare to found an overseas mission. His colleagues advised him to publish a pamphlet and present his case to the churches. After Carey's induction to a church in Leicester he read to his friends as much as he had written of the pamphlet, which he named The Enquiry. The scene is worth visualizing: "The scholarly Ryland (Jnr), cautious Sutcliffe, . . . devout Pearce and others, with Carey pouring his zeal into their hearts." Kettering was the place where the Northampton Association made its chief contribution to the kingdom of God. A preparatory meeting of the leaders was held. Ryland "ran his flag to the masthead" and committed himself to the contemplated venture by preaching from the text, "I the Lord work a work and who shall let it?" (Isaiah 43:13). Most of the others were not as ready as Ryland, but Carey spurred them on and in the end the five men—Carey, Fuller, Pearce, Ryland and Sutcliffe—were unanimous in the faith that they should "hazard" a Missionary Society, even with so humble and feeble a beginning. They agreed that half a guinea should be the minimum subscription for membership. Ryland's name was first on the list with the promise of two guineas, the total initial subscription list adding up to £13.2.6d. The leaders were all young; Ryland was thirty-nine, Carey thirty-one, and the others slightly younger or older, so it was young men who caught the vision and young men who took the plunge.

Many Christians gathered to bid farewell to Carey, missionary elect, including fourteen Baptist ministers. Of these the four already named, and Carey, met to "talk for the last time together of the task which lay, with all its mystery and possibility, before them. Carey drew them into a covenant that, as he went forth in the Society's name . . . they should never cease till death to stand by him, and to this they plighted their troth." In every case the covenant was kept with entire fidelity until death. In Ryland's case this meant for thirty-three years—Carey outliving him by eight years—and during that time he corresponded regularly with Carey. With his own experience as principal of a college in England, whose students he "goaded" into overseas service, he was able to give Carey wise counsel respecting the problems which Carey faced in his college in India, and he was faithful in praying for all that concerned Carey.

On the Society's twentieth anniversary, when friends of the Mission met in London, Ryland preached on the text, "The zeal of the Lord of hosts will perform this" (Isaiah 9:7). He spoke of Carey's joy in his two sons, Felix and William. "But he has a third son," he said, "giving him pain because, although dutiful, he is unconverted." He asked their instant prayers for Jabez. "A deep quiet fell on all and they knew God was near and was hearing." Before they called, God had answered because the next Indian mail brought the news that "with a contrite spirit Jabez had received Jesus as Saviour and Lord."

It certainly seems that of the four original men who were behind Carey when he went as their representative to India it was Ryland who continued to be most closely associated with him and most faithful to him, finding time right to the end of his busy life as college principal and pastor to pray for and write and counsel the one who, because he never returned to England, seems often to have felt somewhat cut off and neglected. When the Lord called Ryland to Himself in 1825 he must have been greatly missed in England, but not less by Carey who, though so far away, still needed all the help his surviving friends could give him.

It deserves to be added that in recognition of his fine scholarship and robust Christian witness, the Brown University of Rhode Island, U.S.A., conferred upon Ryland the degree of Doctor of Divinity in the year 1792.

31

KRISHNA PAL

(1764–1822)

O thou, my soul, forget no more
The Friend who all thy misery bore;
Let every idol be forgot,
But, O my soul, forget Him not.

Jesus for thee a body takes,
Thy guilt assumes, thy fetters breaks,
Discharging all thy dreadful debt:
And canst thou e'er such love forget?

Renounce thy works and ways with grief,
And fly to this most sure relief;
Nor Him forget who left His throne,
And for thy life gave up His own.

(tr. by Joshua Marshman)

ON June 13, 1793, William Carey sailed for India with his wife and family, his wife's sister, Catharine, and a certain John Thomas. As they saw the white cliffs of Dover receding into the distance they said that "men never saw their native land with more joy than they left it." The Baptist Missionary Society was the first-born of British missionary societies, and Carey and Thomas were the first missionaries to sail under its auspices. It has been said that "the light which Carey had kindled spread from hill to hill, like beacon-fires, till every

Christian church, in turn, recognized the signal and responded to the call." Carey's pioneer voyage was a long and difficult one, but the party finally reached Calcutta on November 11th, five months after setting sail.

Carey's companion, John Thomas, has been called "a great human, a great Christian, a great unfortunate and a great blunderer." As a young man he rebelled against home and discipline, ran away to London, did a "medical course," and after many adventures at sea and on land arrived in Calcutta. Having become a real Christian, he confessed Christ boldly, delighted in His Word and sought out the real Christians in Calcutta. Being a compassionate man he was much moved by the conditions of life in Calcutta and Bengal and could find no "missionary-hearted friend" to help him care for the people for whom no one else seemed to care. So he returned to England in order to find such a companion with whom to return. He met the little company of ministers in Kettering who were the nucleus of the first missionary society, and Carey drank in what he told them of his experiences in Bengal. Thomas also read a letter, which was to Carey what the Macedonian call was to Paul. "Have compassion on us," the letter read, "and send us preachers and such as can forward translation."

Men from Britain had gone to India as soldiers, sailors, traders and adventurers but, two hundred years after the East India Company had been formed, Thomas and Carey were the first two Englishmen to go there as missionaries, out of love for Christ and for India. Their stay in Calcutta was beset with difficulties. After a time they left Calcutta and moved to a village where they lived in a bungalow and had a plot of land which needed much hard work to clear before it could be tilled. They then moved on to another village where Carey worked on an indigo plantation but had more time to concentrate on learning Bengali. By 1795 he could preach for half an hour in Bengali so as to be understood, though some complained that he gave them "mental trouble." Although some people were interested

Krishna Pal

in the gospel, none had the courage to pay the cost which they knew they would have to pay if they openly confessed Christ. By that time, in spite of moves and disappointments, Thomas and Carey had translated more than half of the Pentateuch and nearly all the New Testament into Bengali.

At this point encouragement was sent from England in the form of John Fountain, with whom Carey found that he had much in common. Before long several other families came out from England, landing at Danish Serampore. Carey and Fountain also had clear guidance to go there (Thomas had left them though he returned later), taking with them a printing press they had bought for £46. Carey's apprenticeship as a missionary was over and his leadership of what was now a Mission was about to begin.

Serampore was on a highway and on an important river, "a populous, well-ordered, healthful and beautiful town," yet it demanded courage to plant the Mission there as the district was overwhelmingly Hindu with strong Brahmin influence. Zinzendorf had tried to plant a Moravian settlement there without success, and Carey knew that he would have a struggle. He believed that the Moravian plan of communal settlements was the most efficient and economical way to live, so he set himself to mold six families into a community. He was much pleased to change his previous loneliness for congenial company, especially because his wife had suffered from a condition of melancholy ever since arriving in India. Thomas had now returned to them and one day he met a carpenter to whom he spoke of Christ. Krishna Pal had already heard the gospel from John Fountain, but not so directly as from Thomas. At the age of thirty-three Krishna was a guru, teaching others, but he had no peace because he knew that his sin was unforgiven.

He wanted to learn more from these Christian gurus and very soon he was brought into closer contact with them. He slipped during his morning bath and dislocated his shoulder, reached home in great pain and sent for the doctor-padre. Thomas hurried to his help with Marshman, one of the new missionaries, and Carey. Against a tree they set his shoulder and later Thomas and Marshman returned, teaching him and his neighbors a daily devotional chant in rhythmic Bengali:

> *Sin confessing, sin forsaking,*
> *Christ's righteousness embracing,*
> *The soul is free.*

As Krishna was still in pain the next morning Carey took him to the mission station, but soon Krishna went there daily, not for medical attention but for spiritual instruction. Ward, another of the new missionaries, and Felix, Carey's newly-converted son, led him further along the way of salvation. A few weeks later Thomas asked Krishna if he understood what he had learned. He replied, "The Lord Jesus Christ has given His very life for the salvation of sinners, and I and my friend Gokul unfeignedly believe this." "Then you are our brothers," said Thomas. "Come, and in love let us eat together." This meant breaking caste for the former Hindus, but the missionaries were resolved to require of every convert the breaking of caste. Krishna and Gokul sat down with the Mission families and ate with them. A week later, Krishna was baptized, and he and the missionaries kept the Lord's Supper in Bengali for the first time. Krishna was full of praise, and at about 9 o'clock in the evening he returned to the mission station to say that others in his family also wished for baptism. Henceforward Krishna openly accompanied the missionaries, not being shaken by the loathing of his fellows or by the fact that his Brahmin landlord evicted him.

Within a few more weeks the bound Bengali New Testament was ready, the first people's book ever printed in Bengali, and the fruit of seven and a half years of Carey's toil. Ward had taken nine months to print it.

Krishna paid heavily for his Christian allegiance. His eldest child, now thirteen, also learned the love of Christ and revolted against the marriage bond to an idolater who captured her and took her away. Her father was legally helpless to save her and Carey exhorted her to endure the indissoluble marriage and by patience seek to win her husband to Christ. Krishna's meekness through all this was a miracle, as he was naturally fiery. The grace of Christ which had subdued him was his constant theme. He began to compose hymns to Bengali tunes and they were sung everywhere, the spirit of the best known, "O Thou, My Soul, Forget No More," breathing through them all. He would often say,

> I followed the Hindu worship. I bathed in the Ganges, I worshiped dumb idols . . . I visited holy places . . . But it brought me little relief from my sin. Then I heard of Jesus Christ, that He became flesh and dwelt among us, and was as one that served and even for our ransom gave His life. What love, I thought, is this? And here I made my rest.

The women who became disciples with him sought to bring their neighbors to Christ; also his friend Gokul, who had drawn back from baptism, now faced the ordeal, having been conquered by the love shown to him at the mission station and at Krishna's home. The Mission nurtured the group of believers who met in Krishna's home, his whole family having now become Christian. The greatest pleasure the Mission could give a new missionary was to take them to an evening's singing in this transformed Indian home, most of the hymns having been composed by Krishna. Their home became the base of all advances, and Krishna's teaching of other boys with his own children became the nucleus of the free school. Most of the enquirers of the next two years were given their first Christian impressions through this home. They could open their hearts at Krishna's home when at first they were rather shy at the mission compound.

William Carey, attended by one of his pundits

People marveled when Krishna and Gokul broke caste, but they were even more astonished when Kyasts and Brahmins, much higher castes, were also converted and broke caste by eating at the compound and at Krishna's. One of them married Krishna's daughter and the wedding supper, the first of its kind in India, began with a hymn by Krishna.

These gifted converts needed training for the work of evangelism and the missionaries used to take them on their extensive itineraries. Krishna Pal spent many years as an evangelist to his own countrymen, sometimes being mobbed and beaten. For eight months he pioneered gospel work at the foot of the Khasi Hills, where, for the baptism of his first seven converts, a local magistrate welcomed him to his house and set a silver bowl before him, expecting an indoor baptism. But Krishna Pal said he knew nothing of such a method and led his converts to the river, where eight native princes and 600 Khasis assembled to watch the baptisms.

At what seemed to be the height of his usefulness Krishna Pal succumbed to cholera and died in 1822. As he lay dying he was asked if he still loved Christ. "Yes," he replied, "but not as much as He loves me."

How better can we close than with the last three verses of his hymn with which we began?

> *Infinite truth and mercy shine*
> *In Him, and He Himself is thine;*
> *And canst thou, then, with sin beset,*
> *Such charms, such matchless charms, forget?*

> *Ah no! till life itself depart,*
> *His Name shall cheer and warm my heart;*
> *And lisping this, from earth I'll rise,*
> *And join the chorus of the skies.*

> *Ah no! when all things else expire,*
> *And perish in the general fire,*
> *This Name all others shall survive,*
> *And through eternity shall live.*

32

THOMAS KELLY

(1769–1855)

The head that once was crowned with thorns
Is crowned with glory now;
A royal diadem adorns
The mighty Victor's brow. . . .

The cross He bore is life and health,
Though shame and death to Him;
His people's hope, His people's wealth,
Their everlasting theme.

I T has been said that Thomas Kelly was the hymnist of Ireland as William Williams (Pantycelyn) was of Wales and Michael Bruce was of Scotland. Julian, in his *Dictionary of Hymnology*, says that several of his hymns rank with the finest hymns of the English language. The one we have already quoted certainly belongs to this category, as also does:

Look, ye saints! the sight is glorious,
See the Man of Sorrows now,
From the fight returned victorious,
Every knee to Him shall bow:
Crown Him! Crown Him!
Crowns become the Victor's brow. . . .

Hark, those bursts of acclamation!
Hark, those loud triumphant chords!

Jesus takes the highest station:
O what joy the sight affords!
Crown Him! Crown Him!
King of kings and Lord of lords!

Most of Kelly's hymns dwell directly on the work of Christ on the cross for us, the benefits which flow to us through that work, and the glories of heaven. They are the simple and natural expression of the overflowing love of his heart for the One who had died for him and meant so much to him. An example of the simplicity of his hymns is:

Praise the Saviour, ye who know Him!
Who can tell how much we owe Him?
Gladly let us render to Him
All we are and have.

Jesus is the name that charms us,
He for conflict fits and arms us;
Nothing moves and nothing harms us
While we trust in Him.

with its well-known last verse:

Then we shall be where we would be,
Then we shall be what we should be;
Things that are not now, nor could be,
Soon shall be our own.

How excellently fitted to their theme are verses of the hymn:

We sing the praise of Him who died,
Of Him who died upon the cross;
The sinner's hope let men deride,
For this we count the world but loss. . . .

The cross! it takes our guilt away;
It holds the fainting spirit up;
It cheers with hope the gloomy day,
And sweetens every bitter cup.

It makes the coward spirit brave,
And nerves the feeble arm for fight;

> *It takes the terror from the grave,*
> *And gilds the bed of death with light.*

Ever and again Kelly returns to the work of Christ, as in the following hymn on Christ as our great High Priest:

> *The atoning work is done;*
> *The Victim's blood is shed;*
> *And Jesus now is gone,*
> *His people's cause to plead.*
> *He stands in heaven, their great High Priest,*
> *And bears their names upon His breast.*

Most of Kelly's hymns appear in *Hymns on Various Passages of Scripture*. The first edition in 1804 contained only 96 hymns but the tenth edition in 1853 contained 765 hymns. In the preface the author says,

> It will be perceived by those who have read these hymns that, though there is an interval between the first and last of nearly fifty years, both speak of the same great truths and in the same way. In the course of that long time the author has seen much and heard much, but nothing has made the least change of his mind . . . as to the grand truths of the gospel. What pacified the conscience then does so now. What gave hope then does so now.

Thomas Kelly was the only son of Judge Kelly of Kellyville near Athy in Queen's County, Ireland. From school he entered Trinity College, Dublin, and after graduation, being designed for the bar, he entered the Temple in London. Before he was called to the bar the study of Hebrew had led him to the use of Romaine's edition of Calasio's *Hebrew Concordance*. Subsequently he began to inquire about Romaine's evangelical doctrines. While studying these he became convinced of sin and was filled with great anxiety about his state before God. In attempts to remove his distress he tried self-reformation, practiced asceticism, and put his life in jeopardy by fasting. At length he had peace with God through the Lord Jesus Christ by that way of "justification by faith" of which he afterwards became so firm and faithful an advocate. With several other evangelicals he was ordained a minister of the Established Church in 1792.

Kelly met with great opposition from his family, not so much because he became a minister but because he preached the doctrine of justification by faith alone and not by works. He is reported to have said that to have gone to the stake would have been less a trial to him than to have so set himself against those he loved. When Kelly was thirty he married Miss Tighe of Rosanna in County Wicklow, a member of a family remarkable for its wealth and Christian witness.

The gospel was preached in few churches in Ireland in the late eightenth century, and Kelly was greatly encouraged in his evangelistic purposes by the visit of Rowland Hill to Ireland in 1793. Some young evangelical clergymen gave a Sunday afternoon lecture at St. Luke's Church in Dublin until their success awakened the opposition of the rector. They then preached in another church every Sunday morning, but the Archbishop of Dublin, on hearing of

Rowland Hill

the new doctrine, summoned Kelly and his companions before him. He reproved them and issued a decree closing Dublin pulpits to them. In consequence of this they then preached in two non-episcopal churches in the city.

Soon after ordination Kelly had felt scruples about his connection with the Established Church. These scruples increased as he studied the Scriptures until he became a Dissenter, from conviction, not because he had been persecuted by the Established Church. He possessed ample means and built churches in a number of places. They were independent churches, conducted on a congregational basis. He preached in other places but served as pastor at Athy and Dublin. It has been said of him that during the sixty-three years of his ministry he did not seem ever to waste an hour. "His language, his temper, his recreations, as well as his serious studies, were all regulated by the same rule, to 'do all to the glory of God.'"

Kelly was a man of great and varied learning. He was skilled in Oriental languages and possessed real musical talent which, together with his other talents, was consecrated to the glory of God. He became the friend of many good men and the advocate of every worthy cause. His liberality found ample scope in Ireland, especially during the years of famine in the 1840's. In 1854 while preaching, at the age of 85, he suffered a stroke which resulted in his death the following year. His last words were, "Not my will but Thine be done."

Years earlier he had written an evening hymn of two verses which fittingly mark the close of a life spent to the glory of God:

> *Through the day Thy love hath spared us;*
> *Now we lay us down to rest;*
> *Through the silent watches guard us,*
> *Let no foe our peace molest:*
> *Jesus, Thou our Guardian be;*
> *Sweet it is to trust in Thee.*

Pilgrims here on earth and strangers,
Dwelling in the midst of foes,
Us and ours preserve from dangers;
In Thine arms may we repose!
And when life's sad day is past,
Rest with Thee in heaven at last.

33

JAMES MONTGOMERY

(1771–1854)

"Forever with the Lord!"
Amen, so let it be!
Life from the dead is in that word,
'Tis immortality.
Here in the body pent
Absent from Him I roam,
Yet nightly pitch my moving tent
A day's march nearer home.

J AMES MONTGOMERY was born at Irvine in Ayrshire, Scotland, where his father was a Moravian minister. When he was five he went with his parents to Grace Hill, a settlement of Moravians near Ballymena in County Antrim, Northern Ireland. Two years later he was sent to the Moravian seminary at Fulneck in Yorkshire, which was the chief Moravian settlement in England. In 1783 when James was twelve, and still at Fulneck, his parents were sent as missionaries to the West Indies where they both died. At Fulneck the youth received a good education and was under true Christian influence. He acknowledges that his first poetic attempts were sacred poems after the manner of the Moravians. He was a mere ten years old when he began to write such poems, filling a small volume before he was thirteen. He was designed for a preacher but his early devotion to poetry diverted his attention from

James Montgomery

serious study. It was a happy thing that he early recognized his own bent and saw that he could serve the cause of Christ better as a poet than as a preacher. His poetical bent, however, met with sharp reproof at Fulneck. The Brethren saw with concern the visionary habits of their pupil. He was a dreamer who never worked at the proper time! The school diary contains several entries respecting him. He was warned, exhorted and threatened, and at last it was decided to "put him out to business, at least for a time." He became assistant to a baker at Mirfield, near Wakefield. The work was easy and even allowed him time to write verses behind the counter! But after eighteen months, one Sunday morning when his master was at the Moravian chapel, he packed his manuscripts and set out with a few shillings in his pocket in search of more congenial scenes. He soon repented of his impulsiveness and accepted a similar situation at the village of Wath, near Rotherham. A year later he went to London, taking some of his early poems to offer to publishers. Their cold caution destroyed his golden dream of sudden fame and sent him back, almost broken-hearted, to his work at Wath.

In 1792 Montgomery went from Wath to Sheffield as assistant to a Mr. Gales, auctioneer, bookseller, and the printer of a newspaper entitled the *Sheffield Register*. In 1794, when Mr. Gales left England to avoid persecution for his political principles, Montgomery took over the paper, changed its name to the *Iris* and edited it for thirty-one years. As the principles of the paper continued to be too liberal for the government of the day—Montgomery had, for example, reprinted a song commemorating the "Fall of the Bastille"—he was fined £20 and imprisoned in York Castle for three months. He was a very gentle person and it is somewhat amusing to learn that the jury found him to be "a wicked, malicious and seditious person who has attempted to stir up and excite discontent among his Majesty's subjects." He found imprisonment less irksome than he had feared, as he was able to write poems, which were published in 1797 under the title *Prison Amusements*. He wrote many poems, some of considerable length, but apart from the hymns of his boyhood he does not seem to have written many more hymns till much later in life.

Montgomery lived for many years at the *Iris* office, an old house in the middle of Sheffield, but in later years he went to live at "The Mount." He had achieved literary fame by then and many eminent literary people visited him. Like Cowper, Montgomery never married. Also like Cowper he often speaks of unbelief and despondency, and he has in fact been described as "the Cowper of the nineteenth century." An unpublished letter of 1839 indicates that his times of depression continued throughout life: "From whatever cause, I have suffered so much from mental depression that I have spirit for no undertaking beyond daily occupations—and even these are indifferently performed—so that I am compelled to decline every engagement which comes not upon me as an absolute obligation."

It was not until Montgomery was forty-three that he became a member of the Moravian church, having been influenced by the printed sermons of Cennick under whose ministry his father had been converted. As the Moravians had no chapel in Sheffield he worshiped with the Methodists. He was always in sympathy with philanthropic and spiritual movements and occupied himself greatly with their promotion in his later years. He died at the venerable age of eighty-two "amid universal tokens of esteem from his fellow townsmen among whom he had lived and worked and sung, and who recognized 'that his life and his hymns had one music.'"

Montgomery has laid the Christian Church under great obligation by his hymns. In 1825 he published his *Christian Psalmist, or Hymns Selected and Original,* of whose 562 hymns 103 are by Montgomery. It is from this work that most of his hymns are taken. In his "Introductory Essay," which was actually the first English work on hymnology, he has given his account of what a hymn should be. He calls for unity in hymns, gradation and mutual dependence in the thoughts, a conscious progress, and at the end a sense of completeness, and he insists that hymns ought to be easy to understand.

Montgomery's hymns are the productions of a skilled hand and bear traces of the writer's maturity as a poet and a Christian. The most precious truths of Scripture and the richest experiences of the Christian find in them simple but poetic expression. Another important thing about his hymns is that they are very suitable for congregational singing. Julian says,

> As a poet Montgomery stands well to the front. His poetic genius was of a high order. His ear for rhythm was exceedingly accurate and refined. His knowledge of the Scriptures was extensive. With the faith of a strong man he united the simplicity of a child. He is richly poetic without exuberance, dog-

matic without uncharitableness, tender without sen-
timentality. He has bequeathed to the Church of
Christ wealth which could only have come from a
true genius and a sanctified heart.

We trace some of these characteristics as we quote from
two of his finest hymns:

> *Hail to the Lord's Anointed,*
> *Great David's greater Son!*
> *Hail, in the time appointed,*
> *His reign on earth begun!*
> *He comes to break oppression,*
> *To set the captives free,*
> *To take away transgression,*
> *And rule in equity.*
>
> *He shall come down like showers*
> *Upon the fruitful earth,*
> *And love, joy, hope, like showers,*
> *Spring in His path to birth:*
> *Before Him on the mountains*
> *Shall peace, the herald, go;*
> *And righteousness, in fountains,*
> *From hill to valley flow.*

and

> *Go to dark Gethsemane,*
> *Ye that feel the tempter's power;*
> *Your Redeemer's conflict see;*
> *Watch with Him one bitter hour;*
> *Turn not from His griefs away;*
> *Learn of Jesus Christ to pray. . . .*
>
> *Calvary's mournful mountain climb;*
> *There, adoring at His feet,*
> *Mark that miracle of time,*
> *God's own sacrifice complete.*
> *"It is finished!"—hear Him cry;*
> *Learn of Jesus Christ to die.*

His hymn which we have already quoted, "Forever with

the Lord," is full of deep feeling, and few hymns have
been more highly valued. Other well-known hymns of
Montgomery's are:

> Songs of praise the angels sang,
> Heaven with hallelujahs rang,
> When creation was begun,
> When God spake and it was done. . . .

> Heaven and earth must pass away,
> Songs of praise shall crown that day;
> God will make new heavens and earth,
> Songs of praise shall hail their birth.

and the simple communion hymn in which there is much
depth of feeling:

> According to Thy gracious Word,
> In meek humility,
> This will I do, my dying Lord,
> I will remember Thee. . . .

> When to the cross I turn my eyes,
> And rest on Calvary,
> O Lamb of God, my Sacrifice!
> I must remember Thee. . . .

> And when these failing lips grow dumb,
> And mind and memory flee,
> When Thou shalt in Thy kingdom come,
> Jesus, remember me.

We mention other hymns more briefly:

> Stand up and bless the Lord,
> Ye people of His choice,

> Command Thy blessing from above,
> O God, on all assembled here,

> O Spirit of the living God,
> In all Thy plenitude of grace,

and

> *Lift up your heads, ye gates of brass,*
> *Ye bars of iron, yield,*
> *And let the King of glory pass;*
> *The cross is in the field.*

Montgomery's own convictions as to what hymns should be—unified, complete, easy to understand—are exemplified in his hymns. We can also see that Julian's comments on his hymns—their strength yet simplicity, their accurate rhythm, their poetic richness—are very true. The writer has found it profitable to read through a considerable number of Montgomery's hymns, tracing the characteristics mentioned. Perhaps the reader might also find this to be a profitable exercise.

When Montgomery was old and seriously ill he asked a friend to read transcripts of his original hymns to him. He was much affected, but asked his friend to continue, saying,

> It is good for me to feel affected and humbled by the terms in which I have endeavored to provide for the expressions of similar religious experience in others. As all my hymns embody some portion of the history of the joys and sorrows, the hopes and fears of this poor heart, so I cannot doubt but that they will be found an acceptable vehicle of expression of the experience of many of my fellow creatures who may be similarly exercised during the pilgrimage of their Christian life.

REGINALD HEBER

(1783–1826)

Holy, holy, holy, Lord God Almighty!
Early in the morning our song shall rise to Thee;
Holy, holy, holy! merciful and mighty,
God in Three Persons, blessed Trinity.

Holy, holy, holy! all the saints adore Thee,
Casting down their golden crowns around the
glassy sea;
Cherubim and seraphim falling down before Thee,
Who wert, and art, and evermore shalt be.

REGINALD HEBER's family was an ancient one, long settled at Marton Hall in the district of Craven in Yorkshire. His father was a man of intellectual ability, having been both Fellow and tutor at Brasenose College, Oxford. He derived part of his income from the parish of Malpas, Cheshire, and Reginald was born there, in the beautiful "Higher Rectory" overlooking the valley of the river Dee. We are told that, as a child, Reginald was traveling with his parents in the wild, hilly country of Yorkshire when a violent storm broke out, greatly alarming his mother. Reginald said to her, "Do not be afraid, mamma, God will look after us." From childhood he loved books and could read the Bible with ease before he was five. His elder brother used to say "Reginald doesn't read books, he devours them." When he was six he had a severe attack of typhus fever and when convalescent he asked as a special favor that he might be "permitted to learn the Latin grammar"!

Heber received his early education at Whitchurch Grammar school; then at the age of thirteen he was placed under the tuition of a Dr. Bristowe who took private pupils at Neasden, near Willesden, London. In 1800 he went to Brasenose, Oxford, his father's college, and commenced a brilliant university career. In 1803 he won the prize for English verse on the subject of "Palestine," this being up to that time the only prize poem that had won a permanent place in poetical literature; in 1805 he gained the University prize for the best essay on the subject of "The Sense of Honor" and in the same year he was elected Fellow of All Souls College. After leaving the university he traveled for two years, with his friend John Thornton, through Norway, Sweden, Russia, the Crimea, Poland and Hungary, and on his return to England was ordained in the Church of England.

His father had inherited the estate and the living of Hodnet in Shropshire and, the living* having been reserved for Reginald since his father's death in 1804, he at once entered on his duties as a country clergyman and squire, having married Amelia Shipley, the daughter of the dean of St. Asaph. He was much loved at Hodnet and very diligent,

> counseling the people in their troubles, advising them in their difficulties, comforting them in their distress, kneeling often at their sick beds at the hazard of his own health; exhorting, encouraging where there was need; where there was strife, the peacemaker; where there was want, the free giver.

In 1812 he was made prebendary of St. Asaph; three years later he was appointed Bampton Lecturer at Oxford, which gave him the opportunity of establishing his reputa-

---

* The position of vicar or rector with income and/or property.

Reginald Heber

tion as a theologian. In 1822 he was elected preacher at Lincoln's Inn and at the close of the same year he was offered the vacant see of Calcutta, which, after much hesitation, he accepted. *The Life of Henry Martyn* was one of Heber's favorite books. His heroic labors, undaunted zeal and martyr's death had kindled in Heber a profound missionary interest. Before they had any expectation of following Martyn's footsteps, he and his wife, in their peaceful country rectory, had been reading about Martyn, tracing his Eastern journeyings, especially those through the almost unknown Indian Empire. Many of Heber's friends were against his going to India but his reply was, "I have prayed to God to show me the path of duty and to give me grace to follow it; and the tranquility of mind which I now feel induces me to hope that I have His blessing and approbation."

During his short tenure of the vast diocese of Calcutta (which at that time included the whole of India, Ceylon, the Mauritius islands and Australia!) Heber made his mark in various ways. He completed the great work begun by his predecessor, the erection and full establishment of

Bishop's College, Calcutta. He traveled indefatigably
through many parts of his unwieldy diocese, not only per-
forming his episcopal duties diligently but healing differences, cheering the hearts and strengthening the hands of
Christian workers wherever he went. He visited Bombay
and Ceylon, returning to Calcutta in October 1825. In the
early spring of 1826, after visiting Madras and various other
stations, he arrived in Trichinopoly on April 1st. On the
Sunday he preached and confirmed, on the Monday he
confirmed again and visited a native school. Later that day
he suddenly died and was buried in St. John's Church,
Trichinopoly, his wife being still in Calcutta.

Most of Heber's hymns were written during his sixteen
years at Hodnet. He had a desire to improve the services at
his parish church by introducing hymns. He greatly admired the Olney Hymns and arranged a compilation of his
own hymns with a view to using them in his church. He
argued that the hymns used by the Dissenters were a great
blessing to the people, and that as the use of hymns, in
addition to psalms, could no longer be suppressed in the
Church of England, it was better to regulate their use. However, the bishop to whom he submitted his thoughts was
critical and Heber's project had to be dropped.

The best known of Heber's hymns is "From Greenland's
Icy Mountains." On Whitsunday in 1819, Dr. Shipley, his
father-in-law, vicar of Wrexham and dean of St. Asaph,
was to preach in aid of the Society for the Propagation of
the Gospel. On the Saturday evening he asked Heber to
write "something for them to sing in the morning." Heber
sought quietness in another part of the room and after a
little time the dean asked him what he had written and,
reading the verses, said they would do very well. Heber
insisted that the sense was not complete and that he must
write a fourth verse, which is the third in the version we
use today, beginning "Waft, waft. . . ." This hymn is one of
the finest examples of spontaneous hymn-writing we possess. It was written in twenty minutes, and is the expression of the missionary zeal that was the motive power of
Heber's devoted life.

From Greenland's icy mountains,
From India's coral strand,
Where Afric's sunny fountains
Roll down their golden sand,
From many an ancient river,
From many a palmy plain,
They call us to deliver
Their land from error's chain. . . .

Waft, waft, ye winds, His story,
And you, ye waters, roll,
Till, like a sea of glory,
It spreads from pole to pole;
Till o'er our ransomed nature,
The Lamb for sinners slain,
Redeemer, King, Creator,
In bliss returns to reign.

Tennyson, when Poet Laureate, thought the hymn already quoted, "Holy, Holy, Holy," to be very fine; he admired its perfect spirituality and the devotion and purity of its language. The last two verses read:

Holy, holy, holy! though the darkness hide Thee,
Though the eye of sinful man Thy glory may not see,
Only Thou art holy, there is none beside Thee,
Perfect in power, in love, and purity.

Holy, holy, holy, Lord God Almighty!
All Thy works shall praise Thy name in earth
and sky and sea;
Holy, holy, holy! merciful and mighty,
God in Three Persons, blessed Trinity!

This hymn is a paraphrase of Revelation 4:8–11: "And they rest not day and night, saying, Holy, holy, holy, Lord God Almighty, which was, and is, and is to come. . . ." When published in 1861, John Dykes gave his tune to "Holy, Holy, Holy" the significant name "Nicaea." It was at the Council of Nicaea in 325 A.D. that the Church clearly enunciated its belief in the Trinity.

In 1824, when Bishop Heber consecrated a church in India, he says "I had the gratification of hearing my own hymns, 'Brightest and Best,' and 'The Son of God Goes Forth to War,' sung better than I had heard them in a church before." There is a reverent joyousness in the hymn "Brightest and Best":

> Brightest and best of the sons of the morning,
>   Dawn on our darkness, and lend us thine aid;
> Star of the east, the horizon adorning,
>   Guide where our infant Redeemer is laid.

This joyousness reaches its zenith in the grand truth that it is the giver rather than the gift that is acceptable:

> Vainly we offer each ample oblation,
>   Vainly with gifts would His favor secure:
> Richer by far is the heart's adoration,
>   Dearer to God are the prayers of the poor.

It has been said that Heber's hymns do not have "the scriptural strength of our best early hymns, nor the dogmatic force of the best Latin ones. But as pure and graceful devotional poetry they are always true and reverent and are an unfailing pleasure."

35

HENRIETTE AUBER

(1773–1862)

Our blest Redeemer, ere He breathed
His tender last farewell,
A Guide, a Comforter, bequeathed
With us to dwell.

He came in semblance of a dove,
With sheltering wings outspread,
The holy balm of peace and love
On earth to shed.

THE name of Henriette, more commonly known as Harriet, Auber will be remembered in connection with a single hymn, though she did write others.

One Whitsunday, at Hoddesdon in Hertfordshire where she then lived, Harriet was sitting in her bedroom thinking over the sermon she had heard in church that morning, when the lines of the above hymn began to form themselves in her mind. She had neither pencil nor paper, and as she was sitting near a window she took a diamond ring from her finger with which she wrote the words on a pane of glass. It seems that the words remained there for many years, but after the death of the authoress the pane of glass was cut out and stolen.

The hymn is characteristic of the life of the authoress, quiet, devotional, trusting. Harriet's father was rector of Tring in Hertfordshire and she seems to have lived in the same county all her life, at Broxbourne, and later in Hoddesdon where she died. In both places her name and the names of her sisters were for long remembered with affection. She had a valued friend, Miss Mary Jane McKenzie, who lived with her during many of the latter years of her life.

Harriet wrote devotional and other poetry, but only a portion of the former was published in her *Spirit of Psalms* in 1829. This collection consisted mainly of her own work and from it some useful versions of the Psalms have been taken to include in hymnbooks, about twenty appearing in Spurgeon's *Our Own Hymnbook* in 1866.

The hymn, "Our Blest Redeemer," sweet as it is, has much doctrinal content and could almost be used as a treatise on the Holy Spirit and His work. As we take it verse by verse we may find that we have covered at least a part of the ground which theologians would call "The Doctrine of the Holy Spirit."

The first verse clearly takes us into John's Gospel, chapters 14–16, where the Lord is preparing His disciples for the things which must shortly come to pass and which will cause them great anguish. In chapter 14 the Lord tells His disciples not to be troubled. He must leave them to go to prepare a place for them, but He assures them, "I will pray the Father, and he shall give you another Comforter, that he may abide with you for ever; even the Spirit of truth. . . . I will not leave you comfortless: I will come to you" (verses 16–18). In verse 26 the Lord says, "But the Comforter, which is the Holy Ghost, whom the Father will send in my name, he shall teach you all things. . . ." Again, in chapter 16, the Lord tells His fearful disciples that He must go away. "But now I go my way to him that sent me." He knows the sorrow which will fill their hearts, but says, "Nevertheless I tell you the truth: it is expedient for you that I go away; for if I go not away, the Comforter will not come unto you; but if I depart, I will send him unto you" (verse 7). The hymn echoes these words. The Lord further says, "Howbeit when he, the Spirit of truth, is come,

he will guide you into all truth." The Comforter is the most
precious name of the Holy Spirit, speaking as it does of
His ability to heal the broken heart, to turn sorrow into joy
and turmoil into peace. So here in the first verse of the
hymn we have the role of the Spirit in believers' lives: He
is to be their Guide into all truth and their Comforter when
the Lord Himself is in heaven with His Father.

The second verse of the hymn says, "He came in semblance of a dove," and immediately our minds are turned
to the Lord's baptism. "And the Holy Ghost descended in
a bodily shape like a dove upon him, and a voice came
from heaven, which said, Thou art my beloved Son; in thee
I am well pleased" (Luke 3:22). God the Father caused the
Holy Spirit to descend like a dove upon Christ to set His
seal to the fact that Jesus of Nazareth was none other than
the beloved Son of God. Harriet Auber also refers to the
"spread" of the dove's sheltering wings, which is sugges-
tive of the Spirit's ministry in defending the believer against
infernal powers. "As birds flying, so will the Lord of hosts
defend Jerusalem" was Isaiah's message to the believers of
his day, and mention of the Spirit's sheltering wings in our
hymn but revives and reinforces the ancient promise and
reminds us of our need of the Spirit's varied ministry.

> He came in tongues of living flame,
>   To teach, convince, subdue;
> All-powerful as the wind He came,
>   As viewless too.

This third verse takes us straight to Pentecost. The Lord
had commanded the disciples not to depart from Jerusalem, but to wait there "for the promise of the Father, which,
saith he, ye have heard of me. . . . Ye shall be baptized
with the Holy Ghost not many days hence. . . . Ye shall
receive power, after that the Holy Ghost is come upon
you" (Acts 1:4–8). So, "when the day of Pentecost was fully
come, they were all with one accord in one place. And
suddenly there came a sound from heaven as of a rushing
mighty wind, and it filled all the house where they were
sitting. And there appeared unto them cloven tongues like

as of fire, and it sat upon each of them. And they were all filled with the Holy Ghost . . ." (Acts 2:1–4). Thus each disciple received the power to be Christ's witness, enabling him to speak for Christ words that would "teach, convince, subdue." In the same moment the Spirit came as "a mighty wind," the symbol of that cleansing, reviving power needed by the disciples individually and as a company, and by individual Christians and the church as a body ever since Pentecost. The Spirit, too, is the divine Person who brings about the new birth, as John chapter 3 reminds us, and in this respect also the Scripture compares His work to that of the wind.

The fourth verse reads:

> *He came sweet influence to impart,*
> *A gracious willing Guest,*
> *While He can find one humble heart*
> *Wherein to rest.*

We have here described the indwelling of the believer by the Holy Spirit. The divine Guest loves the humble heart. He says that He will dwell "with him that is of a contrite and humble spirit" (Isaiah 57:15).

The Holy Spirit is also a voice within us, speaking through the Word of God and through our consciences. We are told not to quench or to grieve the Spirit. The Spirit Himself, dwelling within us, helps us to obey the exhortations which the Lord gives:

> *And His that gentle voice we hear,*
> *Soft as the breath of even,*
> *That checks each fault, that calms each fear,*
> *And speaks of heaven.*

May we ever be sensitive to this gentle voice and ready to listen and to obey!

> *And every virtue we possess,*
> *And every conquest won,*
> *And every thought of holiness,*
> *Are His alone.*

We link this sixth verse with the fruit detailed in the Epistle to the Galatians. "But the fruit of the Spirit is love, joy, peace, longsuffering, gentleness, goodness, faith, meekness, temperance" (Galatians 5:22–23). We cannot of ourselves bring forth the fruit of the Spirit unless the Spirit first works the fruit in us. The works of the flesh are natural to us, but we would know nothing of "love, joy, peace, longsuffering . . ." if God had not sent the Spirit of His Son into our hearts. To win victory even over one sin we need to be strengthened by His Spirit in the inner man.

It is as wonderful to be able to pray to the Spirit as it is to have access to God the Father (through Christ) and to Jesus Christ, our Saviour.

> Spirit of purity and grace,
>   Our weakness, pitying, see:
> O make our hearts Thy dwelling-place,
>   And worthier Thee.

If such prayer is offered, by faith in God's promise to give the Holy Spirit to those that ask (Luke 11:13), the Comforter will stoop to enter our poor hearts. In one sense our hearts can never be worthy for the Lord to live in them, but in His great mercy He has chosen to do so.

That Christians may live in "the love of the Spirit" (Romans 15:30) and, in all their weakness, bring glory to God by lives indwelt and strengthened by the Holy Spirit, are two of the great aims set before the ministers of God's Word. Just as every servant of the Lord, working in public or in private, cannot but be dependent upon the Holy Spirit of God, so too must the Spirit's ministry operate in the lives of all who would receive blessing "from on high." Many blessings come to us through human channels, but their fountainhead is God Himself; and the indwelling Spirit of God graciously conveys them to us. To all these wonderful truths Harriet Auber gives excellent expression. If it is for one hymn only that she is now remembered, that single hymn is of surpassing worth.

36

JOHN ELIAS

(1774–1841)

And was it for my sin
  That Jesus suffered so,
When moved by His all-powerful love
  He came to earth below?

Thy holy law fulfilled,
  Atonement now is made,
And our great debt, too great for us,
  He now has fully paid.

He suffered pain and death,
  When on the hill brought low:
His blood will wash the guilty clean,
  As pure and white as snow.

(tr. by Noel Gibbard)

ONE Sunday evening about the year 1786 the congregation in a small Calvinistic Methodist chapel at Pentre Uchaf in Caernarvonshire, Wales, was awaiting the arrival of the preacher. Near the pulpit steps an old man sat with a pock-marked boy by his side. The preacher still did not arrive, so the old man told the child to read a chapter out of the Bible to the people. He pushed him into the pulpit and shut the door upon him. The boy was John Elias and the old man his grandfather. To continue in John's own words:

I read a part of Christ's Sermon on the Mount, the people listening attentively. At length I looked over my shoulder and saw the preacher standing at the door of the pulpit; I was greatly alarmed, I closed the Bible and came down as fast as I could. I do not recollect what my age was then—it might have been anywhere from nine to twelve years. This was the first time I entered the pulpit. And neither did I, nor any other person, think I should have the privilege of occupying it so often afterwards.

John Elias was born on May 6, 1774, in a small tenement in the parish of Aber-erch about four miles from Pwllheli in Caernarvonshire. His grandfather was a weaver who also farmed a smallholding. John's father assisted the old man in his trade and lived, with his family, in a small cottage nearby. John was indebted to his grandfather for the instruction and guidance he received in his childhood. He was a churchman, a very upright, moral man, who took great delight in his grandson, teaching him when very young the danger of lying and swearing, taking God's name in vain and defiling the Sabbath. He taught his grandson to read. When he was six he could read the Bible, and when seven he had read as far as Jeremiah.

When still young, John heard that some of the celebrated preachers used to preach at Pwllheli, Pentre Uchaf and other places, and having a great desire to hear them he persuaded his grandfather, after attending the church in the morning, to come with him to hear some Methodist preachers in these places in the afternoon or evening. When, on account of his age, his grandfather was no longer able to go with him, John would go alone.

When a popular preacher from South Wales was expected on his rounds in this locality I would sometimes walk over ten miles on a Sabbath morning in order to hear the first sermon. I would then follow him until nightfall, taking but little food all day. I had great pleasure in listening, though but little spiritual evangelical light had as yet shone upon my mind.

On one occasion he thought of going seventy miles to hear the celebrated Daniel Rowland of Llangeitho, but meanwhile, to John's distress, the preacher died.

John's parents do not seem to have been godly people and no family prayer was offered in the home. John says,

> I was in those days under great trouble of mind because I did not keep family worship. . . . I told [my parents] my distress of mind, and I asked their permission to attempt to read and pray with the family. They allowed me and I began that hour . . . though I had not much encouragement from my family at that time.

When he was eighteen years old he went with a large number of young people to attend a meeting of "the Association" at Bala. They heard many sermons and returned home rejoicing, talking about the sermons, and singing and praying.

> The journey, though forty miles long, seemed to end much too soon—we all walked on foot all the way. I had such enjoyment in the fellowship of these godly people on this journey that I determined to join them.

Dr. Owen Thomas once met an elder who had traveled with them on that journey. At Ffestiniog they held a prayer meeting.

> A request was made for a Bible. . . . At length the quiet, serious young man who was a stranger to most of the company produced one from his pocket. He was asked to read a chapter. "He did so," said the old man, "in such a manner as to make the chapter seem new to us all." He was also urged to offer a prayer. "And if the reading was wonderful," he said, "the prayer was far more wondrous. I have never heard such praying in my life!"

Shortly after this, says Elias,

> in a certain place on the way to Pwllheli, the words
> "the ministry of reconciliation . . ." came to my
> mind with some light which was quite strange to
> me. My soul had such a feast in the words, "God
> was in Christ reconciling the world unto himself,
> not imputing their trespasses unto them"! I saw
> that the way to accomplish this was by imputing
> our sins to Christ, and imputing His righteousness
> to us. The doctrine of imputation has been, since
> that time, of infinite importance in my estimation. I
> felt . . . that I could preach it to my countrymen
> everywhere.

Elias now took steps to join the people of God. He went
to work for a godly man who combined weaving with
farming. In consequence he left his parents' home and lived
with the family of his employer. Through their instrumen-
tality he joined the small Society of Methodists at Hendre
Howel, where he found the people "quiet, kind, brotherly,
of a tender conscience and brokenness of heart. I found
succour there and splendid nourishment." After this Elias
was asked by Griffith Jones, his employer, to engage alter-
nately with him in family prayer. "There was something in
his spirit when praying that caused all that heard to forget
everything but praying." Elias then began to take part in
the ministry at the meetings at Hendre Howel, and as his
preaching was generally acceptable he was persuaded to
attend the Monthly Meeting where on Christmas Day 1794
he was examined for the ministry and given permission to
preach "in those places to which he was invited." In a
short time he became so popular that his services were
sought not only in many parts of Wales but in England
too. Crowded congregations attended his ministry everywhere he went and many were converted. According to all
surviving accounts, "Elias appeared like a comet, in full
blaze, at the beginning of his ministry. He made progress
with regard to the richness of his resources, such as el-
egance of speech, . . . but in force and vigor, warmth and

originality he never surpassed the opening years of his
ministry!"

He records his removal to Anglesey: "In the beginning
of the year 1799, Providence ordered my removal from
Caernarvonshire to Anglesey. It was a sorrowful experience to part with my friends but we separated in love—to
God be all the praise!" Anglesey at that time was a veri-
table Sodom. Drunkenness abounded and the people had
sunk into the lowest depths of corruption and immorality.
The clergy were no better than the people. "Like dumb
dogs they could not bark except at good men like Daniel
Rowland and William Williams who, when they attempted
to preach at Llangefni, were driven from the place." Quar-
reling, fighting, smuggling, and plundering wrecked vessels were other evils in the Anglesey of those days.

Elias endeavored by all means to put a stop to the current of iniquity, encouraged by a few souls who were
grieved by the iniquity of the island. There were several
small Societies, together with a few faithful preachers and
elders, who helped Elias and among whom he soon became a burning and a shining light. Like Daniel Rowland
and Howel Harris he was eminently qualified for "the ar-
duous office of prophesying to a valley of dead bones. . . .
He went forth as a giant to run his course, and the Lord
was with him and prospered him exceedingly in this new
part of the vineyard."

Soon Anglesey appeared a very different county. "A
great thirst for the Word of God was apparent everywhere. . . . The works of darkness . . . began to subside
gradually. Horse racing was given up, through Elias'
preaching against it, and a company of players who ridi-
culed Elias on the stage was driven off the island." Shortly
after his removal to Anglesey, Elias had married Elizabeth
Broadhead who owned and managed a shop in the village
of Llanfechell, near Cemaes Bay, in the northern part of the
island. Two of their four children died in infancy, but the
other two were brought up in the nurture and admonition
of the Lord, and both in later life became members of the

John Elias

church. John Elias' income from preaching was so small that, until her death, his wife continued to manage her shop (at times with her husband's help) in order to help pay their way and educate their children. She was a humble and devoted Christian and would not let her business interfere with her husband's ministerial duties. Even on her deathbed, when she overheard her children say they would send for their father, who had gone on a preaching appointment, she said, "No, by no means; for what is my life to the cause he is engaged in?" Some time after Elizabeth's death, John Elias married a titled Anglesey widow, Lady Bulkeley, and understandably his financial problems met their solution.

It was not only in Anglesey and Caernarvonshire that the wonderful influence of Elias' sermons was felt, but in every part of Wales. Wherever he preached thousands went to hear him. The Word of God was exceedingly blessed and many were convinced and converted. And what a daring preacher Elias was! At the risk of his own life he often preached in the open air and in the strongest holds of the devil. At Rhuddlan in Flintshire the people had for long

years been in the habit of holding an annual fair on a
certain Sunday for hiring servants, selling hooks, scythes
and other things. Drunkenness, debauchery and crime
made the place a sink of iniquity. Although his friends
tried to persuade him not to go, and trembled for his safety,
John Elias went to the place when business and pleasure
were in full swing, and preached the gospel to the ungodly. He sang the twenty-fourth psalm, read the Scriptures and then, with tears streaming down his cheeks, he
poured out his soul in earnest prayer. Not a word was
spoken or a finger raised against him. He never had a
more attentive audience while he preached with amazing
force from Exodus 34:21—"Six days thou shalt work, but
on the seventh day thou shalt rest. . . ." After that sermon
the abominable practices which had been going on in
Rhuddlan for so many years were never repeated. So successful was the ministry of Elias that in the course of time
his converts could be found in nearly every town and village throughout the Principality. And perhaps no man
wrestled more successfully in prayer than he.

In June 1832, when on his way to Bala to preach, Elias
fell out of his carriage and the injury he sustained affected
his health for the rest of his life. While preaching at
Llannerch-y-medd in 1840 he took cold, inflammation set
into one of his feet, and after three months of intense suffering he passed peacefully away in the sixty-eighth year
of his age and the forty-seventh year of his ministry. About
10,000 people followed his mortal remains to the grave,
and throughout the Principality and among the Welsh everywhere the sorrow at his departure was deep and strong.

It is obvious that John Elias was a preacher rather than a
hymn-writer, but it is interesting to read his views on the
subject of hymn-singing in the preface he wrote to the
hymnbook compiled by Richard Jones of Wern, himself a
hymn-writer. Elias says, "It is the particular duty of every
Christian to sing praises to God. . . . But everyone ought
to examine himself *whether he praises God by singing*." He
says that we ought to pay attention to the tune, the words,

and the state of our minds. Regarding the tunes he says, "We should, in order to sing the praises of God, choose those tunes which are the most suitable to cherish sober and devotional dispositions in the mind, and engage all the powers of the soul." As to the words, he says, "The words we use in singing to God's glory . . . should be according to the analogy of faith, agreeing fully with the Word of God; and those who sing the praises of God ought, at least, to consider and understand the words they sing." And in respect to the state of our minds—" 'Singing with the spirit,' 'singing and making melody in your hearts to the Lord.' It is as necessary to sing *to* the glory *of God*, in spirit and truth, as to perform any other part of God's service."

We close with the last three verses of Elias' own hymn of which we quoted the first three at the beginning:

For in His death, our death
Died with Him on the tree,
And a great number by His blood
Will go to heaven made free.

When Jesus bowed His head
And, dying, took our place,
The veil was rent, a way was found
To that pure home of grace.

He conquered blackest hell;
He trod the serpent down;
A host from fetters He'll set free
By grace to be God's own.

The first two lines of this hymn, "And Was It for My Sin that Jesus Suffered So?" are said to echo the question of a maid in the house where Elias was staying, who was in a distressed spiritual condition following a sermon by Elias. His answer to the maid went to her heart and he wrote the hymn, according to tradition, on his way to the "experience meeting" that night.

37

JOSIAH CONDER

(1789–1855)

Thou art the Everlasting Word,
The Father's only Son:
God manifestly seen and heard,
And heaven's beloved One.

> *Worthy, O Lamb of God, art Thou,*
> *That every knee to Thee should bow!*

In Thee, most perfectly expressed,
The Father's glories shine:
Of the full deity possessed,
Eternally divine. . . .

Throughout the universe of bliss
The center Thou, and sun,
The eternal theme of praise is this,
To heaven's beloved One:

> *Worthy, O Lamb of God, art Thou,*
> *That every knee to Thee should bow!*

THIS hymn bears out Julian's commendation of Josiah Conder as one of the best hymn-writers of the first half of the nineteenth century. "His finest hymns," says Julian, "are marked by much elevation of thought, expressed in language combining both force and beauty." They generally excel in unity, and in some (as in the one quoted) the gradual unfolding of the leading idea is masterly. We can trace some of these characteristics in another hymn of Conder's:

> The Lord is King; lift up thy voice,
>   O earth, and all ye heavens, rejoice!
> From world to world the joy shall ring:
>   "The Lord Omnipotent is King!"
>
> The Lord is King! who then shall dare
>   Resist His will, distrust His care,
> Or murmur at His wise decrees,
>   Or doubt His royal promises? . . .
>
> One Lord, one empire, all secures:
>   He reigns—and life and death are yours;
> Through earth and heaven one song shall ring,
>   "The Lord Omnipotent is King!"

Many hymns of Conder's are found in modern hymn-books, including:

> O God, who didst Thy will unfold
>   In wondrous ways to saints of old,
> By dream, by oracle, or seer,
>   Wilt Thou not still Thy people hear?

and,

> How shall I follow Him I serve?
>   How shall I copy Him I love,
> Nor from those blessed footsteps swerve
>   Which lead me to His seat above?

and again,

> Lord, in this blest and hallowed hour
>   Reveal Thy presence and Thy power;
> Show to my faith Thy hands and side,
>   My Lord and God, the Crucified!

Most of Conder's hymns were written as he was passing through the changing experiences, trials and toils of a long and busy life. They are the products of a deeply spiritual mind and are evidently the work of one very familiar with Christian doctrine and well acquainted with the requirements in hymns for public worship.

Josiah Conder was the fourth son of Thomas Conder, a map engraver and bookseller, and was born on Falcon Street, Aldersgate, in the city of London on September 17, 1789. At the age of five smallpox inoculation destroyed the sight of his right eye and, fearing the other eye might be lost, he was sent for treatment to Hackney where he also went to school. At the early age of ten he contributed essays to the *Monthly Precentor* and was awarded two silver medals for his papers. At thirteen he left school and entered the bookselling business of his father, while in his leisure he carried out a system of self-education, for the same purpose talking to the intelligent people who frequented the shop. In 1811 he succeeded to the business, as his father retired on account of ill health. His own literary ability increased, he displayed good literary taste, and when he was twenty-one, articles of his were accepted by the *Athenaeum* magazine. About the same time, with the assistance of poetical friends, he produced a volume of poems entitled *The Associate Minstrels*.

Conder married in 1815 and brought his bride home to his new shop at St. Paul's Churchyard where he lived until 1819. He then disposed of the business, as he had become the proprietor of the *Eclectic Review* in 1814, retaining the management of it until 1837. During his editorship he rendered much service to the dissenting interest. In 1832, on the establishment of the *Patriot* newspaper, Conder was induced to become its editor "to represent principles of evangelical nonconformity." He held this position for twenty-three years. In 1836 he edited the *Congregational Hymn Book: a Supplement to Dr. Watts' Hymns and Psalms*. To this collection he added fifty-six of his own hymns. In 1851 he published a revised edition of Dr. Watts' *Psalms and Hymns,* and in the same year he wrote a special paper on Dr. Watts as "The Poet of the Sanctuary" which was read before the Congregational Union at Southampton.

He was the author of several prose works, some of considerable length. In addition to his exhausting literary labors, he was a lay preacher and was always ready to cooperate in every useful religious or benevolent enterprise. He was also a great letter-writer and kept up a correspondence with James Montgomery, Robert Southey, Robert Hall, and other literary men of his day. The labors of his pen continued uninterruptedly until November 1855 when he suffered an attack of jaundice from which he never recovered.

Before his death he had collected all his hymns into a volume which was nearly ready for the press at the time of his death. It superseded all previous editions and was entitled *Hymns of Praise and Prayer and Devout Meditation*. It was published posthumously in 1856, with a preface by his son, in which he says that many of his father's hymns are "transcripts of personal experience and add to the proofs so often given that God tunes the heart by trial and sorrow, not only to patience but to praise."

Conder's own hymns helped to soothe and cheer him as his path entered the valley of the shadow. His hymns, he said, "while they reproved him, comforted him." He wanted to have those read to him which spoke of the Lord Jesus. A few evenings before his death a hymn which he had composed as a "deathbed hymn," not found in hymnbooks, was read to him:

> *Upholden by the hand*
> *On which my faith has hold,*
> *Kept by God's mighty power, I stand*
> *Secure within the fold.*

> *Weak, fickle, apt to slide,*
> *His faithfulness I've proved;*
> *Because I in the Lord confide,*
> *I never shall be moved.*

> *Beset with fears and cares,*
> *In Him my heart is strong;*
> *All things in life and death are theirs,*
> *Who to the Lord belong.*

The hymn was read to him three times and he then said

that he had it by heart. "Now you can sleep upon that," said one of his children. "Oh, yes," was the emphatic answer, "and die upon it!" On December 27, 1855, just a few days later, he died.

38

CHARLOTTE ELLIOTT

(1789–1871)

Just as I am, without one plea
But that Thy blood was shed for me,
And that Thou bidd'st me come to Thee,
O Lamb of God, I come!

THE hymn "Just As I Am" is undoubtedly the best-known of the many hymns written by Charlotte Elliott. It is much used evangelistically and it might be thought that Miss Elliott wrote it soon after her own conversion. However, when the seven verses of the hymn are read more thoughtfully, it becomes apparent that the words used and the depth of experience expressed are much more those of a mature Christian than of a new convert. Miss Elliott was converted in 1822 through a well-known minister of those times, Dr. César Malan of Geneva. It has been said that when she asked Dr. Malan to tell her how she should come to Christ he replied, "Come just as you are," so although the hymn was not written until twelve years later, in 1834, these words may have recurred to her mind, thus becoming the refrain of the hymn.

We are indebted to Handley Moule, a godly bishop of Durham and relative of the Elliott family, for details of how the hymn was written. Charlotte was forty-five and had suffered ill health for many years. While staying with her brother, an Anglican minister, she was unable to help with a sale of work he had arranged. This caused her to lie awake all night thinking of her uselessness. She even began to question the reality of her spiritual life. The next day everyone but Charlotte left the house to go to the sale and, to quote Bishop Moule,

> the troubles of the night came back to her with such force that she felt they must be met and conquered in the grace of God. She gathered up in her soul the great certainties, not of her emotions, but of her salvation, her Lord, His power, His promise. Then she deliberately set down in writing, for her own comfort, "the formulae of her faith."

So, in verse, she restated to herself the gospel of pardon, peace and heaven. What a new light the circumstances in which she wrote the hymn throw on such words as

> *Just as I am, though tossed about*
> *With many a conflict, many a doubt,*
> *Fightings within and fears without,*
> *O Lamb of God, I come!*

Her sister-in-law returned to tell Charlotte of the progress of the sale and, finding the hymn completed, she asked for a copy. So the hymn stole out of that quiet room of suffering to bring untold blessing to the world. Her brother said later, "In the course of a long ministry I hope I have been permitted to see some fruit of my labors, but I feel far more has been done by a single hymn of my sister's." The hymn has been translated into many languages, even into the native dialects of far-away islands.

There are, of course, many stories of how the hymn has been used by the Lord. A boy of fifteen, who later became a missionary in Bengal, was converted through hearing it sung at an open-air meeting. A Roman Catholic woman was admitted to a home for "fallen" women. Her conscience was hardened and her prejudices intense. Through the influence of the hymn she became a humble believer in the Lord Jesus Christ. Only the annals of eternity will reveal how many lives have been influenced by this hymn, with its lines which are so true to the experience of the soul

Charlotte Elliott

convinced of its sin and helplessness.

The poet Wordsworth had one daughter, Dora. He loved her, calling her his "one and matchless daughter." She was dying. The words of the hymn were sent to her husband and when he read them to his wife she said, "That is the very thing for me." The first day he read them to her ten times, then morning and evening each day until she died. Her mother also was affected by the hymn which she said formed part of her "daily, solitary prayer." The poet, however, "could not bear to have it quoted in his presence," but he was thankful for the comfort it had brought to his daughter.

The writer is taking the liberty of interjecting a personal note here. Under deep conviction of sin she had sought the quietness of a Welsh hillside in order to seek the Lord. The reading of the whole of a Scripture Gift Mission *Gospel of John* did not bring the relief she sought, but there were hymns in the back of the little Gospel and it was while singing the hymn "Just As I Am" that the burden of sin was loosed from her back and rolled down the hillside. In much ignorance of the gospel, but with her whole heart, she joined in the chorus "O Lamb of God, I come!"

The recorded events of Charlotte Elliott's life are few. She was born in 1789 and died in 1871, so that in spite of lifelong ill health she lived to be eighty-two. On her mother's side she was related to Henry Venn, one of the leaders of the evangelical awakening of the eighteenth century. She was more or less an invalid from early years until she finally became housebound. She revived somewhat during the summer months and was able to visit friends who appreciated "her charming conversation and her vivid imagination." Her letters and poems show that she loved the beauties of nature and entered into the joys and sorrows of those she loved. She possessed gifts in music and drawing and was altogether an attractive and accomplished person. She felt that the One who loved her with an everlasting love knew the snare of the company into which her intellectual and artistic abilities were drawing her. She saw her ill health as the Lord's means of delivering her from the snare and of bringing her to Himself.

In her illness and seclusion she became conscious of the evil of her own heart. Until this time, when she was thirty-three, she had no real understanding of the fullness and freeness of the grace of God in the Lord Jesus Christ and suffered much mental distress, thinking she could never be saved. God provided a spiritual teacher in Dr. César Malan. As a skillful spiritual physician he probed her wound and led her to simple faith in God's own Word. As the Spirit of God applied his teaching to her need the burden was lifted from her weary spirit and, though her suffering body at times weighed her down, from the memorable day of her conversion her spiritual horizon was for the most part cloudless. Henceforward the Bible was her principal study and her gift of poetry was consecrated to spiritual use. Her constant testimony was, "I know whom I have believed. . . ."

In 1834 she accepted the editorship of *The Christian Remembrancer Pocket Book*. She prepared this little volume annually for twenty-five years, though it often cost her much painful effort to do so. She also revised *The Invalids' Hymn Book*, adding more than a hundred hymns of her own. These included some hymns which we find in our hymnbooks today. For example:

> *My God, is any hour so sweet*
> *From blush of morn to evening star,*
> *As that which calls me to Thy feet,*
> *The hour of prayer?*

and

> *Christian, seek not yet repose;*
> *Cast thy dreams of ease away;*
> *Thou art in the midst of foes:*
> *Watch and pray.*

During the last two years of her life she was virtually bedridden. But her mind was clear and her affections as tender as ever. She loved the sunsets and the cloud formations she could see through her window. For many years her "motto" had been the verse

> *Lord Jesus, make Thyself to me*
> *A living bright reality,*
> *More present to faith's vision keen*
> *Than any outward object seen,*
> *More dear, more intimately nigh,*
> *Than e'en the sweetest earthly tie.*

As the years passed it was more and more translated into her own experience. She used to say that she was like a limpet on a rock, clinging to her Saviour.

We return again to the hymn with which we started. What a wealth of truth and experience is found in the seven verses of the hymn "Just As I Am!" As we read them

again, and dwell upon each phrase, we see their compre-
hensiveness. They cover every need, every problem, every
experience of the human heart, in coming to Christ and in
living a life consecrated to Him. It *is* a conversion hymn
but it is much more. It is a hymn for the whole of the
Christian life.

39

HENRY FRANCIS LYTE

(1793–1847)

Abide with me; fast falls the eventide;
The darkness deepens; Lord, with me abide!
When other helpers fail, and comforts flee,
Help of the helpless, O abide with me!

Swift to its close ebbs out life's little day;
Earth's joys grow dim, its glories pass away;
Change and decay in all around I see:
O Thou who changest not, abide with me!

THIS well-known and much-loved hymn is certainly an evening hymn. But it is clearly meant for the evening of life, not for inclusion in the "Hymns for Evening" section of a hymnbook. It had been the desire of Henry Francis Lyte to write something which would be of permanent blessing and value to mankind and to the Christian Church. In the judgment of many his desire has been abundantly fulfilled in his hymn "Abide with Me." It was written at a time of much physical weakness, as he was nearing the end of his life and ministry. It has been described as an "immortal" hymn and it has strengthened and consoled many people in all their varied needs and circumstances. We cannot envisage a time when it will not be included in hymnbooks and so continue in its ministry to generation after generation, particularly as believers come within sight of Immanuel's land.

Henry Francis Lyte was born near Kelso, in Scottish border country, the son of an army officer who died when Henry was quite young, and a godly, talented mother who seems to have had much influence on him. He went to school in Ireland, then graduated at Trinity College, Dublin. While there he three times won the prize for the best English poem of the university year, so his poetic gift manifested itself early in his life. He was a distinguished scholar and had a great aptitude for making friends. Some of his early friendships remained firm through life and were a source of comfort and strength during his years of sickness.

Lyte thought of becoming a doctor but changed his mind and went "into the Church." After ordination and a short curacy near Wexford in the south of Ireland, he moved to Marazion in Cornwall where two important events took place. The first event was his conversion. Up to this time he had lived a worldly life, even as a Christian minister. Divine grace intervened in the following way. A neighboring minister sent for him, feeling that he was dying and that he was unpardoned and therefore unprepared to die. Together he and Lyte searched the Scriptures, particularly Paul's Epistles; together they gained a knowledge of Christian doctrine and came into possession of the pardon and peace which Christ alone can give. The other minister died, happy in the knowledge of sins forgiven and acceptance with God. Lyte, now also a converted man, went on to live a busy, useful, but fairly short life, beset by much illness. Even at the time his ministerial friend died his health was poor, and the help it was necessary for him to give to the bereaved family proved too much for his weak constitution. Only a prolonged holiday on the Continent restored him to a measure of health.

The second important event which took place in Marazion was that he met the lady who became his wife. She was the daughter of a Methodist minister and was herself a staunch Methodist. Neither did she change on marriage! On leaving Marazion, Lyte accepted the "perpetual curacy" of a church in Brixham, South Devon. Here

Henry Francis Lyte

his wife used to go to the Methodist church while her husband went to take the service at his church, All Souls. This division must have caused difficulties, but in other respects the marriage seems to have been a happy and united one. She entered fully with her husband into the work of serving the people of Brixham.

For twenty years Lyte worked among the rough seafaring population of the town. It was an important fishing port and well-known historically because it was at Brixham that William of Orange landed in 1688 to claim the English throne from James II, his father-in-law. Unhappily the location of a military station in Brixham, and occasional visits of naval vessels, seriously affected the morality of the town. So Lyte faced a difficult situation, but he was used to difficulties and was not daunted by them. He soon became "a power for good and a person much-loved." In fact Brixham knew him as a Mr. Greatheart, serving the people in things both temporal and spiritual. Many sailors came

Facsimile of the first part of "Abide with Me," as originally written to church out of respect for him, and their hazardous occupation made him all the more concerned to meet their spiritual needs.

Lyte worked unceasingly. His feeble frame constantly protested, but although doctors urged him to rest more he carried on with his indefatigable labors. He educated his own children and also a number of "gentlemen's sons." He was constantly writing. The psalms were like a spring of living water to his soul and his first book consisted of psalms which he set to meter. Several of these are still found in our hymnbooks, for example:

> *Pleasant Are Thy Courts Above (Psalm 85)*

and

> *God of Mercy, God of Grace (Psalm 67)*

The very popular hymn "Praise, My Soul, the King of Heaven" is a loose paraphrase of Psalm 103. His hymns too were beginning to find their way into hymnbooks.

Difficulties in the church hastened the deterioration in his health. Summoning all his energy he preached a sermon especially prepared to secure peace and unity, and he must have felt sad as he realized he must soon leave the people and church he loved. The Lytes lived at Berry Head House which had been given to them by King William IV when he visited Brixham. Lyte loved this house which was "beautiful for situation," not least the terraced gardens which went right down to the sea.

As years passed Lyte had to spend each winter on the Continent, for the English climate played havoc with his weak lungs. He spent time in Naples, the Tyrol and Switzerland, but he spent more time in Rome than anywhere else. That city's climate seemed to suit him and he had friends there. When possible he would return to Berry Head House, which was always home to him, in summer time. He seemed to know intuitively that the summer of 1847 would be his last in Brixham. He wrote, "I am meditating flight again to the South; the little faithful robin is every morning at my window, warning me that autumnal days are at hand. The swallows are preparing for flight and inviting me to accompany them, and yet, alas! while I talk of flying, I am just about able to crawl!"

That same autumn he made one last attempt to preach to his congregation; he spoke solemn words and ministered at the Lord's table. Later that evening he gave his daughter the hymn "Abide with Me," with the music he had adapted to it. The hymn had been written earlier, probably in France. Its words and phrases are the true expression of a heart deeply feeling the need of Christ's presence and firmly assured that it will not be denied. There is an impassioned earnestness in the hymn and a familiarity with the Master altogether free from presumption.

That same week the enfeebled writer left home for Europe with his wife, his second son and a faithful friend. On arrival in Nice he became very ill, but during his intense sufferings he rested calmly in God, saying that "he had nothing and was nothing in himself." In his heart of hearts he gloried only in the cross of Christ. In his active years Lyte had thought with distress of the act of dying, but the God who had given him grace to live gave him grace to die. He died in Nice and was buried there.

> I fear no foe with Thee at hand to bless;
> Ills have no weight and tears no bitterness:
> Where is death's sting? where, grave, thy victory?
> I triumph still, if Thou abide with me.

On the day that news of his death reached Brixham, the fishermen who loved him so much asked that "Abide with Me" should be sung in All Souls Church. The Devonshire people loved Lyte's hymns. Long after his death they used to walk along the shores of Torbay singing favorite verses in the moonlight. The fact that his hymns are still loved so many years after his death demonstrates their abiding "immortal" quality.

40

HUGH STOWELL

(1799–1865)

From every stormy wind that blows,
From every swelling tide of woes,
There is a calm, a sure retreat:
  'Tis found beneath the mercy seat. . . .

O let my hands forget their skill,
  My tongue be silent, cold, and still,
This bounding heart forget to beat,
  If I forget the mercy seat.

TWO hymns by Hugh Stowell are found in most of the hymnbooks in present-day use. They remind us of the godliness of one of the leading evangelical ministers of the Church of England during much of the first half of Queen Victoria's reign. Although his ministry was exercised substantially in the North of England, he was born on the Isle of Man, where his father was an Anglican rector. There is good evidence that a love of Scripture, of Reformation truth and of godly living were distinguishing marks of the Stowell family. One of Hugh's cousins, in whose company he probably spent much of his boyhood, later wrote a History of the Puritans, edited the works of the Puritan Thomas Adams, and wrote booklets for the Religious Tract Society.

Entering Oxford University at the age of nineteen and graduating in 1822, Hugh Stowell became noted among his fellow students for his poetical gifts and his "almost unrivaled powers as a public speaker." He excelled in the University Debating Society.

> His language was remarkable for its purity and elegance; he used no vulgarisms, and the most captious hearer could not say of him that his shibboleths betrayed him, though the sentiments he uttered, and which he was never at the slightest pains to conceal, always showed that he meant to impress upon his hearers what he held to be the grand evangelical doctrines. His animation roused his audience very often into raptures of enthusiasm, and he sat down amidst the tears, or transports, of his hearers.

Throughout his entire life he maintained that "the Bible is God's Word from first to last, or it is not God's Word at all. There is no heresy more dangerous, more deadly, and more desperate than that which denies the plenary inspiration of Holy Scripture."

In his day Stowell was one of the leading churchmen who opposed Tractarianism, that is to say, the Romeward movement in the Church of England led by such men as Newman, Pusey and Faber. He declared that in consequence "the battle of the Reformation had to be fought again"—a sentiment that well befits this latter part of the present century—and on many occasions he spoke at public meetings in support of the great Protestant principles enumerated by sixteenth-century Reformers. He saw an inseparable connection between Britain's safety and a God-given prosperity in church and state on the one hand, and her faithful adherence to Protestant principles on the other. When the country was assailed by Tractarianism he stated with all boldness:

> You know what became of Samson after he had been lulled to sleep on the harlot's lap, and when she had shorn off the locks wherein his great strength consisted. What these locks were to

Hugh Stowell

Samson, Protestant principle is to England. It is the lock of her strength, the nerve of her arm, the sinew of her frame, the jewel of her crown. Rifled of this, her strength is gone, her arm is paralyzed, her crown is fallen, her glory is departed! Oh that the genuine mantle of Protestant zeal might again descend upon us, to guide and direct us, and keep and support us in these days of blasphemy and rebuke!

If such a word was needed in 1840, how much more is it needed in this late twentieth century!

A further great question of the Victorian era on which Stowell frequently spoke was that of national education. He urged that education should be made available for all and that it should be closely linked with the Christian faith. On one occasion he spoke to a vast city audience and held their "breathless attention" for three hours on this subject, although it was generally supposed that "the education of the masses was one of the most dry and difficult themes that could be chosen for a public address."

As already mentioned, it was in the North of England that Stowell exercised by far the greater part of his ministry, for in 1831 he was appointed to a parish in Salford, Lancashire, and there he remained until his death thirty years later. Manchester and Salford together, lying as they do cheek by jowl, form one vast center of population. The Industrial Revolution had left its mark upon them both. In Manchester in particular great commercial enterprises were located, even though it was not until the close of the century that the famous Ship Canal, linking the city with the world's oceans, brought great mercantile vessels to Manchester's docks. Salford possessed factories and mills, and a multitude of smaller workshops. Stowell responded admirably to the challenge presented by a workaday population. He never forgot to remind his hearers that "man shall not live by bread alone, but by every word of God," and under his fervent ministry sinners were converted and believers were edified. When he died it was as though the whole of Salford went into mourning, and the city of Manchester seemed to "sit solitary." All members of the public realized that a man of God had gone to his rest.

Stowell's hymn, "From Every Stormy Wind That Blows," very clearly links the mercy seat of Old Testament Scripture with the Person and work of Christ. Its verses in turn relate the mercy seat to trials, to joys, to Christian fellowship, to sufferings and temptations, to blessings descending from heaven; they close with the believer urging his own hands and tongue and heart never to forget the mercy seat.

Another of Stowell's hymns is that beginning:

> *Jesus is our Shepherd,*
> *Wiping every tear;*
> *Folded in His bosom*
> *What have we to fear?* . . .

Obviously it, too, has a completely biblical background. Almost every line reminds us of verses found in Scripture. It was written for children, and appears in hymnbooks in the section devoted to the young, but believers of all ages will find in it that which appeals to their heart affections. Doubtless many, as they have faced the final strife, have been rendered happy in singing

Jesus is our Shepherd:
Guarded by His arm,
Though the wolves may raven,
None can do us harm;
When we tread death's valley,
Dark with fearful gloom,
We will fear no evil,
Victors o'er the tomb.

Truly "The memory of the just is blessed!" (Proverbs 10:7).

41

HORATIUS BONAR

(1808-89)

Here, O my Lord, I see Thee face to face;
Here would I touch and handle things unseen,
Here grasp with firmer hand the eternal grace,
And all my weariness upon Thee lean. . . .

Too soon we rise; the symbols disappear;
The feast, though not the love, is past and gone;
The bread and wine remove, but Thou art here,
Nearer than ever, still my Shield and Sun.

HORATIUS BONAR was not a "son of the manse" but one of the three sons of an Edinburgh solicitor of excise, all of whom became ministers of the gospel. They were a remarkable trio, all educated at the high school and then the University in Edinburgh. The loss of his father when Horatius was only twelve years old was mitigated by the fact that his older brother quietly assumed his father's place in the home. He owed much to the gentle influence of his mother who taught her three sons their first lessons in the faith.

There is no record of when Horatius was converted or of when he began to write verse, though this must have been no later than the age of nineteen when one of his poems appeared in a students' magazine. He was a diligent and distinguished student at the University, and also at the Divinity Hall, where he came under the influence of Tho-

Horatius Bonar

mas Chalmers, then Professor of Divinity. Horatius was greatly influenced by him, considering him the greatest man he had ever met. His fellow students, including Robert Murray McCheyne, recognized Horatius' intellectual power, his poetic ability and the intense earnestness with which he contended for the faith.

Horatius Bonar held three ministerial appointments. His training-ground was in a church at Leith where, as assistant minister, he worked among young people in a very rough area, took services, engaged in house-to-house visitation, and was in charge of the Sabbath school. His second appointment, in 1837, was as ordained minister of the North Parish Church in Kelso. While there he married Jane Katherine Lundie, by which means she returned to the home of her childhood, her father having been a minister in Kelso.

During the ten years which preceded the "Disruption" of 1843 a great wave of evangelical revival swept over

Scotland. Bonar and his church were much involved in this. The keynote of his preaching, whether in his own church or in his wider ministry in the Border counties, was "Ye must be born again." Many people were born again under his ministry. Bonar preached "the whole counsel of God," with particular emphasis on the doctrines of grace and the Second Coming of Christ. It was felt in Kelso that a new power had come to stir the life of this old Border town.

There were stirrings in the Church of Scotland too, but of a distressing kind. At the Disruption, many ministers, including Bonar, could no longer remain in the Established Church and came out of it to form the Free Church of Scotland.

After twenty-nine years in Kelso, Bonar's third ministerial charge was that of the Chalmers' Memorial Church in Edinburgh. In 1883, towards the end of his long ministry there, Bonar was elected Moderator of the General Assembly, the greatest honor the Free Church can bestow. From this time his physical strength declined and frequently he was unable to preach. The death of his wife and son-in-law affected him greatly, and at last, when his strength was

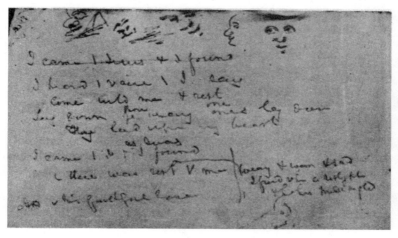

Facsimile of an early draft of the first
verse of "I Heard the Voice of Jesus Say"

quite shattered, his successor was appointed. All through his last, lingering illness he had in front of him a text which was his constant comfort, "Until the day break and the shadows flee away."

It was in Leith that Bonar first began to write hymns, with the motive of arousing the young people out of their listlessness during services. He replaced what he judged to be the unsuitable metrical psalms and hymns which were being used by his own hymns set to more attractive tunes. The habit of expressing himself in poetry and hymns grew gradually on him. He always had a notebook with him so that when traveling or walking he could jot down any idea or fragment of verse which came to his mind. Many of the hymns which he wrote have found an abiding place in the hearts of the redeemed. Most hymnbooks include several of Bonar's hymns—"I Heard the Voice of Jesus Say," "I Hear the Words of Love," "Thy Way Not Mine, O Lord," are just three of these. Bonar kept no record of when he wrote his hymns, with the exception of the hymn chosen here for special mention, "Here, O My Lord, I See Thee Face to Face." It was his custom to go to help his brother, Dr. John Bonar, with the annual communion service in his church at Greenock. The communion service in the Free Church of Scotland is a very special occasion, as it occurs once, or at most twice, in the year. This hymn was written at his brother's request, to be read aloud at the close of the service.

All of Bonar's hymns, not least this one, show his grasp of the whole spectrum of divine truth. He often dwelt on the doctrine of substitution, as in the verse—

> *Mine is the sin, but Thine the righteousness;*
> *Mine is the guilt, but Thine the cleansing blood!*
> *Here is my robe, my refuge and my peace—*
> *Thy blood, Thy righteousness, O Lord my God.*

Another example of his emphasis on substitution and divine grace is found in two verses of the hymn—

All that I was, my sin, my guilt,
    My death was all my own;
All that I am, I owe to Thee,
    My gracious God alone. . . .

Thy grace first made me feel my sin,
    And taught me to believe:
Then, in believing, peace I found,
    And now in Christ I live.

There is much doctrine in Bonar's hymns, but it is doctrine which throbs with warmth and life. Although many of his hymns deal with the personal experience of the believer there is no unhealthy introspection in them. His interest in prophetic truth also is reflected in his hymns. To him the Second Advent was always "that blessed hope," casting its light on the darkest days of earthly trial and conflict.

In 1855 Bonar had a very special experience. With others he spent five months in the Middle East. From Egypt they traveled by camel through the desert of Sinai to Palestine. It was all very fascinating to him and the visit made an impression on him which influenced all his subsequent preaching and writing. An example of this is found in his long poem "Mount Hor," written on the theme of the death of Aaron as described in Numbers 20:23–29. This poem shows how deep was the impression that the scenery and the atmosphere of Palestine had made upon him:

They have left the camp, with its tents out-spreading,
    Like a garden of lilies, on Edom's plain;
They are climbing the mountain, in silence treading
    A path which one shall not tread again;
Two aged brothers the way are leading,
    There follows a youth in the solemn train. . . .

Alone and safe, in the happy keeping
    Of rocks and sand, till the glorious morn,
They have laid thee down for thy lonely sleeping,
    Waysore and weary and labour-worn:
While faintly the sound of a nation's weeping
    From the vale beneath thee is upward borne.

Hymns of Faith and Hope, in which this poem and many others are found, has long been out of print, but if a copy can be found it is a treasure indeed.

We have followed Bonar through his three ministries; we have seen the spiritual value of his hymns and his poetic gift. But what was he like as a man? He was a true Scot in that he was reticent, making little display of emotion. He was, nevertheless, an affectionate man who loved his family, young children in particular, and his friends. His writings, both poetry and prose, show the depths of feeling that were in his heart. He worked indefatigably. It has been written of him that "The light burned late in his study window and he was at his desk early. Members of his household heard his voice in prayer far into the night."

His interests were wide-ranging. Early in life he had shown great liking for English literature, ancient classics, and Greek and Latin hymns of the early church—subjects he pursued through life. He liked sketching, was interested in geology and was an avid reader of books on history and travel. He loved holidays, and especially delighted to be on some lonely wave-beaten beach in Arran, East Lothian or Fife. He had a strong sense of humor, but this he allowed little license, except in the family circle. He was very much amused on being told of a lady in Torquay who met a member of his congregation. "What!" she exclaimed, "Is Bonar the hymn-writer still alive? I always thought he was a medieval saint!" He was a saint indeed, but, happily, of modern days.

42

CECIL FRANCES ALEXANDER

(1818–95)

There is a green hill far away,
Outside a city wall,
Where the dear Lord was crucified
Who died to save us all.

We may not know, we cannot tell
What pains He had to bear;
But we believe it was for us
He hung and suffered there. . . .

O dearly, dearly has He loved,
And we must love Him too,
And trust in His redeeming blood,
And try His works to do.

THIS is perhaps the most famous of all children's hymns, written by Mrs. Alexander who has every right to be considered the best of hymn-writers for children. Her hymns were usually written for her Sunday School class and were nearly all read over to her scholars before being published. It is said that there was a green hill outside the old walls of the city of Derry where Mrs. Alexander lived; it used to remind her of Calvary, thus suggesting the hymn, which was written while sitting by the bedside of a sick child. The little girl was dangerously ill, but recovered, and ever after referred to this hymn as her own possession. Gounod, who wrote a tune for the

Cecil Frances Alexander

hymn—not the one usually sung to it today—affirmed that it was the most beautiful hymn in the English language, its greatest beauty being its simplicity. The hymn was first written with the word "without" in the second line, but the word "outside" was substituted for it after the author-ess had been asked by a very small child what was meant by a green hill not having a city wall.

We agree with Gounod that the great beauty of Mrs. Alexander's children's hymns is their simplicity, and prob-ably fewer questions have been asked by children regard-ing their meaning than in the case of any other author. Among Mrs. Alexander's other children's hymns are "Once in Royal David's City," which ranks second in popularity to "There Is a Green Hill," and "All Things Bright and Beautiful," which is an exquisitely descriptive hymn on the verse, "God saw everything that he had made, and, behold, it was very good":

All things bright and beautiful,
All creatures great and small,
All things wise and wonderful,
The Lord God made them all.

Each little flower that opens,
Each little bird that sings,
He made their glowing colors,
He made their tiny wings: . . .

The cold wind in the winter,
The pleasant summer sun,
The ripe fruits in the garden,
He made them every one: . . .

He gave us eyes to see them,
And lips that we might tell
How great is God Almighty,
Who has made all things well.

Cecil Frances Humphreys was the daughter of Major John Humphreys who served with distinction in the Royal Marines and fought at the Battle of Copenhagen in 1801. On leaving the Army he became a landowner in Wicklow and Tyrone and a land agent in Northern Ireland. Frances began to write poetry at the age of nine, choosing tragic subjects like the death of Nelson and the massacre of Glencoe. In 1846 she wrote *Verses for Holy Seasons*, which was edited by a Dr. Hook whom she had met at the house of a friend and who inspired her with a lifelong conviction of the truth and necessity of the English Reformation in the sixteenth century. In 1848 a tiny volume of thirty pages was published, her *Hymns for Little Children*, for which John Keble wrote the preface. This volume reached a sixty-ninth edition in 1896.

In 1850 she was married to Rev. William Alexander, rector of Termonamongan in County Tyrone, "a parish in a wild area scattered over bogs and mountains for many miles." Mrs. Alexander often walked several miles to meet her husband returning from some distant tramp. It was said of her at this time:

Many a gleam of golden sunshine would she kindle as she entered a desolate home where penury and sickness struggled for the mastery. No inclemency of weather, or distance of travel, or visits of friends, were permitted to interfere with the ministrations of condolence, counsel or charitable help. The good she did, the help afforded, her gentle, loving, self-effacing ministry in this parish will never be known "until the day break and the shadows flee away."

In 1855 the Alexanders moved to the beautiful parish of Upper Fahan on the shores of Lough Swilly, then on to Strabane from 1860 to 1867 when Rev. William Alexander was called to the bishopric of Derry. In her new position Mrs. Alexander was brought into contact with new duties and with people of various social levels. She performed all duties of hospitality with an ease and natural dignity which made her a first-rate hostess. Predominantly her life was one of humble service. In Derry she occupied herself with a Home for Fallen Women and paid quiet, regular visits to very lowly homes in back streets. All her good works were done in a spirit of humility and with no desire for applause.

Although Mrs. Alexander was a churchwoman through and through, she came into contact with many nonconformists, especially Presbyterians, with whom she enjoyed fellowship. She died in 1895. Her funeral was attended by multitudes representing many denominations. "The streets through which the long procession wound its way to the cemetery were thronged with crowds of people. She was laid in her grave amidst the tears of a great community."

Children's hymns were not Mrs. Alexander's only compositions. Her best-known hymn for adults is:

Jesus calls us o'er the tumult
Of our life's wild restless sea,
Day by day His sweet voice soundeth,
Saying, "Christian, follow Me." . . .

> *In our joys and in our sorrows,*
>   *Days of toil and hours of ease,*
> *Still He calls, in cares and pleasures,*
>   *"Christian, love Me more than these."*

> *Jesus calls us: by Thy mercies,*
>   *Saviour, may we hear Thy call,*
> *Give our hearts to Thy obedience,*
>   *Serve and love Thee best of all.*

She also wrote:

> *The golden gates are lifted up,*
>   *The doors are open wide;*
> *The King of glory is gone in*
>   *Unto His Father's side.*

and

> *Spirit of God, that moved of old*
>   *Upon the waters' darkened face,*
> *Come, when our faithless hearts are cold,*
>   *And stir them with an inward grace.*

Her best-known poem is "The Burial of Moses" which had a wide circulation. Of this work Tennyson said that it was one of the poems by a living writer of which he would have been proud to be the author.

Of Mrs. Alexander's hymns her husband says that she "had always practically present to her mind the definition of a hymn given by Augustine. . . . It must be *sung* or capable of being sung; it must be *praise*; it must be *to God*." She enlarged this by the less frequently quoted rule of Jerome that "those only are to be called hymns which set forth in measure the power and majesty of God and are fixed in perpetual admiration of His benefits or His doings."

Several of Mrs. Alexander's hymns have been translated into other languages. A member of the Universities Mission to Central Africa says that he heard her hymns sung by half-clad Africans in a language she had never known. Then, too, the Bishop of Tasmania bore witness to the teaching power of her hymns in the bush area of that island.

Missionary bishops of South Africa and various parts of India have recognized the suitability of her hymns for teaching the elementary truths of the gospel. A great English mission preacher whose work often lay with congregations of highly educated men has written that when these philosophically minded men stumbled over some statement of doctrine, the matter was often made clear to them in the form in which it was presented to them in one or other of Mrs. Alexander's hymns.

In his preface to her *Poems* her husband writes, "To the writer the thought often occurs that these eternal words . . . form themselves into a constant memorial of her before God. The memorial will continue; for the preacher's influence is of a few years, the hymnist's for all time."

43

WILLIAM WALSHAM HOW

(1823–97)

O Word of God incarnate,
O Wisdom from on high,
O Truth unchanged, unchanging,
O Light of our dark sky,
We praise Thee for the radiance
That from the hallowed page,
A lantern to our footsteps,
Shines on from age to age.

SHREWSBURY is a beautiful old town and William Walsham How was born there in a house standing a little back from the road as one ascends College Hill. His father belonged to an old Cumberland family but practised as a solicitor in Shrewsbury. William's love for his childhood home and its pleasant surroundings found expression in his earliest childhood verses.

After his days at Shrewsbury School were over, William went on to Wadham College, Oxford, where he graduated B.A. in 1845 and M.A. in 1847. After a theological course at Durham he was ordained in the Church of England and became curate at St. George's, Kidderminster, which proved excellent training for his future ministerial work. For family reasons he returned to Shrewsbury as a curate in 1848. The following year he married a rector's daughter and became rector of Whittington in Shropshire, remaining there for twenty-eight years.

William Walsham How

Walsham How soon became known as a devotional writer and an acceptable conductor of parochial missions, quiet days and "retreats," while his growing reputation led to various offers of preferment at home and abroad. But he was in no hurry to accept advancement and in turn declined the bishoprics of Natal, New Zealand, Cape Town and Jamaica, besides several more important livings* in England. Ultimately he agreed to become suffragan to the Bishop of London, with episcopal supervision of East London. He was instituted in the living of St. Andrew's Undershaft which supplied his income as bishop. The same year he was created D.D. both by the Archbishop of Canterbury and Oxford University. In London he was known as the "omnibus bishop" because "he scorned the private coach he could afford" and used public transport alongside his poor parishioners in London's East End.

The spiritual desolation of East London at this time was appalling and he sought remedies by all means in his power. He filled the gaps in the ministry, secured drawing-room meetings in the rich West End to help the poor

---

* The position of a vicar or rector with income and/or property.

East End, and awakened interest in rich watering-places like Brighton and Tunbridge Wells, also in public schools and universities. He was very soon recognized as a spiritual force and attracted spiritually minded people around him. He worked in very close contact with his helpers, welcoming them to his home and spending as much time as possible with them. The work he loved best was among children and there was no title he valued more than that of "The Children's Bishop." None of his compositions was written with greater zest than his volume of sermons to children.

His wife had taken a large share of his work, and her death in 1887 doubtless affected his decision to accept the offer of the new bishopric of Wakefield in the following year. He soon became as great a power in the north as he had been in the south, and although he met with many troubles in his new sphere, his earnestness, tact and geniality enabled him to overcome them. His death while on holiday in Ireland in 1897 was as much regretted in Yorkshire as in London.

In 1854 Walsham How, in conjunction with T. B. Morrell, had published a compilation of *Psalms and Hymns*. He also devoted a great deal of time and labor as one of the original compilers of *Church Hymns* which was published by the SPCK in 1871, and was much interested in a children's hymnbook which he helped to revise.

Bishop How takes his place without challenge among good hymn-writers. He wrote hymns for all occasions and seasons of the year. He loved the simple things of life: simple trust, simple character, simple childhood. His popular children's hymn is loved and sung by Christians of all ages:

> *It is a thing most wonderful,*
>   *Almost too wonderful to be,*
> *That God's own Son should come from heaven,*
>   *And die to save a child like me.*
>
> *And yet I know that it is true;*
>   *He came to this poor world below,*

And wept and toiled and mourned and died,
Only because He loved us so. . . .

It is most wonderful to know
His love for me so free and sure;
But 'tis more wonderful to see
My love for Him so faint and poor.

And yet I want to love Thee, Lord;
O light the flame within my heart,
And I will love Thee more and more,
Until I see Thee as Thou art.

His hymn, "For All the Saints," gives utterance to the collective joy of the Church triumphant. The great host of God's serving, struggling, martyred, yet triumphant children seemed to pass before his view as he wrote the words:

For all the saints who from their labors rest
Who Thee, by faith, before the world confessed
Thy Name, O Jesus, be for ever blest,
Hallelujah! Hallelujah!

Thou wast their Rock, their Fortress and their Might;
Thou, Lord, their Captain in the well-fought fight;
Thou, in the darkness drear, their one true Light,
Hallelujah! Hallelujah! . . .

The golden evening brightens in the west;
Soon, soon to faithful warriors cometh rest,
Sweet is the calm of Paradise the blest,
Hallelujah! Hallelujah!

In writing of Bishop How and his hymns Julian says that those of his hymns which have taken the firmest hold upon the Church are his "simple, unadorned, but enthusiastically practical hymns." These characteristics are found in the hymns we have quoted, not least in the one first quoted, which concludes with two fervent prayers:

O make Thy church, dear Saviour,
A lamp of burnished gold,
To bear before the nations

Thy true light as of old.
O teach Thy wandering pilgrims
  By this their path to trace,
Till, clouds and darkness ended,
  They see Thee face to face.

Another very simple hymn found in many hymnbooks is:

O my Saviour, lifted
  From the earth for me,
Draw me, in Thy mercy,
  Nearer unto Thee.

Lift my earth-bound longings,
  Fix them, Lord, above;
Draw me with the magnet
  Of Thy mighty love.

And I come, Lord Jesus;
  Dare I turn away?
No! Thy love hath conquered,
  And I come today.

Bringing all my burdens,
  Sorrow, sin and care;
At Thy feet I lay them,
  And I leave them there.

There is a sweet simplicity and beauty in How's incarnation hymn:

Who is this, so weak and helpless,
  Child of lowly Hebrew maid,
Rudely in a stable sheltered,
  Coldly in a manger laid?
'Tis the Lord of all creation,
  Who this wondrous path hath trod;
He is God from everlasting,
  And to everlasting God.

In his biography of his father, Bishop How's son says, "For the good hymn-writer three qualities, not always found in combination, are requisite. These are good sense, devotional feeling, poetic sense and cultivated taste." It can hardly be doubted that these qualities are found in combination in Bishop How. His son also says that "it is the fate of a hymn-writer to be forgotten. The hymn remains, the name of the writer passes away." Bishop Walsham How was prepared for this; his ambition was not to be remembered, but to be useful. "It was enough for him if he could enlarge the thanksgiving of the church, or minister by song to the souls of men. To be praised is the ambition of the world; to be a blessing is the abundant satisfaction of those who, like Bishop Walsham How, sing because their hearts are full, and who, like their Lord, find their joy in loving service of their fellow-men."

44

JOHN ELLERTON

(1826–93)

Saviour, again to Thy dear Name we raise
With one accord our parting hymn of praise;
We stand to bless Thee ere our worship cease,
Then, lowly kneeling, wait Thy word of peace.

Grant us Thy peace upon our homeward way;
With Thee began, with Thee shall end the day;
Guard Thou the lips from sin, the hearts from shame,
That in this house have called upon Thy Name.

THIS is the most beautiful and tender of the hymns which John Ellerton wrote. It was originally written for a Festival of Parochial Choirs at Nantwich and ranks with Bishop Ken's "Glory to Thee, My God, This Night" and Keble's "Sun of My Soul, Thou Saviour Dear" as one of the greatest evening hymns of the English church. It has been said of Ellerton's hymns that

> the words which he uses are usually short and simple, the thought is clear and well stated, the rhythm is good and stately. His sympathy with nature, especially in her serious moods, is great; he loves the fading light and the peace of eve, and lingers in the shadows. . . . His verse is elevated in tone, devotional in spirit, and elegant in diction.

Perhaps we can trace some of these characteristics in the

last two verses of the hymn already quoted:

> Grant us Thy peace, Lord, through the coming night,
> Turn Thou for us its darkness into light;
> From harm and danger keep Thy children free,
> For dark and light are both alike to Thee.
>
> Grant us Thy peace throughout our earthly life,
> Our balm in sorrow, and our stay in strife;
> Then, when Thy voice shall bid our conflict cease,
> Call us, O Lord, to Thine eternal peace.

Another well-known hymn of Ellerton's found in the "Evening Hymns" section of hymnbooks, and showing the same simple characteristics of the above, is:

> The day Thou gavest, Lord, is ended,
> The darkness falls at Thy behest;
> To Thee our morning hymns ascended,
> Thy praise shall sanctify our rest. . . .
>
> As o'er each continent and island
> The dawn leads on another day,
> The voice of prayer is never silent,
> Nor dies the strain of praise away. . . .
>
> So be it, Lord! Thy throne shall never,
> Like earth's proud empires, pass away,
> Thy kingdom stands, and grows for ever,
> Till all Thy creatures own Thy sway.

Two other hymns of his in current use are his hymn about the Lord's Day:

> This is the day of light:
> Let there be light today;
> O Dayspring, rise upon our night,
> And chase its gloom away.
>
> This is the day of rest:
> Our failing strength renew;
> On weary brain and troubled breast
> Shed Thou Thy freshening dew. . . .

> *This is the day of prayer:*
> *Let earth to heaven draw near;*
> *Lift up our hearts to seek Thee there,*
> *Come down to meet us here.*

and a hymn on marriage and the home:

> *O Father, all-creating,*
> *Whose wisdom, love and power*
> *First bound two lives together*
> *In Eden's primal hour,*
> *Today to these Thy children*
> *Thine earliest gifts renew:*
> *A home by Thee made happy,*
> *A love by Thee kept true.*

A spirit of deep reverence runs through Ellerton's hymns, and no writer was more careful not to put into the lips of a congregation words which, as Christians, they could not make their own. Hence his hymns were eminently congregational.

John Ellerton was the elder son of George and Jemima Ellerton. Born in London in 1826, he came of a Yorkshire family, and Ellerton Priory, a house in Swaledale, near Richmond, indicates the locality from which the family derived its name. As John's brother was eleven years younger than he, for most of his boyhood he was an only child. The memory of his parents was a most sacred and precious thing throughout his life. "I used to feel," he said, "how happy my father and mother were, even more than how good they were; and yet I knew even then, and know still better now, that they had many sorrows and anxieties." It was to his mother especially that the shy, sensitive boy was indebted for the guiding of his opening mind into those channels of thought which it never afterwards forsook. She herself was a woman of considerable literary ability.

John's boyhood was spent in London. "On the whole," he writes, "the religious world at that time was rather gloomy. The great fight against slavery had been won.

John Ellerton

There was no great social or theological battle to fight." In those days he was sometimes taken to the great religious meetings in Exeter Hall and was always especially delighted when a "real missionary" spoke. The family inherited a house in Ulverston, then in Lancashire but now in Cumbria, and settled there in 1838, John being sent to King William's College on the Isle of Man. He remained there until his father's death in 1844 (his younger brother died in the same year), then spent a year under private tuition in Ambleside before going on to Trinity College, Cambridge.

His mother was so devoted to him that she could not bear to be away from him for long, and on his graduation from Cambridge she followed him to his first curacy after he had been ordained, which was at Easebourne, now a suburb of Midhurst, Sussex. In this spot they spent three happy years, his mother helping in the schools and he combining parochial work with diligent study. His next appointment as curate was to St. Nicholas, the parish church in Brighton, and was combined with an appointment as Evening Lecturer at another church. It was for the children of St. Nicholas that his earliest hymns were composed. For the Brighton National School he compiled a small hymnal entitled *Hymns for School and Bible Classes*. These hymns do not come up to the standard of later years but they "breathe the same devout spirit of thanksgiving, hope and love."

In 1860 he became vicar of Crewe Green, Cheshire, and in the same year he married. The population of Crewe Green consisted partly of mechanics employed in the works of the Railway Company and partly of farmers and laborers working for the most part on the estate of Lord Crewe, to whom Ellerton was appointed domestic chaplain. The charm of his preaching soon began to attract many, including university men who came to spend their Sundays at Crewe Green, frequently being guests for the day at the hospitable vicarage.

On the main road between the two Shropshire towns of Market Drayton and Newport lies the village of Hinstock, nestling among low hills. It was to this quiet parish that Ellerton went as rector in 1872. Some thought that to send a man who had achieved renown as a sacred poet, a preacher and a scholar to an obscure parish was to consign him to "a living grave." Ellerton may well not have agreed with this conclusion because it was here that the greater part of his *magnum opus*, the *Notes and Illustrations to Church Hymns*, was written. Here too he composed the article "Hymns" in the *Dictionary of Christian Antiquities*, a piece of writing which cost him many journeys into Cambridge. Matthew Arnold said that in his day Ellerton was "the greatest of living hymnologists," and although he had not stopped writing hymns his work was more and more in the field of hymnology. It was at about this time that, with his friend William Walsham How, he compiled *Children's*

Hymns and School Prayers, the forerunner of the more important *Children's Hymnbook.*

After five years in the seclusion of Hinstock, Ellerton became rector of Barnes, Surrey, a large, populous and important parish. One of the results of his coming nearer London was that he was able to take a more intimate and personal share in the affairs of the SPCK for which he had already done much good work. By the time Ellerton came to Barnes his influence had impressed itself indelibly on the hymnody of the Church. To estimate at its true value the part he took in the development of hymnody we must glance at the situation some half-century before his time. There were countless hymnbooks. Between 1820 and 1850 Julian enumerates at least seventy-eight as having appeared, differing vastly in their quality. In fact, as far as the clergy was concerned, every man did that which was right in his own eyes in the matter. Many who could afford to do so compiled a collection for their own congregation and it was difficult to find two churches in the same town using the same book.

Ellerton did a great deal to remedy this by his work in the editing of *Church Hymns* published by SPCK. Also, with great labor, he prepared an introduction which contained an account of every hymn in the collection, its authorship and history, a work which Ellerton tells us in his preface "occupied pleasantly such leisure time as could be given to it during nine years of a busy life." However, his many works connected with hymnology, combined with the incessant calls of a populous parish, told on his health and at last he broke down under the burden.

He sought restoration of health in Switzerland and was able to return to England as rector of White Roding in Essex. The demands of the parish were not excessive, leaving him leisure to devote his pen more freely than before to the service of the Church. In 1891 his health finally began to break down, further work was impossible, and he retired to live in Torquay. There he seemed to rally, taking a great interest in Dr. Julian's newly published and magnificent *Dictionary of Hymnology*. But his health worsened, his mind became clouded and, as he lay peaceful and happy, there came back to his memory in endless succession fragments of the hymns he so dearly loved. His funeral was unique. "He was buried amid his own hymns," all six hymns used being from his own pen. The six pallbearers were representatives of the chief aspects of hymnody to which Ellerton had given so much of his life.

Hymns were Ellerton's joy and delight. It was impossible to mention a hymn, whatever its origin—Greek, Latin, English, French, German—but at once he told you its author and history. We have said little of Ellerton as a man. It seems that the most remarkable trait of his character was his intense "lovingness"—always making the best of and doing the best for others, never thinking of himself. Good men loved him and his friends generally spoke of him as "dear Ellerton."

45

CHARLES HADDON SPURGEON

(1834–92)

Amidst us our Beloved stands,
And bids us view His pierced hands;
Points to His wounded feet and side,
Blest emblems of the Crucified. . . .

If now, with eyes defiled and dim,
We see the signs, but see not Him,
O may His love the scales displace,
And bid us see Him face to face!

Our former transports we recount,
When with Him on the holy mount,
These cause our souls to thirst anew,
His marred but lovely face to view.

IN the early years of his ministry Charles Haddon Spurgeon wrote verse, and even before this time he gave proof of ability in this direction. When he was eighteen he wrote a poem which, as far as we know, has never appeared in any hymnbook, but which shows that if his life had not been so busy we might have had more of his hymns in present use. The poem is entitled "Immanuel" and we quote the first and last verses:

When once I mourned a load of sin;
When conscience felt a wound within;
When all my works were thrown away;
When on my knees I knelt to pray—

Then, blissful hour—remembered well—
I learned Thy love, Immanuel. . . .

When tears are banished from mine eye;
When fairer worlds than these are nigh;
When heaven shall fill my ravished sight;
When I shall bathe in sweet delight;
One joy all joys shall far excel—
To see Thy face, Immanuel.

In 1866 Spurgeon compiled a hymnbook primarily for the use of the congregation at the Metropolitan Tabernacle, London, hence its title, *Our Own Hymnbook, a collection of Psalms and Hymns for public, social and private worship.* He says in his preface to the hymnbook:

> Our congregation has long used two hymnbooks, the comprehensive edition of DR. RIPPON'S SELECTION and DR. WATTS' PSALMS AND HYMNS. . . . We believe that the store of spiritual songs contained in these two volumes is not excelled by any compilation extant; and we should probably have been very well content with those books had it not been for difficulties connected with the remarkably complex arrangement of their contents. To strangers it was no small task to discover the hymn selected for singing. . . . The providence of God brings very many new hearers within the walls of our place of worship and many a time have we marked their futile researches and pitied the looks of despair with which they have given up all hope of finding the hymns. . . . We felt that such ought not to be the state of our service of song and resolved if possible to reform it. . . . We thought it best to issue a selection which would contain the cream of the books already in use among us, together with the best of all others extant up to the hour of going to press. . . . May God's richest blessing rest upon the result of our arduous labors! Unto His glory we dedicate OUR OWN HYMNBOOK.

Charles Haddon Spurgeon

Spurgeon humbly adds,

> The editor has inserted with great diffidence a very few [hymns] of his own composition, chiefly among the Psalms, and his only apology for so doing is the fact that of certain difficult Psalms he could find no version at all fitted for singing and was therefore driven to turn them into verse himself. As these original compositions are but few it is hoped that they will not prejudice the ordinary reader against the rest of the collection, and possibly one or two of them may gratify the generous judgment of our friends.

Perhaps the writer may be forgiven for quoting one of Spurgeon's hymns which does not appear even in *Our Own Hymnbook* (presumably having been written later than its publication) or in any other hymnbook. The same love to Christ which was the burden of the hymn written by the youth of eighteen is the theme of the mature Christian pastor, who had meanwhile become the most popular preacher in England. "Those who were present at the College Conference of 1890 are not likely to forget the thrilling effect of this hymn when sung to the tune 'Nottingham' by 500 ministers and students." It contains nine verses, of which we give five:

> *All my soul was dry and dead*
> *Till I learned that Jesus bled;*
> *Bled and suffered in my place,*
> *Bearing sin in matchless grace.*
>
> *Then a drop of heavenly love*
> *Fell upon me from above,*
> *And by secret, mystic art*
> *Reached the center of my heart. . . .*
>
> *All within my soul was praise,*
> *Praise increasing all my days;*
> *Praise which could not silent be:*
> *Floods were struggling to be free. . . .*

> *Hallelujah! O my Lord,*
> > *Torrents from my soul are poured!*
> *I am carried clean away,*
> > *Praising, praising all the day.*

> *In an ocean of delight,*
> > *Praising God with all my might,*
> *Self is drowned. So let it be:*
> > *Only Christ remains to me.*

In addition to the hymns of his own composition, Spurgeon added to the hymns of others; for example, he wrote verse three of the hymn, "Come Ye Who Bow to Sovereign Grace":

> *Buried with Him beneath this flood,*
> > *We glory in His death:*
> *We own our great incarnate God,*
> > *And rise with Him by faith.*

The hymn

> *Why should I sorrow more?*
> > *I trust a Saviour slain,*
> *And safe beneath His sheltering cross*
> > *Unmoved I shall remain.*

is ascribed jointly to William Williams and Spurgeon.

❧

Charles Haddon Spurgeon was born in the quiet, picturesque village of Kelvedon in Essex on June 19, 1834. His father, John Spurgeon, was "equally efficient at conducting his business during the week and at ministering regularly to his congregation of villagers on the Lord's Day." He was known as a man of strong character and unimpeachable integrity. As he was not much at home it fell to Charles' mother to instruct her children, so her influence on him was the greater.

When Charles was old enough to leave home he went to live with his grandfather, who for many years had been minister of the Independent Church at Stambourne, Essex. On one occasion a minister had come to preach on behalf of the London Missionary Society. He was especially drawn to Charles and before he left the manse he made a remarkable prophecy destined to be literally fulfilled. He said, "I feel a solemn presentiment that this child will preach the gospel to thousands and God will bless him to their souls." At the age of seven Charles went to live in Colchester, where he went to school and acquired some knowledge of Latin, Greek and French. Before he left Colchester he passed through the greatest change of his life. He had been convinced of sin in his childhood, and himself said:

> I lived a miserable creature, finding no hope, no comfort, thinking that surely God would never save me. . . . My heart was broken in pieces. Six months did I pray and never had an answer. I resolved that in the town where I lived, I would visit every place of worship in order to find out the way of salvation. . . . At last, one snowy day, I could not go to the place I had determined to go to. . . . I turned down a court and there was a Primitive Methodist chapel. I had heard of these people and how they sang so loudly that they made people's

Birthplace of C. H. Spurgeon, Kelvedon, Essex

heads ache; but that did not matter. I wanted to know how I might be saved, and if they made my head ache ever so much I did not care. So, settling down, the service went on, but no minister came. At last a very thin-looking man came into the pulpit and opened his Bible and read the words, "Look unto Me and be ye saved, all the ends of the earth." Just setting his eyes upon me, as if he knew all my heart, he said, "Young man, you are in trouble. . . . You will never get out of it unless you look to Christ." And then, lifting up his hands, he cried out, as only a Primitive Methodist could do, "Look, look, look!" "It is only look," said he. I saw at once the way of salvation. Oh how I did leap for joy at that moment! "Look"—what a charming word it seemed to me! Oh, I looked until I could almost have looked my eyes away; and in heaven I will still look in joy unutterable.

Although brought up among the Independents he was led by his studies in the New Testament to change his views on the subject of baptism, and on May 3, 1850, he was baptized in the river Lark, near the village of Isleham. His mother was somewhat upset and is reputed to have said to him, "Ah, Charlie, I have often prayed that you might be saved, but never that you should be a Baptist." To which he replied, "God has answered your prayer, Mother, with His usual bounty, and given more than you asked."

In 1851 Spurgeon moved to Cambridge where he became an usher in a school and a member of the Baptist Church. It was here too, while still under sixteen, that he began to preach, and at eighteen he became minister of the little Baptist church at Waterbeach, six miles from Cambridge. There was a possibility that he might go to college, but instead, early in 1854, he was engaged for a preparatory period of three months at New Park Street Chapel, one of the oldest Baptist chapels in London, which was then in a state of serious decline. Long before the three months had passed London was ringing with his name. The chapel, which held 1200 people, was crowded an hour before service time, and all over London the question was being asked, "Have you heard Spurgeon?" Even after the chapel was enlarged the following year, it was not capable of holding the crowds who thronged to hear him, and services were held in various larger buildings until the building of the Metropolitan Tabernacle which was opened in March 1861. From the beginning of his ministry there until his death, this noble edifice was thronged, very often with as many as 6,000 people. His sermons were printed week by week, the circulation of them rising to about 25,000. "It was the enunciation of the simple gospel of the grace of God, together with their clearness of style and freshness of thought, that gave to his sermons the power they had and made them so acceptable in all the languages into which they were translated."

A number of institutions were founded by Spurgeon, but none of them was more dear to his heart than the College "inaugurated to train for the ministry the many earnest young men who were springing up around him and who felt an irresistible impulse to preach the gospel."

For nearly forty years Spurgeon's voice was heard in London, proclaiming the unsearchable riches of Christ. Long periods of enforced rest sometimes kept him from his much loved work, and the Downgrade Controversy in which he was involved towards the end of his life had an adverse effect on his health. He became dangerously ill in the summer of 1891 and seemed at the door of death for weeks. He recovered sufficiently to go with his wife to the sunny shores of the Mediterranean, which he had visited for years to recover strength. It seemed at first as if he were going to recover, but at length as Sunday, January 31, 1892, was passing away he gently "fell to sleep and was gathered with his fathers." On Thursday, February 11, he was buried in a plot of land in Norwood cemetery which he himself had chosen years before. Then he would know the reality of the last verse of his hymn which we quoted earlier:

> *Thou glorious Bridegroom of our hearts,*
> *Thy present smile a heaven imparts;*
> *Lift the veil, if veil there be,*
> *Let every saint Thy beauties see!*

So the great preacher passed away, leaving a gap not only among his own people but throughout the whole religious world. As long as the English tongue is spoken, among the most treasured of its names will be that of the Essex boy who turned many to righteousness, and witnessed in Britain, and through his writings to the ends of the earth, to the power of the gospel of the grace of God.

46

FRANCES RIDLEY HAVERGAL

(1836-79)

Take my life, and let it be
Consecrated, Lord, to Thee;
Take my moments and my days,
Let them flow in ceaseless praise. . . .

Take my voice, and let me sing
Always, only, for my King;
Take my lips, and let them be
Filled with messages from Thee.

C HARLES Haddon Spurgeon was not the only person who said that Frances Ridley Havergal "sang like a seraph," or words to similar effect. An Irish schoolgirl of no particular fame once expressed the same opinion. With others she had been invited to a house where Frances was staying, and the girls were very excited at the thought of meeting "the little English lady."

In a few seconds Miss Frances, caroling like a bird, flashed into the room! Flashed! yes I say the word advisedly, flashed in like a burst of sunshine . . . and stood before us, her bright eyes dancing, and her fresh, sweet voice ringing through the room. I shall never forget that afternoon, never! I sat perfectly spellbound as she sang chant and hymn with marvelous sweetness, and then played two or three pieces of Handel which thrilled me through and through!

Frances Ridley Havergal

Of many hymn-writers we have very little, if any, information as to the circumstances in which their hymns were written. This is not so with several of the hymns of Frances Havergal. We know the whole story of the one we have quoted, which we will give in her own words:

> Perhaps you will be interested to know the origin of the consecration hymn "Take My life." I went for a visit of five days to. . . . There were ten persons in the house, some unconverted and long prayed for, some converted but not rejoicing Christians. He gave me the prayer, "Lord, give me all in this house!" And He just did. Before I left the house everyone got a blessing. The last night of my visit, after I had retired, the governess asked me to go to the two daughters. They were crying. . . . Then and there both of them trusted and rejoiced. I was too happy to sleep, and passed most of the night in praise and renewal of my own consecration, and these little couplets formed themselves and chimed in my heart one after another till they finished with

Take my love—my Lord, I pour
At Thy feet its treasure store;

Take myself, and I will be
Ever, only, all for Thee!

On another occasion, when visiting a friend, Frances walked with him to the entrance gate of a boys' school, and while he went in she leaned wearily against the playground wall to await his return. Ten minutes later he found her busily scribbling on an old envelope. The result, which she handed him, was the hymn:

Golden harps are sounding,
Angel voices sing,
Gates of pearl are opened,
Opened for the King;
Christ, the King of glory,
Jesus, King of love,
Is gone up in triumph
To His throne above.

All His work is ended,
Joyfully we sing;
Jesus hath ascended!
Glory to our King!

Of yet another hymn we know the origin. As the hour of midnight struck on New Year's Day, 1859, the bells of St. Nicholas Church, Worcester, of which Frances' father was rector, began to peal. Frances and her sister Maria were sleeping in the same room in the nearby rectory. Maria roused her sister to listen to the bells, at the same time quoting to her, as a New Year's motto, the text, "As thy days thy strength shall be." Frances did not reply for a few minutes, then gave back to her sister the same thought in the form of two verses which she had composed in the few moments of silence. The next day she added two more verses, thus forming a hymn which, though it appears in some American hymnbooks, does not seem to have been included in English ones. Three of the four verses run:

"As thy days thy strength shall be!"
This should be enough for thee;
He who knows thy frame will spare

Burdens more than thou canst bear.

When thy days are veiled in night,
  Christ shall give thee heavenly light;
Seem they wearisome and long,
  Yet in Him thou shalt be strong. . . .

When thy days on earth are past,
  Christ shall call thee home at last,
His redeeming love to praise,
  Who hath strengthened all thy days.

Frances Ridley Havergal was born in the village of Astley, Worcestershire. She was the daughter of William Henry Havergal, a man of genuine piety and great gifts who, in his day, was acknowledged to be a first-rank authority on church music and psalmody. It was his devotion to the ministry of the gospel which led him to refuse a professor's chair in music at Oxford University. Frances loved her name "Ridley" because she bore it from one descended from the godly and learned Bishop Ridley of the noble army of martyrs. By the time she was four years old Frances could read the Bible and any ordinary book correctly and had learned to write. French and music were gradually added to the curriculum, but great care had always to be taken not to tire her or to excite her somewhat precocious mind. The treasured little book in which she wrote her childhood hymns begins with verses written when she was seven:

Sunday is a pleasant day
  When we to church do go;
For there we sing and read and pray
  And hear the sermon too. . . .

And if we love to pray and read
  While we are in our youth,
The Lord will help us in our need
  And keep us in His truth.

It was from Astley that her father went as rector to St. Nicholas Church, Worcester. Frances wrote,

It was in very great bitterness that I bade adieu to my pleasant country life and became, as I remember dear father called me, "a caged lark." But at St. Nicholas Rectory I had a tiny room all my own; its little window was my "country" and soon the sky and the clouds were the same sort of relations to me that trees and flowers had been.

Her mother died in 1848, when she was a girl of twelve. In 1850 she was sent to school before her father's second marriage the following year. She speaks of the day she went to school as "perhaps the most important of my life." The school's proprietress, Mrs. Teed, was nearing the end of her teaching days and was very much concerned about the spiritual welfare of her pupils. Many girls were converted and spiritual conversation was heard everywhere. Frances' heart used to sink within her because, although she prayed and sought, she seemed further away from the Lord than girls who had only just begun to think of religion. Finally she confided in an older friend, telling her how she longed to know that she was forgiven. With her help Frances came to assurance of salvation.

She went abroad with her parents in 1852, spending the winter in Dusseldorf, where she went to school, and afterwards she boarded for a time with the family of a German pastor. Her confirmation day, which took place shortly after her return to England, was to her a very solemn occasion, full of meaning. She always kept the anniversary of this day and later renewed her confirmation vow in the verse:

> Now, Lord, I give myself to Thee,
> I would be wholly Thine.
> As Thou hast given Thyself to me,
> And Thou art wholly mine;
> Oh take me, seal me as Thine own,
> Thine altogether, Thine alone.

She remained at home until she went to live with her sister near Stourport, where she superintended the educa-

The Epistle of PAUL the Apostle to the HEBREWS.

"Better."

Facsimile of a page of Frances Ridley Havergal's Bible

tion of her nieces for nine years, until the last of them went to school in 1867. She then returned to her father's vicarage, now at Shareshill, near Wolverhampton. Her father understood the high-strung, excitable temperament of his daughter and tried to curb her exuberant mental powers in order to cause her less strain and nervous exhaustion.

It was late in her short life that she began to use her beautiful voice. In instrumental music her touch on the piano was "marvelously clear, crisp and full of refined expression." Her volume, *The Ministry of Song*, she dedicated to her father. The poems it contains are "rich in thought, full of pathos and heart knowledge, earnest in purpose and musical in expression, forming a real combination of religion, genius and art." Frances herself tells us how she wrote her hymns:

> Writing is *praying* for me, for I never seem to write even a verse by myself, and feel like a little child writing: you know a child would look up at every sentence and say, "And what shall I say next?" That is just what I do; I ask that at every line He would give me not merely thoughts and power, but also every *word*, even the very *rhymes*. Very often I have a most distinct and happy consciousness of direct answers.

Her father, with whom she was very much one in spirit and in gifts, died of apoplexy in 1870.

Although Frances was so joyous in spirit, and so fully consecrated to the service of her Lord and Master, she also knew depression, doubt and gloom. After these times passed, when she again found joy in spiritual things, she drew forth the lessons she had learned in the dark, difficult places, refreshing other weary and thirsty ones with her words of sympathy and understanding. She carried on a large correspondence, seeking by this means to be of spiritual help to others. But it was not only by the pen that she sought to serve her Master. For many years she held several weekly Bible classes for which she prepared care-

fully, and which were often followed by personal inter-
views with those who sought her help. She visited cottages
and farmhouses till her strength failed her and a series of
breakdowns left her prostrated with exhaustion. The toil
and excitement of all she sought to do was too much for
her highly-strung nature. She fell into a nervous fever and
thought herself to be dying, but although she recovered
she was never strong again, being subject to severe head-
aches, followed by much nervous depression.

After the death of her stepmother, Frances and her un-
married sister went to live at the Mumbles, near Swansea.
For many years she had paid visits to Switzerland, North
Wales and Scotland, with friends or to visit friends, rejoicing in the scenery and returning refreshed to carry on her
literary and other work.

Many of her hymns still delight Christian congregations:

> *I Am Trusting Thee, Lord Jesus*
>
> *Like a River Glorious*
>
> *Who Is on the Lord's Side?*
>
> *Master, Speak! Thy Servant Heareth*
>
> *I Bring My Sins to Thee*

One hymn in particular seems to sum up many of her
heart-longings:

> *Lord, speak to me, that I may speak*
> *In living echoes of Thy tone;*
> *As Thou hast sought, so let me seek*
> *Thy erring children lost and lone. . . .*
>
> *O teach me, Lord, that I may teach*
> *The precious things Thou dost impart;*
> *And wing my words, that they may reach*
> *The hidden depths of many a heart. . . .*
>
> *O use me, Lord, use even me,*
> *Just as Thou wilt, and when, and where,*
> *Until Thy blessed face I see,*
> *Thy rest, Thy joy, Thy glory share.*

That time was soon to come, for in May of 1879 she caught a chill which was followed by congestion and inflammation of the lungs. Her brother Frank, to whom she was much attached, was called. Her testimony to the vicar and the doctor was radiant, and to her sister she said, "Not one thing hath failed." Later in the day she asked her brother to sing "Jerusalem, My Happy Home," to her father's tune "St. Chrysostom." Only a few minutes before her death she sang, clearly though faintly, to a tune she composed herself, the first verse of her hymn:

> *Jesus, I will trust Thee,*
>   *Trust Thee with my soul;*
> *Guilty, lost and helpless,*
>   *Thou canst make me whole.*

> *There is none in heaven,*
>   *Or on earth like Thee:*
> *Thou hast died for sinners—*
>   *Therefore, Lord, for me.*

Shortly afterwards her brother commended her departing spirit into her Redeemer's hands and she calmly and gently passed away. Her death took place at Caswell Bay, Swansea, but she was buried in her father's grave in Astley churchyard, Worcestershire.

47

ANNE ROSS COUSIN

(1824–1906)

The sands of time are sinking;
The dawn of heaven breaks;
The summer morn I've sighed for,
The fair, sweet morn, awakes:
Dark, dark hath been the midnight,
But dayspring is at hand,
And glory, glory dwelleth
In Immanuel's land.

THE hymn of which this is the opening verse was composed by Mrs. Anne Ross Cousin, wife of a Free Church of Scotland minister of Melrose, Roxburghshire, but its content, its phrases and imagery are those of seventeenth-century Samuel Rutherford, being based upon sayings found in some thirty-six of his famous letters, so that we may rightly claim that the hymn is as much his as hers. Of Mrs. Cousin herself very little need be said. A doctor's daughter, with literary gifts, she wrote 107 hymns in all, the one here receiving comment being first published in the *Christian Treasury* of 1857. It contained nineteen verses in all, all but six being omitted from most hymnbooks. We urge readers to seek them out, for not only do they reach a high level of excellence but, in a sense, form the best of all introductions to the 365 letters of Rutherford—which rank among the finest of their kind ever published. Spurgeon once said that they are "as near to inspiration as any writings outside Scripture itself." Extravagant praise possibly, but at the same time worthy of note!

Samuel Rutherford was a native of Roxburghshire and became a graduate of Edinburgh University, where he was appointed to the post of "regent of humanity." In his earlier days he seems to have paid but scant attention to the needs of his soul. "Like the fool I was," he wrote, "I suffered my sun to be high in the heaven and near afternoon . . ."; actually he was about twenty-seven years of age before repentance toward God and faith toward the Lord Jesus Christ entered his life. Sadly did he realize that his youth had been misspent, a fact which caused him later to write: "There is not such a glassy, icy, slippery piece of way betwixt you and heaven as youth; the devil findeth in youth dry sticks and dry coals and a hot hearthstone; and

Samuel Rutherford

how soon can he with his flint cast fire, and with his bellows blow it up!"

Rutherford's conversion was soon followed by his entrance upon the work of the ministry. From 1627 to 1636 he was pastor of the parish of Anwoth "among the soft green hills of Galloway overlooking the Solway Firth and the hills of Cumbria." To his dying day Anwoth held his heart fast:

> *Fair Anwoth by the Solway,*
> *To me thou still art dear!*
> *E'en from the verge of heaven*
> *I drop for thee a tear.*
> *Oh! if one soul from Anwoth*
> *Meet me at God's right hand,*
> *My heaven will be two heavens*
> *In Immanuel's land.*

The ivy-clad walls of Anwoth's ancient but now ruined church building are still visited by those who like to keep in memory men and women of whom the world was not worthy.

As a minister Rutherford was a paragon of diligence. Rising regularly at three in the morning, he spent the early hours in prayer, devotions and study. His afternoons were occupied in visiting the sick and afflicted, and in catechizing his widely scattered flock. "For such a piece of clay as Mr. Rutherford," said one who knew him well, "I never knew one in Scotland like him. He seemed to be always praying, always preaching, always visiting the sick, always teaching in the schools, always writing treatises, always reading and studying." Sabbath days were his high days, his congregation including some of the principal families in that part of Galloway. As a preacher he had "a strange utterance, a kind of a skreigh; of which I never heard the like," said one of his friends. "Many a time I thought he would have flown out of the pulpit when he came to speak of Jesus Christ." He was "a little fair man," warm of temper, sometimes even fiery towards his opposers, ever full of love and zeal in the cause of his Saviour. For him to live was Christ; he was fully convinced that death would be his gain. At times he even spoke of Christ in his sleep, and dreams were sometimes the ladder by which his lively soul ascended to the Lord who stood above it.

An English merchant, visiting Scotland, tells how in one place he heard a preacher, "a well-favored, bearded, proper old man, who showed me all my heart." Later, he continues, "I heard a sweet, majestic-looking man and he showed me the majesty of God. After him I heard a little fair man [Samuel Rutherford] and he showed me the loveliness of Christ." And it is the loveliness of Christ that was the hallmark, so to speak, of Rutherford's ministry. That theme pervades the letters that flowed from his pen. It was as though, from time to time, their writer was caught up into paradise in order that he might catch a glimpse of the "Altogether Lovely," and impart that knowledge to the Lord's flock on earth.

To his life's end Rutherford retained his love for his first parish. Its very birds he counted blest. Within its bounds he experienced all that in an earthly body he was able to experience of the love of Christ. Within its confines Christ "built a heaven of His surpassing love, a little New Jerusalem like to the one above." But changes came contrary to his desires and designs. He found himself at odds with the ecclesiastical "powers" of the time and they sent him into exile in far-off Aberdeen. As Shimei was confined to Jerusalem by sentence of Solomon (1 Kings 2:36), so must Rutherford not fail to regard the granite walls of the northern city as his confine; to disregard the "powers" might mean imprisonment or even death. He called Aberdeen his "sea-beat prison." But in it the Lord and he "held tryst."

> And aye my murkiest storm-cloud
> Was by a rainbow spanned,
> Caught from the glory dwelling
> In Immanuel's land.

Correspondence helped to fill the prisoner's days, for

220 of his letters were despatched from his "prison," chiefly
to his Galloway friends.

Rutherford's confinement to Aberdeen, and his prohibi-
tion from preaching the gospel of his loved Saviour and
Lord, lasted for about two years (1636-38) and then deliverance came from an unexpected quarter. Scotland was
convulsed by widespread dissatisfaction with the royal
(Stuart) policy to which Archbishop Laud gave expression.
It gave rise to "the covenanting revolution." A Scottish
housewife seated in St. Giles Cathedral, Edinburgh, threw
her stool at the occupant of its Anglican pulpit, crying,
"Will ye read that book [Common Prayer] in my lug?"
Jenny Geddes' courage met glad, but angry, response
throughout Scotland. A nation rose to its feet. A Covenant
was signed; English religion must be resisted. Taking advantage of the uproar and of the strong public sentiment
which he fully shared, Rutherford hastened back to
Anwoth to resume his ministry. But his fame was much
more widespread than formerly, and eventually he succumbed to a pressing invitation to become Professor of
Divinity at St. Andrews University on the coast of Fife, an
appointment which would give him much influence over
candidates for the ministry of Scotland's Presbyterian
Church.

Rutherford's contacts with England and its Puritan ministers came about chiefly through his membership in the
Assembly which drew up the famous Westminster Confession
of Faith. The English Long Parliament had broken with the
king (Charles I); civil war commenced in 1642. In 1643 the
Scots came into the war on Parliament's side, one condition of help being "reform of religion." The reform was
entrusted to the Westminster Assembly of Divines,
Rutherford being one of those chosen to represent the
Church of Scotland. He remained in London four years,
preaching several times before Parliament. In 1648 he returned to St. Andrews and spent his remaining years in
ceaseless striving for the purity of the Church of Christ
and the faithful preaching of the Word of God! "I had

rather be in Scotland with angry Jesus Christ than in any Eden or garden on earth," he said.

His troubles continued to the last. In 1660 came the Stuart Restoration, following upon the Cromwellian Commonwealth. Rutherford was charged with treason and summoned to answer for himself at the bar of Parliament. But he received the summons as he lay on his deathbed. "Tell them," he said, "that I have a summons already from a superior Judge and judicatory, and I behove to answer my first summons; and ere your day arrives I shall be where few kings and great folks come." And so he crossed the River and passed through the pearly gates into the City, there to see the King in His beauty. The "little fair man" entered the land where no inhabitant ever said, "I am sick" (Isaiah 33:24).

Among Rutherford's deathbed sayings is the following: "I shall shine; I shall see Him as He is; I shall see Him reign, and all the fair company with Him, and I shall have my large share. Mine eyes shall see my Redeemer and no other form. This seems to be a wide word, but it is no fancy nor delusion; it's true, it's true!" Jesus Christ was his "kingly King," his "blessed Master." "Let my Lord's Name be exalted; and if He will, let my name be ground to pieces that He may be all in all. If He should slay me ten thousand times ten thousand times, I'll trust."

> *With mercy and with judgment*
> *My web of time He wove,*
> *And aye the dews of sorrow*
> *Were lustred with His love.*
> *I'll bless the hand that guided,*
> *I'll bless the heart that planned,*
> *When throned where glory dwelleth*
> *In Immanuel's land.*

48

EDWARD HENRY BICKERSTETH

(1825–1906)

Peace, perfect peace, in this dark world of sin?
The blood of Jesus whispers peace within.

Peace, perfect peace, by thronging duties pressed?
To do the will of Jesus, this is rest. . . .

Peace, perfect peace, our future all unknown?
Jesus we know, and He is on the throne. . . .

It is enough: earth's struggles soon shall cease,
And Jesus call us to heaven's perfect peace.

I N August 1875 Edward Henry Bickersteth, then vicar
of Christ Church, Hampstead, was staying with his
family in Harrogate. One Sunday morning he heard
the vicar of Harrogate preach from the text, "Thou wilt
keep him in perfect peace, whose mind is stayed on thee"
(Isaiah 26:3). He alluded to the beauty of the phrase "perfect peace" as the best rendering of the repeated word
"peace, peace" in the original Hebrew. That afternoon
Bickersteth went for a solitary walk on the moors. It was
his custom at Sunday tea-time to ask each of his family to
repeat a hymn, doing the same himself or reading out some
new composition of his own. That Sunday tea-time he read
the hymn he had just composed on the moors, "Peace,
Perfect Peace." In singing the hymn it is all but impossible

to convey the fact that it really consists of questions and answers. Probably no music can ever be written to the hymn which indicates this, though one composer added to his tune the odd direction, "To be sung in an enquiring spirit," without any indication as to how this was to be done. It has been much loved and widely sung, and is said to have been a favorite hymn of Queen Victoria's. It has been translated into many languages, and in his later years Edward Bickersteth heard it sung in Japanese and Chinese when, as bishop, he was on a missionary tour in the Far East.

Bickersteth was born in 1825 in Islington, London, which was then on the edge of fields which stretched away to the rising ground of Highgate and Hampstead. He was five years old when his father went to be rector of Watton in Hertfordshire. He was brought up in a thoroughly consistent spiritual atmosphere. Life was real and earnest in Watton Rectory, which was likened to a beehive, so busily occupied were its inmates. His sister Emily wrote in her *Recollections*:

> At 5:30 every morning an alarm clock went off and aroused Edward who tumbled half asleep into his shower-bath and soon roused all his sisters by vigorous knocks on their doors. In an hour's time all were downstairs, the boys at work with their tutor. . . . The rector himself spent part of this time in a retired walk, engaged in his devotions. At 7:50 he returned from his walk and gathered his children into his study where each one repeated passages from the Holy Scriptures of their own choosing, some of them learning whole books of the Bible.

Edward himself learned the last twenty-eight chapters of Isaiah in his boyhood, probably in this way.

Edward was educated at home until he went to Cambridge, his father's curate being his tutor. Many years later, when he was Bishop of Exeter, he told a small group of chaplains the story of the struggles which reached their climax in his conversion, the conscious surrender of himself into his Saviour's keeping, and the enjoyment of the peace which he came to possess. This experience seems to have come to him while he was reading Krummacher's *Elijah the Tishbite* one Sunday afternoon when he was about fourteen years old. That same evening he told his father the joyful tidings. Very soon afterwards he knew that his calling in life was to be the ministry, and with this end in view he entered Trinity College, Cambridge, in 1843. His years there were characterized by diligence in work and fidelity to the religious principles in which he had been brought up and which he had made his own.

In 1848 he was ordained by the Bishop of Norwich, preaching his first sermon on the following Sunday to a crowded congregation at Watton, from 1 Corinthians 1:30— ". . . who of God is made unto us wisdom, and righteousness, and sanctification, and redemption." A few weeks later he was married to his cousin, Rosa Bignold, and shortly afterwards they moved to Banningham in Norfolk, where Edward became curate in charge of the church. After three years' diligent pastoral work there and a brief curacy in Tunbridge Wells, he was called to be rector of Hinton Martell, near Wimborne, Dorset, until in 1855 he went as rector to Christ Church, Hampstead. The large old-fashioned house to which he then brought his family was to be their home for the next thirty years. It was a great change to have a parish of 3,000 at Hampstead after a few hundred at Hinton Martell, but he entered on his new work with characteristic enthusiasm. Services, classes, meetings of all kinds were held and movements set on foot to help many foreign and home missions. He also began open-air preaching on Hampstead Heath. He was a welcome visitor in the homes of both rich and poor and would go at once to any home where there was trouble. He had a gift for bringing people together and inspiring them with the desire to work, both in the church and in outside activities, while he himself was called upon to do much work outside his parish. He took part in missions, served on the committees of various societies, and was the first to introduce "retreats" and "quiet days" among evangelical clergy and laity. Bickersteth was a man of wide sympathies which went out to all Christians with whom he felt at one on the fundamental truths of the faith. He maintained that missions should be sent to Roman Catholics in Ireland and elsewhere, holding it to be the duty of those "who had the fuller and purer light of the Reformation, to diffuse it amongst those who were still in the darkness."

In 1884 his name was brought forward as one fitted for higher office in the Church and at the age of sixty he became Bishop of Exeter, an office he held for fifteen years. Any page from his book of engagements would show how he abounded in the work of the Lord. He made strong and persistent efforts for the promotion of Sunday observance, lifting up his voice in Convocation against resolutions which he felt would weaken a cause so dear to his heart. He used to say, "There are two sacred ordinances which have come down to us from Eden, Holy Marriage, the bond of human love, and the Holy Day of Rest, binding men to God." Bishop Bickersteth greatly delighted to fulfill the apostolic precept, "A bishop must be given to hospitality." For many years he entertained large gatherings of various kinds at his home—churchwardens and their wives, Sunday School teachers, organists and choirs, nurses, nonconformist ministers, bell-ringers, policemen, old people. All resident in his diocese partook of his hospitality.

In 1877 his eldest son, a Fellow of Pembroke College, Cambridge, went out to India as the founder and first head of the Cambridge Mission to Delhi. Never did a father give up a much-loved son more willingly to God's work. He said, "Ought not the Church of England to double her missionary forces before the twentieth century dawns, and account this as only an earnest of far greater things? Is it too much to say that if we give one-tenth of our clergy . . . to mission fields, England's church would be the gainer, not the loser?" Bickersteth's missionary interest was like a thread which ran through the whole of his life. It was said of him that "no bishop of our time has been so devoted to the foreign missionary enterprise and so identified with its interests as Bishop Bickersteth." He paid visits to India, Japan (where another son was a missionary bishop) and to Palestine, because he wanted to see for himself "how his brethren did in the mission field." The most exciting experience of the whole tour was a terrible earthquake which occurred while he and his wife were staying with friends in Japan. The previous evening their host had asked Bickersteth to take family prayers, and he had chosen to read Psalm 91 and "said a few words on our home in God, its security and blessedness." The next morning the house, though substantially built, "shuddered and trembled and swerved to and fro." His son Edward went out into the garden and found the earth reeling under him. Bishop Bickersteth said that it was delightful to see his host's beautiful spirit of childlike trustfulness and thankfulness.

Bishop Bickersteth possessed a marked poetic gift and was recognized as one of the sweet singers of the Israel of God in his day. Julian, in his *Hymnology*, says,

> There is a soothing plaintiveness about his hymns which gives them a distinct character of their own. His thoughts are usually with the individual and not with the mass, with the single soul and his God. . . . Hence, although many of his hymns are eminently suitable for congregational purposes . . , yet his finest productions are those which are best suited for private purposes.

His missionary hymn is undoubtedly meant to be for congregational use:

> *"For My sake and the gospel's, go*
> *And tell redemption's story";*
> *His heralds answer, "Be it so,*
> *And Thine, Lord, all the glory!"*
> *They preach His birth, His life, His cross,*
> *The love of His atonement,*
> *For whom they count the world but loss,*
> *His Easter, His enthronement.*

> Hark, hark, the trump of jubilee
> Proclaims to every nation,
> From pole to pole, by land and sea,
> Glad tidings of salvation.
> As nearer draws the day of doom,
> While still the battle rages,
> The heavenly Dayspring through the gloom
> Breaks on the night of ages.

So, too, is his hymn on the theme of the Lord's Supper:

> Not worthy, Lord, to gather up the crumbs
> With trembling hand that from Thy table fall,
> A weary heavy-laden sinner comes
> To plead Thy promise and obey Thy call. . . .
>
> My praise can only breathe itself in prayer,
> My prayer can only lose itself in Thee;
> Dwell Thou forever in my heart, and there,
> Lord, let me sup with Thee; sup Thou with me.

The poetic taste of Bishop Bickersteth qualified him for the work of hymnology. In 1870 he compiled *The Hymnal Companion to the Book of Common Prayer*, and twenty years later he brought out a third edition which within a few years had superseded the large number of private compilations which had been in use in evangelical parishes in England. In 1866 *Hymns Ancient and Modern* had been published and this compilation appealed to much of the churchmanship of the day, but the evangelical school in the Church continued almost without exception to use Bickersteth's *Hymnal Companion*.

In 1900 he was greatly weakened by an attack of influenza; his summer holiday did not bring its wonted renewal of vigor, and in September he tendered his resignation. The pain of parting from many whom he loved weighed heavily upon his spirit, but the stronghold to which he had resorted for so long was his place of refuge and "he took shelter there as the shadows of life's evening gathered around him." He himself had said earlier, "Now that I am treading the border land of old age, the mighty

verities of the Cross and the Resurrection seem more im-
pregnable and necessary. When flesh and heart must at the
longest fail, the Crucified and Risen Incarnate God is alone
our strength and portion forever."

In December 1900 he moved to London and it was hoped
that a period of complete rest might restore him to a measure of strength. For a time it seemed that this expectation
would be realized, but the improvement was not maintained and the illness which was to last for more than five
years gradually became worse. He accepted the will of
God concerning him with perfect submission and childlike
trust and was fond of repeating lines of John Newton's:

> *He that has helped me hitherto*
> *Will help me all my journey through,*
> *And give me daily cause to raise*
> *New Ebenezers to His praise.*

On May 16, 1906, the gentle, loving spirit of Edward
Henry Bickersteth took its flight and went home to God. A
simple but beautiful service was held in London at Christ
Church, Lancaster Gate. His hymn, "Peace, Perfect Peace,"
was sung and he was laid to rest among his kindred at
Watton.

> *When the weary ones we love*
> *Enter on their rest above,*
> *Seems the earth so poor and vast,*
> *All our life joy overcast?*
> *Hush, be every murmur dumb;*
> *It is only "Till He come."*

49

FRANCES JANE VAN ALSTYNE

(1820–1915)

All the way my Saviour leads me:
What have I to ask beside?
Can I doubt His tender mercy,
Who through life has been my guide?
Heavenly peace, divinest comfort,
Here by faith in Him to dwell!
For I know whate'er befall me,
Jesus doeth all things well.

FANNY JANE CROSBY was descended from an intrepid family who emigrated to New England in the seventeenth century. She was born in 1820 in New York State, and when only six weeks old, having inflammation of the eyes, a doctor recommended hot poultices—which destroyed her sight. When speaking of this in later years Fanny said, "I have not for a moment felt a spark of resentment against him, for I have always believed that the good Lord, in His infinite mercy, by this means consecrated me to the work that I am still permitted to do. When I remember how I have been blessed, how can I repine?"

Her father died before she was a year old, and her mother, grandmother and a Christian lady in whose house they lived, were her first instructors. Her longing for knowledge became a passion and when still a child she learned by heart the four Gospels and a large part of the first four books of the Old Testament. She did not long for restoration of sight but for mental enlightenment. She loved her home, but was ready and willing to go away to be educated. When she was told that she was going to the Institution for the Blind in New York she clapped her hands, saying, "Thank God! He has answered my prayers." So at the age of fourteen she made the long journey to New York City, remaining in the Institution for twenty-three years, eight as a pupil and fifteen as a teacher.

Fanny was converted at a revival meeting in a Methodist church. She had been concerned about her spiritual condition for some time and that evening the hymn "At the Cross," with the opening words "Alas! and did my Saviour bleed, And did my Sovereign die?" was sung. When the line "Here, Lord, I give myself away" was reached, she said, "My very soul was flooded with celestial light. I sprang to my feet shouting 'Hallelujah!' and then for the first time I realized I had been trying to hold the world in one hand and the Lord in the other."

With others, Fanny was taken to Congress to demonstrate the good results attending systematic teaching of the blind, and she held her audience captive by the recitation of a poem she had written for the occasion. From that time she was a friend of United States presidents, including Abraham Lincoln, but especially Grover Cleveland who was Secretary to the Institution for the Blind. She was brought more into contact with him and often went to him when she wanted a sympathetic friend.

Fanny had written little poetic pictures since the age of eight. She said, "When I gathered flowers and caught their fragrance I wanted to say something poetic about them. . . . As I wandered down to the brook with my grandmother, listening to the rippling of the waters, I felt something in my soul that I wanted to say about the river."

At the age of thirty-eight Fanny married Alexander Van Alstyne, a gifted blind student whom she had known at the Institution for fifteen years. She said of him, "He is a firm, trustful Christian, a man of kindly deeds and cheering words. Our tastes are congenial and he composed the

music of several of my hymns." They lived happily together for forty-four years, she surviving her husband by
another thirteen years. Fanny herself was a loving, sympathetic woman, always ready to minister to those in sorrow
and to give pleasure to others. Joyousness was one of the
characteristics of her life. When she was but a child she
resolved that her blindness should not make her unhappy
or prevent her from being useful in the world; she never
allowed those around about her to pity her because she
was blind. She wrote, "Darkness may throw a shadow over
my outer vision, but there is no cloud that can keep the
sunlight of hope from a trustful soul."

Fanny had written a large number of secular and religious poems, but her writing of hymns really began when
she left the Institution and became associated with some
notable Christian leaders. Altogether she wrote 8,000
hymns and poems, one of the best known being "Pass Me
Not, O Gentle Saviour." Ira D. Sankey said, "No hymn in
our collection was more popular than this one at the meetings in London in 1874. It has been translated into many
languages." Her hymn "Safe in the Arms of Jesus" has an

Moody and Sankey at the Agricultural Hall, London

Fanny Jane Crosby

interesting story attached to it. A friend coming to her house and saying that he had forty minutes to catch his train asked her to write words to music which he played to her. She left the room and, returning after twenty minutes, read to her friend the words of "Safe in the Arms of Jesus."

One day, in conversation with a friend, Fanny said, as she took a little New Testament from her bag,

> During these many years my love for the Holy Bible has not waned. Its truth was bred into my life. My mother and grandmother took pains that I should know the Bible better than any other book. All that I am and all that I ever expect to be, in literature or life, is due to the Bible.

And at ninety years of age she again said,

> My love for the Holy Bible and its sacred truth is stronger and more precious to me at ninety than at nineteen. This book is to me "God's Treasure House"; there is nothing I love better than to have my friends read to me from the sacred page. I am

living in the sight of Eternity's sunrise. . . . My simple trust in God's goodness has never failed me during these many years. There is nothing in this wide world that gives me so much joy as telling the story of my Saviour's loving mercy.

In a verse of her hymn "Saved by Grace," she wrote:

> *Some day the silver cord will break,*
> *And I no more, as now, shall sing,*
> *But oh! the joy when I shall wake,*
> *Within the palace of the King!*
> *And I shall see Him face to face,*
> *And tell the story—saved by grace!*

The "silver cord broke" on February 12, 1915, and Fanny Crosby went to be with Christ. She was rich in faith, hope and love, and some of her hymns will live forever.

During the last seven years of Frances Ridley Havergal's life she and Fanny Crosby wrote to each other. In answer to her inquiry about the famed American singer a friend had said to Miss Havergal, "She is a blind lady whose heart can see splendidly in the sunshine of God's love." She was deeply touched by this reply and wrote Fanny Crosby the following beautiful lines:

> *Sweet blind singer over the sea,*
> *Tuneful and jubilant! how can it be,*
> *That the songs of gladness which float so far,*
> *As if they fell from the evening star,*
> *Are the notes of one who never may see*
> *"Visible music" of flower and tree,*
> *Purple of mountain, or glitter of snow,*
> *Ruby and gold of the sunset glow,*
> *And never the light of a loving face?*

Many of Fanny Crosby's hymns are full of joy and praise to the Lord. For example:

> *To God be the glory—great things He hath done!*
> *So loved He the world that He gave us His Son;*

Who yielded His life an atonement for sin,
And opened the Life-gate that all may go in.

and

Praise Him! praise Him! Jesus, our blessed Redeemer!
Sing, O earth, His wonderful love proclaim!
Hail Him! hail Him! highest archangels in glory,
Strength and honor give to His holy Name! . . .

Some of her hymns, however, are in a quieter, more pensive vein, as:

Here from the world we turn,
Jesus to seek;
Here may His loving voice
Tenderly speak.
Jesus, our dearest Friend,
While at Thy feet we bend,
O let Thy smile descend!
'Tis Thee we seek.

and

Jesus, keep me near the cross:
There a precious fountain,
Free to all, a healing stream,
Flows from Calvary's mountain.

The last verse of the hymn we quoted at the beginning of this chapter is a fitting close to this account of the life of one whose hymns have been a blessing to so many:

All the way my Saviour leads me:
O the fullness of His love!
Perfect rest to me is promised
In my Father's house above.
When my spirit, clothed immortal,
Wings its flight to realms of day,
This my song through endless ages:
Jesus led me all the way.

50

FRANK HOUGHTON

(1894–1972)

Thou who wast rich beyond all splendor,
  All for love's sake becamest poor;
Thrones for a manger didst surrender,
  Sapphire-paved courts for stable floor.
Thou who wast rich beyond all splendor,
  All for love's sake becamest poor. . . .

Thou who art love beyond all telling,
  Saviour and King, we worship Thee.
Immanuel, within us dwelling,
  Make us what Thou wouldst have us be.
Thou who art love beyond all telling,
  Saviour and King, we worship Thee.

T HIS hymn about the Incarnation of Christ took shape in the mind of Frank Houghton when he was traveling in the mountains of Szechwan, far inland in Western China. The text "Though he was rich, yet for your sakes he became poor" had been in his mind for a long time, but his thoughts had not crystalized into verse until that journey. There were no railways in East Szechwan in the 1930's and few roads; certainly there would be none in the mountainous hinterland. So Frank might have been walking or he might have been traveling by *huakan,* an improvised sedan chair which resembled a deck-chair slung between two poles. It was a leisurely form of travel, providing time for reading, meditating and perhaps even for writing.

It was in 1920 that Frank had offered himself to the China Inland Mission. Previously his own doctor had told him that as he had been debarred from military service because of the condition of his heart, so this same condition would prevent him from being accepted for overseas service. He was finally accepted by the C.I.M. for "sedentary work." Negotiating the mountainous terrain in Szechwan was far removed from sedentary work but his heart did not seem to be adversely affected.

Frank Houghton was born in 1894 at Stafford, England, where his father, Thomas Houghton, was curate for a time. He was the fourth of eight children, five of whom, including himself, became missionaries. He came to know and love the Saviour when quite young, and when still a boy began his lifelong custom of expressing himself in verse, using this gift to the glory of God. When he was fourteen, after hearing a sermon on Luke 1:78–79, ". . . the dayspring from on high hath visited us . . . ," he wrote the poem:

> The night is dark, and over all the world,
> The banner of the foe has been unfurled.
>   The fight is fierce and long—
>   The foe is strong. . . .
>
> The Sun of Righteousness Himself appears,
> Dispels the gloom, and drives away our fears;
>   In all His power He reigns,
>   And peace maintains.

In the same year he and his brother were saved from drowning, but only just in time, for they were unconscious when found. The same evening they read in *Daily Light*, "He brought me up out of an horrible pit . . . praise to our God." The whole experience had a profound effect on their later missionary service.

During his schooldays in Weston-super-Mare, Frank bore a clear witness to the saving power of Christ, leading several boys to Christ. After theological training at the Lon-

Frank Houghton

don College of Divinity (now St. John's College, Nottingham) and ordination in 1917, he went as curate to St. Benedict's, Liverpool, later moving with his vicar to Preston. Many of the boys in his Bible class, whom he led to Christ, themselves went into Christian service at home or abroad.

At that time Frank read and reread the life of Hudson Taylor. He was somewhat relieved when his doctor told him he would not be accepted for overseas service, but the conviction that God had called him constrained him to apply to the C.I.M., and after being accepted, as we said, for sedentary work, he sailed for China in November 1920.

Frank Houghton's spirit was very much akin to that of Hudson Taylor, the founder of the Mission. He wanted to be all things to all men and especially to identify with the Chinese, treating them, on the human plane, as equals and brothers. The Chinese language did not present difficulties to him—as a student Greek too had come easily, and throughout life he used the Greek New Testament—and when later he moved to the far western province of Szechwan he readily adapted to the western Mandarin dialect.

Life was becoming very unsettled in China. A Republic had been set up in 1912 after the overthrow of the Manchu dynasty, and the resultant regional rivalry had brought much suffering to the land. Missionary work continued in spite of everything, but a verse written at this time indicates Frank's conflict of heart:

> Ring'd around by Satan's power,
> Ceaselessly at grips with sin,
> Battle-stain'd and faint within—
> "Father, save me from this hour!"
>
> Nay—it was for this I came!
> Heard afar God's trumpet-call,
> Heard and answer'd, rose, left all—
> "Father, glorify Thy Name!"

In 1923, after serving for some time in Suiting, Szechwan, Frank married Dorothy, one of the daughters of Bishop Cassels of West China. This same year there was looting and raping in Suiting by a bandit army, and refugees filled the Mission premises. The following year Frank became Principal of the Theological College in Paoning, Szechwan, and gave himself to its young men, befriending them and helping them spiritually. Both Bishop and Mrs. Cassels died as a result of visiting students when an epidemic broke out in the college the following year.

When the Houghtons returned to England on furlough in 1926 they had no thought of not returning to China. But it happened that, in London, the Mission unexpectedly needed a new Editorial Secretary, and as Frank possessed the essential qualities he was invited to accept the post.

> Was it His Voice that called?
> Here where the roads divide,

Faintly I heard the summons
Far up the mountain side.

But as I stood perplexed
I heard the Voice close by—
His well-known Voice in the darkness—
Follow, for it is I.

So Frank accepted, and was Editorial Secretary for nine years, editing *China's Millions*, whose pages in those days contained "strong, interesting and inspiring material." He was involved with informing supporters at home of the work in China and with the calling out of reinforcements for that work. To support the appeal in 1929 for 200 missionaries in two years, he wrote this challenging hymn in 1931:

Facing a task unfinished,
    That drives us to our knees,
A need that, undiminished,
    Rebukes our slothful ease,
We, who rejoice to know Thee,
    Renew before Thy throne
The solemn pledge we owe Thee
    To go and make Thee known.

Meanwhile, in China there was brigandage, famine and fighting; two Finnish ladies were killed and the thoughts of missionaries were turned back to the Boxer Rising of 1900 when scores of missionaries were martyred. Frank summed up all that needed to be said in verse:

Trust that triumphs when fear dismays,
Light that shines in the darkest days,
Peace and power, and a song of praise!
When I remember Thee.

In 1934, when Frank had been Editorial Secretary for seven years, he felt the need to revisit China to see present conditions for himself. Before he began his tour of the country a missionary had been taken by the Communists and not heard of again; Hayman and Bosshardt had been cap-

tured and released after 413 and 560 days respectively; and
John and Betty Stam, two American missionaries, had been
captured and beheaded. Frank went on his tour regardless
of these deteriorating conditions, and before it ended he
was asked if he would be willing to return to China as
Bishop of East Szechwan. He accepted the challenge and
took up office in 1937.

There followed four years of constant travel in dangerous conditions. In December 1938 the Mission Council met
in Shanghai to "seek the Lord's face" as to the future of the
Mission in view of the uneasy peace in Europe and the
two-year-old war between China and Japan in which the
Japanese had captured the long coast of China with its
ports. As war broke out in Europe, Frank wrote to his wife
from a wayside inn in China to tell her that he had agreed
to be nominated for election as the Mission's General Director. He was formally appointed to this task, which could
only be fulfilled by a very courageous man with great faith
in God, in October 1940.

His workload and his responsibilities were great, but
still he expressed himself in poetry:

> From Thee is all my expectation, Lord,
>   O speak the word—
> Thy servant waits for Thee.

Frank did not wait for the Lord in vain, and with His
help he carried his responsibilities and united his fellow
missionaries in a warm harmonious fellowship which must
have helped them in the trials of the increasingly difficult
war years. Many of the missionaries were interned by the
Japanese after they entered World War II at the time of
their devastating attack on the American Pacific Fleet at
Pearl Harbor. With John Sinton, the Deputy Director, Frank
Houghton bore all the burdens and emotional stresses of
leadership. Singapore fell to the Japanese, but missionaries
still undertook pioneering projects. Funds were low, ra-
tioning was severe, and a telephone call asking if a few
bags of flour would be useful, just when the Mission's last

flour had been used, was an example of the Lord's faithfulness in providing for them. One of the graces which Frank wrote was often used in those days:

Thy gracious provision has spread us this board;
Help us to eat to Thy glory, O Lord.

When the long nightmare of war came to an end, both in the Pacific region and in Europe, headquarters returned to Shanghai from Chungking. China was accessible again and there was much to do in recontacting and helping churches and in planning for advance. "Our aim," Frank wrote, "is to assist in building up the Church throughout the land. The Mission engages in pioneer evangelism where no church exists, with a view to establishing new churches which in turn will spread the light." After his death the Assistant Director recorded that Frank Houghton's "vision for the church when he became General Director has really formed the present policies of the Mission."

The next difficulties came from Communists, who began to advance from their headquarters where they had been reserving their strength for action when the Japanese were defeated. The Mission held on, but by May of 1949 Shanghai had fallen to the Communists, and late in 1950 Bishop Houghton issued the very important statement, "Cooperation with the Chinese Church has ceased to be possible—the majority of missionaries must plan to withdraw." Many thought that this would be the end of the C.I.M.—and so it was, in a way, but only to give place to the Overseas Missionary Fellowship which in years to come worked in countries from Thailand to Japan. The plan of God was not to close the Mission but to reform it and attack again. Frank's spirit rose to the challenge of new frontiers, but at an important conference of Directors

with agonizing heart-searching and tears, in which every strong man shared, there came the realization that Frank Houghton, who had borne so many years of crisis and heartache, could not be asked to continue as leader in the new era. Frank's serenity when the shattering decision was made was impressive. He was faint, perplexed and no doubt heartbroken, but trusting and even radiant in his acceptance of the will of God.

Even so, it was not surprising that his spirit was dismayed when he found himself out of missionary service. But the Lord strengthened him and opened a way for him into pastoral service in England, first in Leamington Spa, then in a quieter living* near Banbury, until in 1963 he retired and he and his wife went to live in Parkstone, Poole, where he helped a vicar who had no curate. The lease of their flat expired and, the future being again uncertain, Frank wrote four poignant lines:

> Dark and dim is the road ahead—
> "How can I plan for the journey?" I said.
>
> "Did you not know, on the road ahead,
> I'm planning for you?" the Master said.

The Lord was indeed planning for them and provided a flat which was more suitable than the one they had left. Frank continued serving the Lord and writing poems till his health finally failed and he was taken to Cornford House, Tunbridge Wells, the Mission's home for retired workers. There, on January 25, 1972, Frank Houghton "heard the call to meet Him whom he had loved and to be with Him forever. The words of the Apostle Paul, 'For to me to live is Christ and to die is gain,' were true also for Frank Houghton."

Most of the information in this chapter is taken from *Faith Triumphant* by kind permission of the Overseas Missionary Fellowship and Mrs. Frank Houghton.

---

* The position of a vicar or rector with income and/or property.

HYMN TITLES & FIRST LINES

A

B

I

J

L

M

N

O

This book was produced by the Christian Literature Crusade. We hope it has been helpful to you in living the Christian life. CLC is a literature mission with ministry in over 45 countries worldwide. If you would like to know more about us, or are interested in opportunities to serve with a faith mission, we invite you to write to:

Christian Literature Crusade

P.O. Box 1449

Fort Washington, PA 19034